Taming Tigers

Praise for *Taming Tigers*

'The antidote to self-help' – **Richard Dunwoody, *horseracing legend and polar explorer***

'A shrewd, inspiring and practical blueprint for anyone determined to find greater and deeper satisfactions in life' – **Alec Wilkinson *of the* New Yorker**

'Engaging, challenging, inspiring and hilarious . . . a practical, compelling model for achieving results' – **Gary Hoffman, *Group Vice-Chairman, Barclays Bank***

'Truly inspirational and more importantly 100% effective' – **Phil Boyle, *General Manager, BT Major Business***

'Challenging and inspiring' – **Ian Dyson, *Finance Director, Marks and Spencer plc***

'Thought provoking, empowering and entertaining' – **Mike Green, *Deputy Group Finance Director, ITV plc***

TAMING TIGERS

Do things you never thought you could

Jim Lawless

158.1
LAW

2 4 6 8 10 9 7 5 3 1

Published in 2012 by Virgin Books, an imprint of Ebury Publishing
A Random House Group Company

Copyright © Jim Lawless 2012

Jim Lawless has asserted his right under the Copyright, Designs and
Patents Act 1988 to be identified as the author of this work.

Every reasonable effort has been made to contact the copyright holders of
material reproduced in this book. If any have inadvertently been overlooked,
the publishers would be glad to hear from them and make good in
future editions any errors or omissions brought to their attention.

www.randomhouse.co.uk

Addresses for companies within The Random House Group Limited can be found
at www.randomhouse.co.uk/offices.htm

The Random House Group Limited Reg. No. 954009

A CIP catalogue record for this book is available from the British Library

ISBN 978 0 753 53991 0

The Random House Group Limited supports The Forest Stewardship Council®
(FSC®), the leading international forest certification organisation. Our books
carrying the FSC label are printed on FSC® certified paper. FSC is the only forest
certification scheme endorsed by the leading environmental organisations,
including Greenpeace. Our paper procurement policy can be found at
www.randomhouse.co.uk/environment

Printed and bound in CPI Group (UK) Ltd, Croydon, CR0 4YY

To buy books by your favourite authors and register for offers visit
www.randomhouse.co.uk

Contents

To the Horse and to the Sea

To Maddie and to Gee

To be free
as wild animals are.
To dive naked as a dolphin,
Swift, silent, serene
into the depths of the sea.
To fly high up into the infinite blue of the sky,
And glide quietly over modern man's shabby world
To blend in with the air,
Or melt into the water,
Becoming one with Nature
And re-discovering the 'Self'.
This is my motto

Jacques Mayol, the first human being to dive to 100 metres on a single breath and the inspiration behind Luc Besson's film **The Big Blue**, *1988*

Acknowledgements

Many inspirational people have helped me to get *Taming Tigers* to this stage.

First, thanks must go to Blaire Palmer and my great team at Taming Tigers, all of the audience members, workshop delegates and people on major corporate change programmes who have given invaluable comment and advice and, often, stayed in contact.

The gallop to the racetrack in one year would not have been possible without the help of Gee Bradburne (née Armytage), Michael Caulfield, Tina Fletcher, Graham Fletcher, Mark Bradburne, Martin and Sarah Bosley, Charlie Morlock, Jason Cook, Roddy Griffiths, Henry Daly, Jamie Osborne, Andrew Balding, Charles and Meregan Norwood, Georgie Browne, Hayley, Gary and Jayne Moore, Theatre of Life, Mr Music Man, the wonderful Airgusta, and many other people and horses.

I could not have become the first Briton to pass the 100m mark in freediving without the support and commitment of Debbie Metcalfe, Andrea Zuccari, Marco Nones, Jon Pitts and the team at Alchemy, the yoga centre, in London.

Thanks to Brian Lawson for his dogged insistence that I try to deliver a 'motivational speech' and to Yann Martel for inspiring 'the Tiger' in his inspirational book *Life of Pi*.

I am extremely grateful to the people who contacted me after seeing a Taming Tigers presentation and agreed to have their stories included in this book. Thank you for your honesty, generosity and time.

A special thanks is due to Richard Dunwoody for all of his help and support along the way and for being kind enough to write the foreword to this book.

Thanks to my editors, Ed Faulkner and Clare Wallis of Virgin Books, and Richard Collins and to my literary agent, the inimitable Robert Kirby – their comments and advice have been invaluable.

Huge thanks are due to my friends and family for permitting me to shut myself away for weeks on end to create this book and for tolerating my adventures.

Finally, I would like to thank Gee Bradburne (nee Armytage) for all of her time and energy and pure hard work – in all weathers – to get me to the racecourse; and thanks to Gee, to Anita, my best friend and partner and to my daughter Maddie for their faith in me.

Foreword

Taming Tigers is an important book. Life is for living – and living well. Taming Tigers is all about setting ourselves free to do just that – at work or at home.

Taming Tigers is the antidote to self-help. For one thing, the approach is completely practical. If you follow the Ten Rules you'll find very few 'short cuts' but a lot of excitement and challenge and opportunities to surprise yourself. But also Jim lives the philosophy. He doesn't just talk about it.

I rode nearly 2,000 winners during my career, including success in two Grand Nationals and a Cheltenham Gold Cup. I still hold the record for the number of racecourse falls – six hundred and seventy-two! Every day I rode there were Tigers to be tamed but nothing compared with the Tigers that attacked when I was told by an American kinesiologist, out of the blue, that my career was over. After seventeen years working on a racetrack, I was immediately running a business – sat in an office for twelve hours a day. That was a far bigger personal challenge than riding Desert Orchid around any racecourse.

Facing change, whether we choose it or it chooses us, is a huge test but also a huge opportunity. And the battle is won or lost in our heads. This book unravels that battle.

Racehorses are a handful. And the few people who make it to ride in public on a racecourse have generally worked for many years with easier animals before they take a racehorse on. Their highly strung nature, coupled with their strength and speed, makes sitting on their backs, even on the gallops, an acquired taste. There is no brake, just 'negotiation' and if they decide they've had enough of you, more than likely you're off!

When I first heard about a man from London who had arrived in Lambourn and was falling off and being run away with around the neighbourhood, I didn't fancy his chances. When Jim got in contact and asked me to help I couldn't resist and it was great to help him set his own record – fastest jockey from non-rider to track – and to be part of proving Taming Tigers.

Early in 2008, to support Sparks, Racing Welfare and another charity close to my heart, Spinal Research, Doug Stoup, an American guide, and I completed a route from the coast of Antarctica to the Geographic South Pole that had only been completed in tractors and Sno-cats some fifty years ago. We became the seventieth and seventy-first people to reach the South Pole un-resupplied and without animal, machine or wind assistance. Our expedition was, without doubt, the toughest challenge I have ever taken on.

Having seen Jim speak a few weeks before I left the UK, I had his voice and Rule 10 ringing in my ears as things began to get really tough as we neared the Pole.

I'll be continuing to attempt to tame my Tigers and I wish you every success with Taming yours. Rule 1 – Act Boldly Today. Who knows where it could lead you!

Richard Dunwoody MBE
Three Times Champion Jockey, Polar Explorer
Speaker and Author
2011

Author's Foreword

The Ten Rules for Taming Tigers is a re-structuring and a re-statement of truths that you already know. I didn't invent them, but I did observe them, experience them and experiment with them. And I have done my best to prove them by putting myself in some tricky situations with only the Ten Rules for company. I've now put them into a guidebook which I hope is useful to you and which gives the great adversary in our heads a name – 'the Tiger'.

Most 'self-help' books promise to tell the reader how to live. Many suggest that you 'can do anything you put your mind to'. I have no idea how you should live and I am quite sure that humans cannot do 'anything' they put their minds to. I will never leap a building in a single bound. I was very happy when Richard Dunwoody described Taming Tigers as 'the antidote to self help'.

I do believe that the meaning of life is whatever you make it. *Taming Tigers* is an invitation to move past your natural fears of change and growth in order to make of life something that is meaningful to you and that you can enjoy, share and be proud of. No more, no less.

I've been privileged to share the Ten Rules for Taming Tigers with over 200,000 people through keynote addresses and major corporate change programmes around the world. Now you can join our online community, use our finely tuned coaching tools and gain encouragement and advice from others in our Campus at tamingtigers.com. The Taming Tigers Campus is entirely free to join and to use.

The stories of people, on the Campus and in this book, who have used the Ten Rules, tamed their Tigers and achieved great things for themselves and others convince me that we're on to something worthwhile here.

Tiger taming never stops. So I wish you every success in taming your Tigers and I hope you'll wish me the same with mine. Please share your experiences in the Campus to help us improve the rules and to encourage others to make the leap and tame their Tigers.

Jim Lawless
Berkshire, England
2011

Introduction

Bring out your dead!

Seven thirty on a June morning in 1998. Bang on time Richard, one of the finance team, walked into the office. I was sitting, invisible to anybody else, in my partitioned 'pod' in the large open-plan office of the IT multinational where I was employed as an international legal counsel. Richard gave an audible groan and said to the apparently empty office: 'Oh well, only four years, two months, three weeks and two days to go.' I stopped working on the latest contract and did a quick calculation. I had thirty-four years, five months and a few days to go – if I could afford to retire at sixty-five, that is.

The office complex where I worked in unfashionable Slough, to the west of London, was good for the motorways and Heathrow airport but little else. Slough did me a life-changing favour, though. My desk was by a window on the ground floor, next to a side street. Somewhere nearby was a funeral parlour. Every morning as I started work the hearses would come past me bearing their loads. Every lunchtime they would return empty. This, along with my calculation that I had nearly thirty-five years of my sentence still to run, got me thinking: 'What if this is as good as it gets?'

The genie was out of the bottle. If this was my life, what on earth was I doing with it? When was it going to get started?

At thirty, maybe it already had. I had spent six years training as a lawyer and in four years of practice had moved from the City to international IT. The stark reality was that I had not enjoyed many work days during that time.

The terrifying truth was becoming apparent. I had to make a change. The Tiger began to roar at me to stay put. Battle was about to commence.

A year later Optimise (now Taming Tigers) was born. Initially, we taught business people to inspire their audiences rather than club them with tedium when making presentations. We were soon invited to support leaders of large companies who needed to inspire their people to face up to change.

One fateful day, the telephone rang; the caller was inviting me to give a motivational presentation. I immediately refused. I thought that loud razzmatazz American-style speeches were an appalling idea. I had nothing to speak about in any case.

The caller was persistent: 'Do it better if you don't like the American style.' Fair comment. I accepted the job.

Speech day came. I was to deliver sixty minutes of motivational genius. After thirty minutes I thanked the audience and bowed to their slightly surprised applause. I'd been so nervous that I'd missed out great chunks of material – all carefully timed at home to meet the required hour – and I'd stood there, mute, with thirty minutes still left to go. To my amazement, as I tried to get out of the place, one of the audience members approached me, said how much she had enjoyed it and asked if I would polish it up and deliver it again in a month's time.

The Tiger roared again . . .

The story of your life

You are writing the story of your life. You must be, mustn't you? Who else could possibly be holding the pen? You are writing a sentence of your story now, as you read this book. I am writing a sentence of my story now, as I write these words to you. Our stories are about to collide through these sentences of ours, the decisions that I have taken and the decisions you are about to take. You and I are very similar when we come to the subject of the Tiger, as we shall discover.

If you have the good fortune to be living in the free world, you are the one writing the story of your life. The very beginning of your story was dictated by genetics and environment, of course. Later, you made of that what you chose to make of it. No excuses. You and I took our decisions, acted accordingly and got our results. We're still doing that today.

Your story is the sum of all of the decisions you have made so far. That is how we write our story:

We take decisions that lead to actions that lead to sentences in the story.

You decided that you would try for that exam, but not for this one. You decided to go for this job, but not that one. You decided to push this little idea through at work but perhaps you decided not to risk that big career-making innovation. You decided to say hello to this beautiful person one fine day, but not that one. Now you are married to this one – *and you never even spoke to that one?*

Think about it! You decided to attend that social gathering – but not the more intimidating one the day before. You decided to speak with this attractive person, not that one. You decided to ask them on a date or to accept their invitation. You decided to show up on the date. You wake up thirty years later with three teenage children and a caravan. It makes you think about the consequences of these critical little decisions without which the big ones do not present themselves, doesn't it? Were they your decisions or the Tiger's?

How you take these decisions, whether they are taken to write your own meaningful story or merely to avoid the Tiger's roar, is what this book will help you to explore.

So here is the question for you. The only one that matters to you and me at the moment.

How much of your story so far is yours, the one you wanted to write, and how much of your story is a second-rate, fear-bound tale – dictated by the Tiger?

YOUR STORY AT WORK

This book is primarily about the story you are writing at work. Your work is probably the second greatest adventure of your life after the one involving family and friends. Do you agree? Perhaps it is currently the greatest adventure for you. Perhaps it does not feel like an adventure at all at present – we'll change that together if you are up to the challenge. Work is an arena in which we can all come to know ourselves, discover who we really are, connect with and impact upon others, find opportunities for growth and development, make a difference to many and create a legacy. It is also the arena in which many people sleep. *Taming Tigers* is about waking up, living the adventure.

You live in a uniquely prosperous, healthy and opportunity-filled moment in the history of mankind. Your potential to connect across the globe is greater than ever before. You live in a time when healthcare is better than at any point in our history. You live in a time of great change in industry where meritocracy, recognising and rewarding performance is becoming daily more important and urgent. This is a time when the creativity of the individual is valued at work more than ever before, when you can create your own opportunities – when 'they' *need* you to create the opportunities. We'll explore that together later in this chapter.

Whatever age you are, there has never been a better time to wake up, enter the New Economy and ride the wave of change to your advantage. Another advantage you have is that you are reading this book. Many will not bother to. They already know 'how it all works'. Their 'Rulebook' has been compiled to their satisfaction. They use that as an excuse to remain asleep. Their

Tiger is at work, saving them from the fear and reward of taking a chance, saving them from their fear of humility and of admitting and embracing uncertainty, saving them from the fear, discomfort, triumph and satisfaction of growth and achievement. Saving them from the tools that you and I will be employing to live our adventures.

Let's you and I not join them.

Who is writing your story? You or your Tiger?

WHAT IS THE TIGER?

The Tiger is the invisible force within you that stops you acting. But you knew that already, didn't you? The Tiger roars at you when you consider doing or saying something that will require you moving into unknown waters, taking a personal risk, living your adventure.

Why do I refer to this universal internal force as the Tiger? Because it often feels real and external. It is a big and powerful presence. Because it is loud, even louder at night, and seems to have real teeth. Because it feels as if our very survival may be at stake when we encounter it. Because it causes our adrenaline to be released and this makes our physiology and our thought processes alter in a very real way. Because we want to flee from it unless we are prepared for battle.

The Tiger is a metaphor, of course. It isn't really there. You created it yourself, so you can tame it. Many people have moved past it and you can, too. This book will give you the weapons to combat the Tiger, but you will have to go into battle yourself. Only you can defeat your Tiger. That is where this book will differ from self-help books. There are no quick fixes. You are the guru, not me. I've simply been down the path before you and I'd like to share the lessons I learned. I'd like to hear what you have learned, too. Contact the Taming Tigers team through the Campus at tamingtigers.com and we can swap notes.

The sleepy folk don't refer to this as their Tiger. They know that they can justify, intellectually, why they do not move beyond the impasse. It's nothing internal for them – they will look for and blame external forces at work that stymie them. They are merely victims of the cruel world. They can list all the reasons why they could not do something. They never allow others (or themselves) to see that they are actually justifying a lack of action caused by fear. Fear of the unknown. Fear of getting it wrong. Fear of the joy of getting it right, fear of the effort involved in living fully. They will never know the great reward of being awake either.

This book is not about 'Success!!' in the tired, self-help sense. It is not about making more money or achieving the perfect relationship, although it will help you with both. Nor is it about affirmations or mantras. This book does not include a CD that claims to change your life while you are asleep – I believe that is tosh, designed to exploit the desperate. I'm banking on you being smarter than that. If that's what you're after, return this book to the bookshop before you crease the cover or break the spine and get your money back.

THE TIGER IN ACTION

Let me give you an example of the Tiger in action from my own experiences. I wanted to set a new British freediving record. I was (and still am) intrigued by the sport; I love being in the water and feel strangely at home by, on or in the sea. I had taken some lessons as a tourist on holiday. I believed that I could step up a gear and thought that that would be an excellent way of testing Taming Tigers theories. But I kept putting off making a commitment – that is the moment of making an unbreakable promise to myself – that I would attempt the record. The reason for the hesitation was fear – but not the fear that you might expect. I was not afraid of the depth or of the risks. I knew that

I would work slowly through the depths, becoming comfortable at each as I trained.

I run a successful business and I have a family. The fear was of striking a line through the first week of my diary for every month from February to August 2010. The first week would have to be spent in Egypt training in deep water. Time would have to be spent away from family and from work during a global downturn, for eight months. Would we be OK? Would we pay the bills? Would my competitors win work and a reputation that I should have won? Would my clients tolerate my absence? Decision time. The battle raged. Would the Tiger win? Intriguing. I had to dig deep and use the Ten Rules that I will shortly introduce you to in order to move past the Tiger and achieve the record.

Meet Your Tiger

Here's a question for you: how often do you dream about the great things that you would like to do with your life? Really. Think about it. Daily? Weekly?

How often do you have great ideas that you are quietly confident that you could implement? Ideas about:

- the people you would like to spend time with – developing and nurturing their talent and confidence

- the time you would like to spend creating the vision and the strategy

- the technological innovations you think should be explored

- the processes that need re-engineering

- the clients you think could benefit from your organisation's expertise

- the ways you could earn more money

- the staff that need to be inspired and communicated with and given the opportunity to contribute to the greater plan

- the work that you would like to delegate (that great Tiger-tickling leap of trust) to give you time to do this

What about the ideas to reduce environmental impact, to create more social good as a result of the business's activities, to lobby governments and create positive change for your industry, for society? What about the plan to strike out on your own – to prove that you can do it better, as you so often think you can?

Why is it so rare for you actually to do anything about it?

Have you ever found yourself in conversation – with yourself or with others – about your plan and heard yourself say something along the lines of:

- yes, it is a great idea and I could probably pull it off, but the wife/husband/partner would never let me go for it

- yes, but it might go wrong and then what would happen?

- some chance: people with my education/background don't get opportunities like that

- do you think for one moment that [insert name of senior person] would let me actually do something like that?

- that's just not how we do it round here – 'they' wouldn't go for it

- not until the mortgage is paid and the kids have left home

- I saw [insert name of person] try that x years ago – his career never recovered

- smarter men and women than me have tried and failed

- at my age? You can't teach an old dog new tricks

If you have ever said any of these things without first having a long conversation with the wife, husband or boss or the person who failed, without preparing the business plan for your innovation and presenting it quietly to trusted colleagues for advice, without questioning why, exactly, this is the 'way we do things around here', without working out what would happen if it went wrong and whether the risk is manageable and so on, then, yes: you *have* met your Tiger.

Your Tiger dictates that you avoid these preparatory explorations. It roars at you to stop. And the reason why you make the decision you make is fear. Fear of entering the unfamiliar. Fear that it may be possible. Fear that the effort may be uncomfortable. Fear that we may discover that there is no barrier except our Tiger. If we admit that then there would be nowhere to hide, would there? Time to get on with it or to admit that you are not big enough to try; and then have the decency to shut up about it. Ouch!

Why have I written *Taming Tigers*?

The Ten Rules for Taming Tigers will bring you greater success in many areas, certainly. But that is not why I have become fascinated with them, tested them rigorously and now locked myself away to write them down for you. Let me tell you the reason: we all have a great story to write, a path to follow, one that is unique to us. Most of us never find out what it is because of the Tiger's roar. That is a tragedy and I believe that *Taming Tigers* is one powerful route to avoiding that tragedy.

One day you and I may be in a nursing home somewhere. Let's go there together for a moment.

You're ninety years old. Your life is a little less frenetic. You have less paper left on which to write your story. You have less ink in your pen. And you won't be writing with the same vigour in those distant days as you can at the moment. Perhaps your biggest concerns as you wander off to breakfast in the morning will be: 'Will I win at cards today?' 'Did I remember to put any pants on?' and 'Do I smell of wee?'

Wouldn't it be devastating to look at that old character in the mirror – you – and say, after seventy or eighty years of sheer, incredible opportunity, 'What was the problem? Why didn't I wake up? Why didn't I do it? Why didn't I get involved?' The question in the nursing home will not be *Did I have a great story in me?* We all have a great story in us. It will be: *'Did I write my story or did I let my Tiger dictate my story to me?'*

What do you have to do today (that's right, *do* and *today* – wake up, it's happening now) to know that when you face that old man or woman in the mirror you can grin devilishly? To say, after eighty long years of opportunity and possibility: *'I lived! I got out there and made an impact. I made a difference. I lived my live to the full. I wrote my own great story. I loved, I won, I lost. There is nothing to regret. I was awake!'*

I have created and written down the Ten Rules for Taming Tigers because I firmly believe that each of us has a tremendous story to write and that these Ten Rules will help you to write it.

I believe that every person who looks back with regret and sadness at what might have been, who dies with their story unwritten, is a great loss to our collective story: to humanity and to the planet. The impact of people at their daily work is the single largest influence on both humanity and the planet. You have a part to play. A story to write. Your story.

And your story will touch many thousands of others.

I believe that there is a clear, identifiable difference between those who will look back at a great story and those who will look back full of regret, or perhaps still be playing the resentful, deluded victim.

One set tamed the Tiger. The others let the Tiger dictate their story to them.

Wake up! The Tiger has no teeth. It is a brilliant, powerful trick of the mind. Your mind. You are in charge of it. You can change it.

How can I be so sure that *Taming Tigers* will help you write your story?

The Ten Rules are different from self-help ideas because, before committing them to paper for you, I have tested them rigorously. I have tested them in my own business activities running the Taming Tigers group; in the boardrooms of major organisations; in schools; in my journey to the racetrack on horseback and in my quest to become Britain's deepest freediver. I will share my stories in this book to help you see how the rules can work. Clients of mine have also been generous in sharing their own stories, all motivated, solely, by the desire to pass on to you what they have learned and gained from the Ten Rules.

I've delivered Taming Tigers as a keynote presentation across the globe. I've been trusted as an adviser to hundreds of individuals and teams and boards within companies from all sectors in the twelve years since I established Taming Tigers. My team and I have refined the Ten Rules as a result of our experiences. Here are some of the realisations that I see time and time again when people are introduced to the Tiger:

- I now see that it's not because of my background/ education . . .

- I *do* have time to do these things – the Tiger stops me trusting and delegating!

- I can communicate effectively – the Tiger made me scared to try – it was easier to say 'I just can't'

- it's not the boss's fault after all. When I prepared carefully and I had a 'real' conversation with her – it was fine

- they actually *want* me to be a full-time leader – not to micromanage them – that'll make my life so much easier and more stimulating – but it's a hard habit to break

- I thought I had reached the top of my game – but I haven't, I had reached the extent of my imagination – I've just seen a whole new level to play in!

Taming Tigers is different because it does not attempt to hide the hard graft and scary moments associated with writing your story and creating your successes. No short cuts here. I have attempted to deal with reality, not what is 'nice' to hear. And that reality brings us deep satisfaction and lasting rewards that no quick fix can deliver.

There is one caveat, however. From this book knowledge is available – but not wisdom. Wisdom is not acquired by reading. Wisdom is what results when you incorporate this knowledge into your personal experience. You are the only one who can create that fusion and bring yourself greater wisdom. You have to experience your Tiger, experience facing up to it and, eventually, taming it. The sooner we start you off doing that, the more chance there is that your encounter with this book will lead to great adventures in your life – and not merely to another trophy on your bookshelf. Enjoy the ride!

What do riding on the racetrack and freediving have to do with you or with work?

The first thing to point out is that both of those challenges were far more mental than they were physical. Freediving is the only extreme sport in which adrenaline will kill you. A sudden panic at 100 metres means that you will use the oxygen in your system very quickly – far too quickly for you to make it to the surface before it runs out. A racehorse will detect any other animal pumping adrenaline on its back before the animal knows it has released adrenaline. Just think 'fear' and it'll bolt with you. Both sports are excellent ways of experimenting with how the mind and the body work and interact under pressure. But there are a great many other similarities with your challenge of moving forward in the workplace that have made them an excellent testing ground for the Ten Rules. Here is a selection:

1. Cold-calling influential strangers and asking for help with an innovative, risky project

2. Slowly building relationships with people who don't initially want to welcome you

3. Dealing with the fear of public, career-damaging failure

4. Dealing with a fear of real financial loss

5. Committing to a goal with no certainty as to its success – but with a personal cost attached

6. Creating a plan, changing it as you meet obstacles

7. Deciding upon new behaviours and sticking to those with discipline

8. Time management (I still had to pay the mortgage)

9. Juggling family commitments

10. Being creative and innovative about how to hit a goal that 'they all' said was not possible

11. Innovating (nobody had done either thing before from my starting point)

12. Building and motivating a team of people far wiser than me to support me

13. Keeping myself motivated to the end and through the down times

14. Being personally accountable for success

15. Having a wonderful, inspiring prize at stake, that is meaningful for you

Who Is writing your story? – you or the Tiger?

As we work together over the next hours, days or weeks, you will begin to understand the Tiger that you and your experiences have created much more clearly than you do at this stage. And as we work together, you will also begin to see the damage that the Tiger is doing and you will, very possibly, start to get angry.

Yes, I did say 'angry'. Anger isn't a taboo word. Understood and used properly, it can be a tremendous springboard to a new chapter in your story and a new approach to your work and wider life. As you begin to see the effect of the Tiger on the years that have passed so far – on the story that has been written to date, however fabulous and successful it is – you will see areas, perhaps small but none the less significant, where the Tiger has dictated and you have diligently written what it commanded. And that will create an emotion. Use it well.

I was taking some air on a lovely summer's afternoon having delivered a presentation to around a thousand people in Amsterdam. One of those attending the presentation was particularly keen to say hello and he followed me out on to the lawn. After saying some kind things about the presentation, he told me how jealous he was of me.

'Why?' I asked.

'Because I have always wanted to be a professional speaker and to inspire others for a living.'

'No, you haven't,' I replied.

He looked stunned. 'Yes, I have! I have always wanted to.'

'No, you haven't,' I said again. 'If you had always wanted to do that for a living you would be doing it. You are doing *exactly* what you want to do for a living.'

He was getting angry now. Clearly, I was supposed to have massaged his ego here.

'That's easy for you to say, you have a story to tell.'

'Sure, but I didn't when I started speaking. And many speakers don't use their personal story.'

'Yeah, but I guess it's different if you are a corporate lawyer first and make your pile before taking a risk on speaking.'

'Well, sorry to disappoint you, but I wasn't a good enough lawyer to have made any money by the age of thirty, which is when I changed tack!'

I gave him my number and an invitation to call whenever he wanted to ask me any questions on getting started in the career he had always wanted to pursue.

He never called, of course. Poor guy: the Tiger ate his story for tea.

Shall we be honest with each other as we journey together?

Honesty will be important during our time together over the coming days. I will be honest with you in this book. I will not write anything that I cannot back up from personal experience. If you are willing to be honest with yourself, you will see a change in yourself. You will meet yourself in a new way. You will wake up.

So let's be honest. If you truly believe that race, upbringing, religion, educational qualifications, gender, the mortgage, the wife/ husband/partner, the kids, the boss, the organisation you work for or the country you live in are the reasons why you are 'unable' to do the things that you want to do, then you need to tame your Tiger. Perhaps today, this very day, is the first day of your life, the one on which you will choose to start being honest about it.

Shall we end this section together with some truly courageous honesty and face another taboo subject?

You will eventually die. I will eventually die. That is the correct starting point for our journey together. Only from that starting point can we begin to give ourselves permission truly to live; to write our own story. Because from that perspective, my fear of missing out on a few weeks' money to try for a free-diving record, or your fear of putting into practice your innovative plan at work in case you publicly fail, become quite laughable, don't they? What are we actually worried about?

What are we waiting for?

Let's live!

The Ten Rules for Taming Tigers

The British record is mine for the taking. Or is it?

Looking down from the cliff top on to the diving platform reassures me that I am at the right place. It bobs in the ocean with a small crane-like structure on the top. That is where I will be going on this bright February day. Once there, I will take my first journey into the ocean on the sled.

'Jim?'

I turn from the sea to the two men approaching me.

'I am Marco but everybody calls me Rasta. This is Andrea.'

Marco is wearing shades and long, heavy dreadlocks hang from the back of his head. Andrea's bare torso is shaped like a perfect inverted triangle and he is taller than Marco. Both are flashing big Italian grins at me and two hands are extended. So these are the guys who run the Only One Apnea Centre, the premier freediving training centre on the Red Sea. Many world and national records have been set here (Andrea himself holds four national records). The world's finest have dived here and Only One has a reputation as a record 'factory'. Now I'm here to attempt to follow in their footsteps. Hmm.

I've not met Rasta and Andrea before but I have emailed them about the plan to get to 101 metres and they have agreed to help me. Paula, Rasta's girlfriend and the centre manager, takes me through some paperwork. I change into a wetsuit and within fifteen minutes we have walked down the steps to the base of the cliff and out to the end of the pontoon that floats inches above the coral reef. The ocean is beneath us and the platform is a 100-metre swim away.

I put my mask on, slide into the water and instinctively look below to check on the sealife. I do not place much faith in omens but some cannot be ignored. At first it looks like a small submarine beneath me, then I realise that I am looking at the dappled markings of a seven-metre-long whale shark. I take a deep breath and dive to her.

She lets me swim with her at a depth of about fifteen metres. We make direct eye contact and time slows. Now the record feels as if it is mine to claim.

Rasta and Andrea join me with the huge, harmless shark until she cruises away and we give up the chase. Training plans in the water are always subject to immediate rescheduling when wildlife comes to pay a visit.

A freedive warm-up begins with quiet time spent bobbing on the water, face down, breathing through a snorkel. Time to calm the mind and the body. Time to slow the heartbeat after the swim. When we are ready, we take it in turns to pull ourselves down the line to around seven metres and there we hang, holding the rope and our breath. This is to awaken the mammalian dive reflex. We all have this. It is as ancient and as beyond our control as the breathing reflex itself. It prepares the body to dive. Proof of our aquatic antecedents, it links us with dolphins and whales. As the dive reflex kicks in, each dive becomes longer and more enjoyable.

'Ready to try the sled, Jim?' Andrea is speaking.

Yes. Very ready.

We are using a tandem sled today. Two divers can descend together and I will be diving with Andrea beside me. Andrea will be checking that I am comfortable with the rate of descent and working the sled until I learn how to do it alone. Rasta will be on the platform above, releasing the sled into the water.

The sled is a metal construction with all sorts of arms coming off its central, hollow spine. Through this central spine the rope passes. The sled is attached to the crane arm overhanging the platform and is weighted with lead. When Rasta yanks on a rope, the attachment is released. The sled then falls into the ocean and sinks at an average speed of 1.6 metres per second along the fixed line. As we descend, our suits and bodies will begin to compress. This will reduce our buoyancy and the speed will start to increase.

On this tandem sled we do not descend feet first but knees first. Positioned beside each other, our knees hook over a bar at the bottom of the structure. We loop our outside arm over a second bar at shoulder level and use that hand to pinch our noses in order to equalise against the increasing pressure. Our inside arm goes round the other diver's shoulder. On the top of the structure is the lift bag and the air tank that will inflate it. The lift bag brings us back to the surface.

Andrea and I arrange ourselves on the sled. Andrea tells me that all I have to do is equalise my ears as we descend, unhook my knees at the bottom and hold on with my hands to the bar my knees are wrapped around. He will deal with the lift bag.

'If you have any problems at all you touch my shoulder and I'll stop the sled – we'll come up immediately.'

'OK.'

We 'breathe up' together for two minutes. My heartbeat is rising rather than falling. Not a great start. I have no idea what to expect so I am feeling as I do at the beginning of a roller-coaster ride: apprehensive and alert. The state of my head is asking my adrenals for a flight or fight hit – just when I don't need it.

Rasta gives us a thirty-second count. I begin to inhale for my final breath at fifteen seconds. I nod at Andrea who nods at Rasta.

Clunk.

My eyes are immediately beneath the water, adjusting. My ears are immediately hurting. I have never equalised them at this rate before – it is a constant effort. My body is rippling under the force of the passing water and the pressure beneath my knees as the bar pulls us into the depths is far greater than I had anticipated.

I have freedived and scuba dived before but never attached to a weight. Now I am being dragged into the sea and I am unprepared for how alien and how dangerous this feels. My stomach and chest start to go into some sort of spasm. It is like hiccups mixed with a gagging reflex – very unpleasant and causing a panicky feeling. I struggle to persuade myself that there is no danger except the danger of my head losing its calm. I have learned this skill from speaking on stage and riding racehorses but now I am on the edge of panicking.

Clang.

We are at the bottom of the line. I detach my knees and hold on to the upper bar, watching as Andrea opens the valve and fills the airbag. We begin to rise then clang back down on to the bottom plate.

What's happening?

The spasms continue and I can hear myself making a strange noise in my throat. Andrea releases more air and we begin to rise. The spasms cease as the pressure decreases. The surface is approaching very rapidly now so I release the sled and decrease the speed of ascent. The sun and the platform burst into sight and Rasta's shades come into view. His face is wearing a big grin.

'Welcome back, Jim! How was it?'

'Er. It was different. I need to get used to it. How deep did we go?'

'Fifteen metres! Congratulations!'

Shit! Fifteen metres?

I guess if it were easy everybody would be doing it. But how can I possibly get from here to 100 metres? I have just experienced an increase in pressure to two and a half times the atmospheric pressure that we all experience at sea level. At 101 metres that pressure will increase to eleven times atmospheric pressure. My lungs have just halved in size. They will be going to an eleventh of their normal size in the record attempt and there will be other big differences as well. Mentally, I will be a long way from home down there – that will take a far steadier head to avoid the adrenaline release that I have just experienced. Then there is the effect of pressure on my ears to cope with.

Who the hell do I think I am even to contemplate this?

This record is certainly not mine for the taking. It will take more than the appearance of my whale shark to bring me good luck. This will be a real test for all of the Ten Rules also. Fear and discomfort are telling me not to write this chapter of my story.

Why bother?

Why bother?

I want to take this test. I want to learn more about the Ten Rules and test them again. I want to know who I am and I want to get closer to the sea. This is my story. I won't sleep through it. I won't run away from it. I won't let the Tiger dictate it.

The Ten Rules for Taming Tigers

It's time now to introduce you to the Ten Rules that have helped businesses and individuals all over the world to achieve extraordinary results; the Ten Rules that took me to the racetrack and to 101 metres under the sea; and the Ten Rules that will help you, if you dare to commit to the adventure, to do things you never thought you could:

Rule 1   Act boldly today – time is limited
Rule 2   Rewrite your Rulebook – challenge it hourly
Rule 3   Head in the direction of where you want to arrive,
         every day
Rule 4   It's all in the mind
Rule 5   The tools for Taming Tigers are all around you
Rule 6   There is no safety in numbers
Rule 7   Do something scary every day
Rule 8   Understand and control your time to create change
Rule 9   Create disciplines – do the basics brilliantly
Rule 10 Never, never give up

Simple? Oh yes. Easy? No – if they were we would all be following them. And we are not. That is one of your great advantages – if you have the courage to act to write your own story. Most people will not be following these rules.

The rules are placed in a particular order and they are in that order for a reason. But they are not part of a linear process and it is important to understand that. These are not 'steps to success'. Be suspicious of anybody who claims to offer this holy grail.

In time, you will learn that in a tricky Tiger-infested moment you may go with whichever of the rules helps you. For now, though, begin to act upon them in the order in which they are presented.

To give structure to the rules and the process that, over time, they will take you through, both the rules and the remainder of this book are divided into four parts:

Part One   The Integrity Rules: Rules 1, 2 and 3
Part Two   The Leadership Rules: Rules 4, 5 and 6
Part Three The Change Rules: Rules 7, 8 and 9
Part Four   The Growth Rule: Rule 10
Epilogue   Tiger-Free Living

Let's have a look at each of these parts.

Part One The Integrity Rules

Integrity n. *wholeness; soundness; steadfastness*

The Integrity Rules do not mean I'm suggesting you lack integrity in the usual sense. They are asking you to look at whether you act in integrity with your true Self – your values, meaning, purpose, desire to connect authentically with others and your need to grow and develop, or whether you are acting on the Tiger's instructions and avoiding fear and discomfort – to the detriment of your true desires.

Are you doing what you want to do with your time on earth? Are you living or working towards the kind of life that you would like to be living? Or is the Tiger dictating your story to you? The Integrity Rules will help you to decide and bring you closer to self-sovereignty.

Rule 1: Act boldly today – time is limited

Rule 1 will ask you to get started. Not plan it. Not Google it. Not buy a book or talk to your friends about it. *But to start it.* And to start it as if you mean it. If you are not sure what to start, it asks you to act boldly today to find out.

Whether you are a CEO or studying for your first school exams, when I ask you to start it like you mean it, you will have to confront why you haven't started so far, and you'll meet the Tiger. That is where the integrity process begins. When you lure the Tiger out of the long grass and into the open and take a long look at him, you will realise how well you know him. You'll realise how closely you have lived together for so long in apparent harmony. Now you have self-awareness. Now you can take charge and move towards integrity. Now you can act in the way you wish to act and not in the way which avoids the Tiger.

Now there is no need to find subtle excuses for inaction: Now integrity is possible.

Now you'll dare to wonder, my fellow Tiger tamer, what adventures might begin if you dared to begin the task of taming him. Today!

Rule 2: Rewrite your Rulebook – challenge it hourly

Rule 2 confronts you with some of your very favourite strategies for remaining out of integrity. The rational sounding, intellectually justifiable fictions that we perceive to be real until we are inspired to challenge them. Fictions shared perhaps by millions, and almost certainly pandered to by friends and family alike.

Rule 2 demands honesty to yourself about the Tiger and the strategies that you are using to avoid meeting the Tiger. All the carefully constructed rules you have about how life works that save you from trying new things, from growing, from being authentic, being yourself. Beginning to notice this, and learning strategies to overcome it, is the purpose of Rule 2.

Rule 3: Head in the direction of where you want to arrive, every day

Now we do some planning and take some steps along the road to only you know where. This is Rule 3. And this is still a part of the integrity process, for two reasons.

First, Rule 3 is about deciding upon and committing to arrive at a place that you yourself and not your Tiger want to arrive at – a place in integrity with who you are and what you want to become. Second, you will be asked to commit to real action with real dates. Action and deadlines will bring you face to face with your Tiger. They will also bring you closer every day to the story that you want to be writing. Closer to integrity.

Integrity is only the starting place for our journey together. We have merely brought on provisions, plotted our course and hoisted our sails. Practical and real though those are, we'll need to sail our little craft when the skies darken and the waves crash over us to the jeers of our detractors. We'll need the second set of rules for that.

Part Two The Leadership Rules

Leadership n. *derivative of leader*
Leader n. *one who leads*
Lead v. *to be in charge; to influence towards action or belief; to draw a person or animal along*

You do not have to be in a leadership position to use the Ten Rules, although all of them will assist you in becoming a better leader of others, whatever your job title. The Leadership Rules, Rules 4, 5 and 6, are primarily about taking the lead in your own life, a prerequisite to successfully taking the lead in anybody else's. To truly take a lead in your own life, it's necessary to recognise and defeat a whole new level of Tiger attack:

The Tiger that our interaction with others will unleash upon us.

How do we prepare for leadership at work? How do we ensure that we, and not the Tiger, are in control, that it is our hand on the tiller and not the Tiger's paw? As we regain control of the rudder, we start to earn the right to lead others. Consider this question: 'What makes you think people would want to follow you?' Would the following feature in your answer?

- I have the ability to be accountable to myself – to choose my own story and set about writing it rather than allowing fear in the moment of decision or action to drive me off course (**Rule 4**).

- I have the confidence and humility to call upon others to assist me, to inspire them to do so and the discipline to treat them right in the process (**Rule 5**).

- I have the integrity of knowing that my actions and decisions are guided by my carefully considered view of what is right and not by fear of the harsh judgement of others (**Rule 6**).

- I have the ability to stand apart from the crowd, exposed, when required to do so – but not to do it just for its own sake (**Rule 6**).

All these attributes can be seen, for example, in a well-adjusted child – but they are less frequently seen in behaviour at work. Yet in the New Economy they are commercially vital, not just 'morally' desirable – and at all levels of the organisation.

A lack of the above traits would bring about early casualties in the leadership credibility race. Leadership 'behaviours' flow from an integrity, a state of mind – from the ability to lead oneself. They do not flow from a list in an MBA textbook or from reading a poster of required values and behaviours in the canteen.

Rule 4: It's all in the mind

Rule 4 equips you to do battle against the 'voices' in your mind. These voices encourage each of us to diminish our ambition when we are contemplating the correct course or to change direction when we are under pressure in the moment of performance. Both voices, which I will introduce to you later as the Headmaster and the Saboteur, are the work of the Tiger.

If we cannot master the conversation in our head, we cannot master our decisions. And we write our story by making decisions, taking action and receiving a result.

Rule 5: The tools for Taming Tigers are all around you

Being able to work with and lead others in order to reach our goals is essential. Little that is truly worthwhile can be accomplished without the assistance of others. In Rule 5 we look at this in depth, consider why we are generally discouraged by the Tiger from asking assistance of others and seek to overcome that fear.

Whoever it is who can most help you in your quest is waiting for your call. Can you afford to shy away from making contact? Are you really leading the creation of your story if the Tiger denies you access to your allies and mentors?

Rule 6: There is no safety in numbers

The greatest jockeys are in the grandstand – not on the race-course. There we find the people who can hold forth for hours on how a horse should have been ridden. Not that they have ever sat on a horse.

All of our heroes were on the track, however. In Rule 6, the personal leadership quality of being able to filter the opinion of others – comes to the fore. Will you stay in the grandstand, unexposed and safe, expressing opinions that you will never invite yourself to act upon or to follow through to triumph? Or will you work through the Tiger's roar to master that tricky skill and be able to ignore the noise of the famous 'water-cooler conversation' in the office? Will you get out onto the track and write your own story?

Now we have to make the new way a habit – to create a change in ourselves over the long term. Rules 7, 8 and 9 are there to help us to do exactly that.

PART THREE THE CHANGE RULES .

Change v. tr. *to make different; to swap; to refresh*
Change v. intr. *to undergo alteration*

Do you want to have a single, open and honest conversation with your boss or develop an open working relationship? Do you want to hit your targets or numbers this month or consolidate and consistently hit stretch? Do you want to inspire the team at the next monthly meeting or do you want consistently to be an inspiration to your ever more successful team?

I want you to feel you can stay in the exciting new place, even move forward from it. I want you to feel confident that you can create a long-term change and not a momentary flash of inspired action. You'll need consolidation and consistency and the next three rules, the Change Rules, for that.

Rule 7: Do something scary every day

Dealing with our fear and discomfort is a learned skill. Rule 7 is all about practising this new skill. Deliberately placing yourself in situations that create small-scale fear and discomfort until the rise of emotion, experienced physically and mentally, becomes familiar – as is the way that you deal with it and act in spite of it.

Your reaction to fear is likely to determine who you will meet and speak to in life. It is likely, therefore, to influence directly the genetic makeup of your children. This matters!

Dealing with fear and discomfort alone won't do the job. We will need a whole new relationship with time if we are to consolidate the change and make Tiger taming a new habit and truly write our own story. What is time but the paper we write that story upon?

Rule 8: Understand and control your time to create change

Rule 8 is not about 'time management'. We have a deep relationship with time but we rarely examine this relationship and very often it is an unhealthy one. Rule 8 is about trans-forming that relationship. Once you have a healthy relationship with time, it is possible to exert control over it. Once you exert control over your time, you can begin to create a Tiger-free way of thinking, of acting and of gaining results.

We don't 'spend' this scarce resource of time in doing things. We 'invest' it doing things. It always brings a return. A life spent watching daytime TV, eating pizza and drinking whisky is invested – it brings a very definite return. What's your investment plan?

If you're investing your time in writing a great story – the story that you have chosen and that will have you leaping out of bed tomorrow morning with a mixture of excitement and healthy apprehension – you'll find Rule 9 a great help.

Rule 9: Create disciplines – do the basics brilliantly

Olympic athletes have disciplines for themselves. They have disciplines around training, around diet, around mental toughness and, usually, around the order in which they will put their kit on. The basics and disciplines are there to enable them to go through the necessary level of discomfort to achieve the prize. Without the disciplines, they do not know the standard that they should hold themselves to in order to attain their prize. They provide clarity. Without defining the disciplines and basics of elite performance, they do not know the standard that they should hold themselves to in order to attain their prize.

Have you ever defined the standard that you wish to hold yourself to?

What is the one thing that, if you did it consistently brilliantly every single day, would make the biggest impact on your chosen story in twelve months?

Think about it. We'll come back to that.

Part Four The Growth Rule

Growth n. *the process of increasing in size; the process of developing physically, mentally, or spiritually; the process of increasing in amount, value, or importance; increase in economic activity or value*

Rule 10 is the Growth Rule. It's about keeping your promises to yourself and to others; it's about finishing; achieving and succeeding; growing in confidence. Seeing it through to the end requires us to go through the stage of fear and discomfort. We cannot do that without growing.

When you embark upon longer-term projects, you have to keep going to keep your promise. That is tough. To achieve something, you have to *do* things and you have to *finish* doing them. That is, you have to carry on doing things until that thing is complete. Not completing has a consequence: 'Fear is temporary; failure is forever'.

This is another area in which *Taming Tigers* moves heavily and determinedly away from traditional self-help. A lot more courage and sweat than 'short cut' and 'affirmation' is required to tame a Tiger and create a permanent change, but the result is all the more exciting and rewarding for it as Tiger tamers around the world have discovered and are still discovering.

The Growth Rule is this:

Rule 10: Never, never give up

Epilogue: Tiger-Free Living

To strive to live authentically at work, to have a Tiger-free career, involves an holistic approach. In this introduction to living Tiger-free we will explore what that might mean with regard to your wider activities. This is not a guide to living your life. I'll leave that to the self-help gurus. This is about identifying areas that impact on your ability to tame your Tigers at work – and about the rewards and achievements that are to be gained from living Tiger-free.

Part One

The Integrity Rules

Rule 1

Act Boldly Today – Time Is Limited

'What have you ever done to tame your Tiger, Jim?'

The second delivery of my motivational speech had been going well, until I heard these words. The problem was that my heckler was the 'general manager' – the big boss of the five hundred people who were all staring at me expectantly.

I told him about leaving law, setting up my own business, the results that we had achieved with clients. He didn't think that was enough.

'Well, what do you have in mind?' I asked. It's a question I would probably not ask a heckler now that I have a little more experience on stage.

'If you don't mind my saying, you are quite short.' I did mind this, but my Tiger was roaring quite loudly, so I stayed quiet.

'And if you don't mind my adding, you are slightly overweight.' I really *did* mind this. I thought that such feedback was better suited to a one-to-one session.

'So I'll bet you a pound that you can't become a jockey, and ride in a televised race under official Jockey Club Rules, within twelve months.'

I was gripping the lectern quite hard to stay upright at this point.

'That's ridiculous.'

'Why?'

'Because I can't ride a horse.'

His face broke into the kind of evil smirk that the baddies have in the movies when they realise they have the hero trapped.

'In that case, it will be a really interesting Tiger to tame, won't it?'

A strange electrical current ran through my mind. He's bloody right. It will be extremely interesting. It will teach me about the Ten Rules; it'll teach me about myself. It'll either prove the rules are spot-on and give them real credibility or it'll show me that I am wrong and that I should kill them off.

If I couldn't achieve something extraordinary with the Ten Rules, how could I expect anybody else even to try?

Could it be done? Could a total sporting disaster at school, now overweight and completely unfit, ride in a horserace, live on TV in a year's time using just the Ten Rules for Taming Tigers?

I had to find out the answer. I grinned back, the way the hero does when he knows he has just the right gadget up his sleeve to help him escape the villain's clutches. I told him I would agree on the condition that I could have one month's prep time to research and to put a plan in place.

He smiled. We shook hands. A new adventure began.

Reality check: on the way home that evening I was feeling pretty good. I had left the house that morning an overweight businessman, off to give a presentation to a bunch of sales-people. I was coming home as a man who, this time next year, would be riding in his first televised horserace.

You never can tell what a difference a day will make!

But things began to look different as I stared out of the train window. I went to a large London comprehensive school and there were no riding stables there that I had ever noticed. Sometimes, after a particularly riotous lunch break, there hadn't even been many usable toilets in the place. I'd been to the races only twice in my life. On both occasions it had been in a corporate hospitality area, and on both occasions I'd enjoyed the hospitality just a little too much to focus on the horses.

I knew nothing about racing. I knew nobody in racing. I could not take time off work to achieve the goal – I had a family and a mortgage to pay. I had no spare cash to throw at the challenge.

My spirits took another knock when I got home, opened a cold beer, fired up my laptop and started to learn about jockeys. Did you know that they get up at five o'clock most mornings and are at work by about six? And – get this – they do that six days a week, twelve months of the year. Winter included!

Did you know that flat-racing jockeys go into their races weighing between seven and a half and nine stone? Now, I didn't own a set of scales at this phase in my life. I did like beer and I really loved curries. I did also have a dim recollection of having weighed in at around twelve stone the last time I had had a medical.

I had to put 25 per cent of myself somewhere else – and I had no idea where to put it!

I learned that jockeys are very fit. This came as a blow as I thought that the horses did all the work. I hadn't done any exercise at all since I had left school seventeen years previously.

I learned that jockeys usually sat on their first horses somewhere between the ages of six and twelve months. Try as I might, I couldn't find any stories of jockeys who had started learning to ride at the age of thirty-five and raced within twelve months. Not encouraging.

By now the Rulebook was working its magic. Beautifully designed to keep me safe, it started to place rational sounding obstacles in my way. I had started a battle that would rage for the next year.

The battle with the Tiger had begun.

Rule 1: Act boldly today – time is limited

Let's cut straight to it. The real difference between those people who look back from the nursing home with a big happy grin, knowing that they wrote their story, and those who look back with resentment and disappointment, knowing that the Tiger dictated their story to them, is that the first lot acted. They stopped thinking and they did something. Do you agree?

We wait too long trying to get the idea right before we act upon it – not staking the company on it or anything as drastic as that – just before we act to explore it. We don't need to get it right or make it perfect. Involve others, get it into the conversation; get advice; get encouragement; accept that there is no such thing as 'right'. Do something different today to explore the idea.

Act!

This all sounds blindingly obvious, of course. So let's explore why it is so rare that we see bold action. Let's also discover whether you are going to take any action today to tame your Tiger, or whether you are going to nod sagely at the blindingly obvious advice, ignore it, and then wonder why you achieved no great change as a result of reading *Taming Tigers*.

Think of the biggest problem you need to solve at work. It does not have to be within your job description, but you want to get it solved. Maybe it is about dealing with non-performing members of your team. Maybe it is about dealing with glitches in the process. Perhaps it is about improving the way your customers are handled. Perhaps it involves taking your bold and innovative ideas for product development through a process designed to prepare them for a presentation to the board. Perhaps it is how to get you a new job or a pay rise.

Now think of a reasonable timescale in which you could achieve this.

Turn the book over for a moment and really think it through.

Now that you have an outcome you want to create and a

reasonable timescale in which to create it, I'd like to make things more interesting. What if I offered you US $10 million to create that outcome in *a third of the time* that you had in mind? How does that change things for you? What is the bold action that would make you put down this book and get up from your chair now in order to do it? Where would you drive to? Who would you telephone? What aeroplane would you board in order to secure your life-altering sum of money?

Stop reading and put the book down.

Think it through. Really. What would you do?

I have some good news and some bad news for you. First, the bad news: I'm not about to part with any of my hard-earned cash.

Now the good news. You don't need my cash in order to perform the bold action that you have just created.

Outside family, our work is the most exciting adventure of our lives. This is the area in which we can put ourselves to the test, make our mark upon the world and leave a huge positive impact on other people.

You don't need a bribe from me to make your next working day live up to that promise of it being your adventure.

Now act.

Now!

Rule 1 tells you to act boldly today. You now know the bold action you need to undertake in order to make an immediate difference to something that needs fixing at work. The timescale in the Rule is 'today'. We agreed at the outset that this was blindingly obvious. At that stage you might even have considered asking for your money back for such trite advice.

So put the book down again and go and do it.

Now!

How did it go?

If you did it, congratulations – you are out of the starting stalls.

You didn't do it?

Why?

Ahhh, I see.

Yes, yes. I understand. We all do. Everybody feels the same way about this. But some people push through that.

The excuses that you are coming up with are simply the Tiger at work. No, it's not too late in the day. Yes, you could find the number if you tried. Yes, this is a great book – but it will still be here after the call and it will mean all the more to you by that stage as we'll both be Tiger fighters then.

Congratulations. You have met your Tiger. Is it familiar now?

Now that you've met the Tiger, push through the fear and discomfort that it is creating in you and do it.

Stop diluting it. Stop doing deals with yourself about doing an even bolder act tomorrow. Do it now. Tomorrow will not be any easier. It will be the same, but with the added knowledge that you wimped out today.

How's the pulse?

Have you done it?

No? Ring a friend! Ring a friend now. A real one, a bold one, one who does things and doesn't just make you feel good by offering platitudes. Ask that friend if he or she can see any reason why you should not do this bold action now.

Ring them now.

Are you writing this sentence of your story or is the Tiger?

Why did you buy this book if not to tame your Tiger? You can buy a nice self-help book with a hypnotic CD if you want to feel warm and fuzzy. Taming Tigers *is about being ALIVE. Are you up for that?*

Once you have completed the bold action, feel free to turn the page. If you wish, log on to the Campus at tamingtigers.com and watch the film entitled 'I don't want to do my bold action!' and I will give you more encouragement.

This is your story – you are about to write a new sentence of it, and who knows where that may take you? That is truly exciting.

Wake up and do it now!

Why am I suggesting that you 'act boldly today'?

Rule 1 brings you five big advantages:

1. It shows you that only the Tiger is stopping you

2. It interrupts your habitual patterns of Tiger appeasement and exposes them to your own gaze

3. It takes you to commitment

4. It often delivers a bold result and causes your story to jump forward

5. It helps you to Wake Up!

In the rest of this chapter, I'll take you through these five advantages.

Rule 1 shows you that only the Tiger is stopping you

When you consider the bold action and you hesitate, you increase your self-awareness. Notice the conversation in your head. Only the Tiger is stopping you. You may imagine all sorts of horrors – that is the Rulebook, the Tiger's great creation – not reality. We will come to the Rulebook shortly.

Be honest. There was nothing stopping you from taking the bold, courageous action you thought of earlier except the Tiger, was there?

Rule 1 is a particularly important and testing rule for me personally. I don't like it – but I need it. It requires me to look in the mirror, to question myself, dance with my demons and admit my insecurities. If I do that work honestly and courageously, I end up having to take the action. When I have finally managed to take my bold action, the result has always been wonderful and the process less scary than I had anticipated. I am confident that you will find the same thing.

After we have the self-awareness to recognise that the Tiger is the only thing stopping us from acting, we know where the enemy is. Once we can recognise the Tiger, we can begin to tame it.

Rule 1 and interrupting patterns

You and I are both creatures of habit. Like a meandering river, we both choose the path that causes us less pain on a daily basis. We notice this no more than a river notices the boulder it has flowed around for millennia. Unlike the river, we can clamber over, tunnel under or smash our boulders.

Rule 1 interrupts our habitual patterns of behaviour. It also makes us aware of these patterns – yet more valuable self-awareness.

Many of our patterns were established in our teens. Often they were vital survival patterns then and are therefore very uncomfortable and scary to change. For that reason, many of us will never address these teenage survival patterns. Once you are aware of them you can reflect honestly on the cost of these habits to you and on the prizes you can win by making a change.

Once your patterns are interrupted and awareness raised, they are more difficult to follow. Once you interrupt the pattern with a bold action (usually involving another human being) this act alone changes things. Other energies are involved. The thing is now bigger than you – deadlines and actions start to be agreed upon, if only for an exploratory conversation. The thing has life outside your head. You no longer control it and therefore your patterns, preferences and habits are of secondary importance to you.

Experiment with interrupting your patterns more. Take a different mode of transport. Use a different supermarket. Introduce some random pattern interruptions and see what you get back. The Tiger is a creature of habit. Habit is sleep-inducing.

You and I are in the waking-up business now.

Acting boldly to get to the racetrack

On the morning after my internet research about the racing bet, I took a bold action. I rang the only person in the world I knew with an interest in horseracing, a man called Stephen. You have to remember that I knew nothing about horseracing. I told Stephen about the bet and asked him for his thoughts.

'I don't think you'll like it very much.'

'Why not?'

'Well, imagine you are standing on the seat of your motorbike. A motorbike that is three times higher than normal. Oh, and you're not allowed to hold on to the handles of the handlebars – you hold on to the middle of the handlebars. Then somebody, not you, twists the throttle round to thirty-five miles per hour and you're off.'

'Hmm. Go on . . .'

'Well, after a while you'll need to speed this bike up a bit if you're going to win the race.'

'Speed it up?' I asked doubtfully.

'Yes. So you start shoving the handlebars to and fro with your hands and moving your backside up and down until you get up to about thirty-eight miles per hour. Then you take one hand off and start waving it around furiously with a heavily padded "stick" in it to keep that speed up until the end of the race.'

'That doesn't sound safe.'

'It's not.'

'So what about Health and Safety regulations? They can't just let people go out and do dangerous things like that on TV. Will I get a protective jacket? A full-face helmet with a visor if I'm going to stand on the seat of a motorbike at that speed?'

'No. You'll get a silk jacket, which you wear over a flimsy body protector. You'll get a skullcap, too, but, to be absolutely honest, that's not much help in a serious fall – especially if you get kicked.'

'Did you say kicked?'

'Oh, that can happen if you fall off, for sure.'

'Oh. Then do the saddles have safety belts fitted to stop you falling?'

'No. And you won't want to be staying on it if there's a collision. You want to be thrown well clear.'

'Do I? At what speed did you say?'

'Around thirty-eight miles per hour. But think about it. There might be fourteen horses each weighing half a ton and each bringing that weight down hard against the turf through their four legs – each of which has a nasty sharp metal shoe on it. If you go and fall off you want to be thrown as far away from that as possible.'

'Do I?'

'Oh yes.'

'OK. Thanks, Stephen. Bye.'

'Bye.'

So that was a good conversation, then. Much better.

Rule 1 and commitment

A commitment is a promise to ourselves or others. Making a promise requires a decision. As we know, the process of making a decision involves meeting the Tiger.

You and I both know that nothing we have achieved in our lives was done without commitment. But how do we reach this mystical moment of commitment? The moment when reverse gear is taken away and we decide that we will go forward. We remain uncertain of how we will do it, but we decide that we will be responsible for ensuring that the thing is done.

It is in this moment that your life changes. These moments have changed our world. Alexander Fleming committed to bringing penicillin to the attention of the public. John F. Kennedy committed to putting a man on the moon. They were just people, too. They had Tigers.

This is the crux of it. This is one of the most important

paragraphs in this book. *How do we reach commitment?* The answer is that commitment flows from a bold action. The bold action does not follow a moment of commitment.

Read that again. Have a little think. Do you agree?

Commitment gets things done. The bold action brings us towards commitment.

Let me explain how the bold action brings commitment (and not the other way around) by sharing with you the story of how I started my journey to the racetrack. I now know that I did not commit to becoming a jockey when I took the bet. I committed a couple of weeks later. When I took the bet, I had burned no bridges; I had made no irreversible change, I had reverse gear available. Then the bold action led me to shake hands with a woman called Gee Armytage and we made a commitment to each other. That changed everything . . .

COMMITTING TO THE RACING CHALLENGE

A couple of days after my bet, I found all twelve stone of me sitting next to a sprightly Sir Keith Mills, founder of Air Miles and Nectar, yachtsman and soon to become one of the architects of the London 2012 Olympic bid. As I tucked into a portion of trifle, he asked me what I was up to at the moment. I told him. He began to chortle. Then he realised that the idea of this twelve-stone trifle-scoffer becoming a jockey was so entertaining that he called the table to silence to tell everybody.

'How long have you been riding?' one of the other guests fired back.

'I've been pony-trekking twice,' I answered.

This really hit their funny spots. I was getting pretty keen for the speeches to start.

A year later, once I had had my first ride, I contacted Keith to tell him. He was generous in his congratulations and I was very pleased to have removed the monkey that I placed on my own back that evening. I had not intended my naïve answer to Keith to be a bold action, but it turned out to be one. The reaction of the table helped me immensely.

I acted boldly that evening by leaving the remainder of my trifle uneaten. Ouch! And I went on a diet from that very moment. I ate fruit only until lunchtime. I refused all biscuits in client meetings and I substituted a walk in the evening for my usual dessert.

I also decided that night that I would have to face up quickly to the other big scary truth. The thought of getting on to a horse terrified me.

'What are your riding goals?' the woman asked as I booked my first riding lesson. I liked her style.

'I'm going to be riding under Jockey Club Rules on the race-track in twelve months.' I was booked in for the following day.

I was sure that I could detect a frisson of excitement as I arrived at the yard the next day. The girls were clearly waiting for someone interesting and seemed to be mistaking me for that person. They started looking a little doubtful the moment I stepped out of the car. It occurred to me later that jockeys generally have a less full figure than I did. Jockeys usually wear britches and riding boots rather than Wellington boots and jeans, too.

'We've all been looking forward to meeting you.' My attractive teacher is beaming at me – I like being a jockey already. 'Tell me, what have you been doing? Where do you ride? Who's your teacher?'

'It's my first day on a horse today!'

I don't know the name of the animal I was supposed to ride that day. He has become known as Trigger in my mind. He let out a whinny of contempt as he was led back into his box and Dobbin was brought out to take his place. The girls got back to their jobs around the yard and I didn't even get a farewell wave after my lesson – which took place at a steady walk.

The following Friday I was in the pub with some friends. As we swapped stories of our weeks I mentioned the bet. Eyes widened.

'So what's the bold action you've done?'

I told them about the trifle, the fruit, the absence of biscuits, the walks and the riding lesson. They were unimpressed.

'That's not bold!'

'I was hungry – and the horse was big – it felt pretty bold.'

'No. Half the country is on a diet and most seven-year-old girls have had a pony riding lesson.'

I cleverly switched the onus back to them. 'What do you suggest then?'

'Obvious – ring up racehorse trainers – get one to take you on and teach you.'

Maybe not so clever.

I don't know how you feel about cold-calling busy and important people who are central to a multimillion-pound industry and asking them for help. I didn't like the thought much. My Tiger was roaring.

Racehorse trainers may be a lot of things – entrepreneurs, salesmen and women, business people, employers, nurturers of talent, animal experts, logistics managers, race readers and tacticians. Idiots they are not.

'Well, I wish you luck, Jim, and you're welcome to come and visit us, have a look about and grab a broom if you like. But it would take a couple of years before I'd be comfortable putting you on to one of my horses.'

That was one of the more polite answers I received. The message was that I was too old, too heavy and I couldn't ride a horse – let alone a racehorse. I decided to ring the Jockey Club and the Racing Schools. I got the same answer there. Nobody was able to tell me why the age limit was there. Nobody wanted to question it either.

This was a very interesting week for the Ten Rules and for the Tiger tamer himself. It was the week when I began to become committed. Where did the commitment come from? It came from emotion. It came from getting way outside my comfortable, habitual area of operating and seeing and realising that I could interact with this world. Currently, I was interacting on their terms. *Would it be possible to change those terms?*

Emotion was also being generated by the off-hand, negative response I received. That had an interesting effect on me. It made me want to prove them wrong.

Something else important was happening. They were giving me the same answer. I knew from working in industry that when one hears the same answer from a group of people as to why something can't be done, the Rulebook is at work. The beliefs and assumptions that grow up in individuals and groups and become, over time, set in stone as reality. All groups have these. It is the outsider's great advantage. It is the main reason that we give consultants our 'watches' and pay them to 'tell us the time'.

When Friday came around again and I met my friends, I ate salad with no dressing and was drinking sparkling water. I asked them for the boldest action they could think of. We decided upon ringing some of the most senior people in British horse-racing during the next week and asking them for assistance. Now the Tiger was really roaring.

Nothing could have prepared me for the reaction I received. Everybody I called either took the call or returned it promptly. Everybody was interested. Everybody wanted to make it happen and offered help. One person I really wanted to speak to was Michael Caulfield, CEO of the Jockeys' Association of Great Britain (now the Professional Jockeys' Association). Surely he knew a thing or two about what was involved in being a jockey.

Only one problem: I had no number for him, so I emailed the JAGB through their website. Ten minutes later a number that I didn't recognise flashed up on my mobile.

'Jim? It's Michael.'

Within a couple of days I was having dinner with Michael and a woman I had never heard of: Gee Armytage.

We were in a pub in a place that I had never heard of either, Lambourn.

By the end of the evening, though, I'd become very aware that Lambourn was one of the three major horseracing centres in England. These were just words at that time of night. Soon enough, I would see the bucking and kicking reality of strings and strings of racehorses in daylight, a sight that I still find as exciting now as I did the first time I saw it.

By the end of the evening I had also learned a little about the tiny and very beautiful Gee, who radiated vitality across the table. It turns out that Gee Armytage is one of the first women to have ridden in the Grand National, the most famous horse-race in the world as well as the most dangerous. She is the first woman to have ridden winners at the Cheltenham Festival (Britain and Ireland's most celebrated jumps meeting) as a professional jockey. She remains one of the most successful female jump jockeys of all time.

I learned that Gee was engaged to Mark Bradburne (they have since married), a professional jump jockey. Mark came second in the Grand National on Lord Atterbury just a few months after we met. He won the Ascot Chase on Hand Inn Hand just a few weeks later. I also learned that Gee now worked as personal assistant to one Anthony Peter (AP) McCoy, MBE.

Of course, I hadn't ever heard of AP McCoy. It turns out that I probably should have done my homework better. He's ridden more winners than any other jump jockey in history and went on to win the BBC's coveted Sports Personality of the Year trophy in 2010, beating the successful Ryder Cup golfers and leading footballers.

I ate a salad and didn't mention the word 'trifle'. Neither Michael nor Gee were eyeing up the dessert trolley either. After dinner, Gee became quiet and thoughtful.

'Okay, then. If you are really up for it, I'll take you on. You need to be down here at 7 a.m. on Saturday. I'll get Candy Morris to open her shop early and we'll kit you out. Then we will go to Martin Bosley's yard to watch them work the horses. After that, I'll see if Tina Fletcher can fit you in for a lesson to get you started.'

You've guessed it: I'd not heard of Candy, Martin or Tina either, but I should have.

'Well, what do you say?'

Oh no. Now I was in trouble. Should I start the car fast and head for London? Or should I shake the hand that this woman had extended across the dinner table? If I did, life would never be the same again and I knew that things would get a lot less comfortable for me in the coming weeks.

We shook hands.

'Excellent. Gotta dash. See you Saturday – 7 a.m.' Gee Armytage was gone.

This was an unbelievable turn of events. The bold action had somehow brought a solid gold racing legend on to the team. And, in the moment I shook hands with Gee Armytage, I was truly committed. Reverse gear had been removed. I was going racing – whatever the challenges ahead.

Game on!

Rule 1 brings you a bold result

My bold result was that within a month of my bold action:

- I was living in Lambourn

- I had Tina Fletcher, a world class showjumper qualified to teach Olympic riders teaching me how to steer and walk a horse

- I had Gee Armytage, a racing legend, as my coach

- I was on a fitness and diet regime crafted by a coach, Jason Cook, who trains professional jockeys in Lambourn

- I was riding racehorses out on the gallops every morning. No, I did not have a hidden talent. Gee had asked the Lambourn community for the safest conveyance in the valley and a great man called Martin Bosley had responded. The horse was doing all the thinking – not me – but I was there every day tacking up, talking to the stable staff and *learning*

That was one bold set of results in my quest to get to the racecourse.

I am assuming that you would like to get things moving, to win rather than just be placed, to score a nice bold result and make life more interesting?

If you take your bold action today, I wonder what your bold result will be. Don't you want to find out?

Rule 1 makes you Wake Up!

All these people had been waiting to help me. All these adventures had been waiting until I woke up, faced my Tiger and began to live them. This is the final, and perhaps the most important, thing that Rule 1 does for us.

Rule 1 makes us Wake Up!

We spend so much of our lives stuck in our own heads with our own fears to keep us company, spending time with similar people who reinforce our view of the world. Rule 1 is the first of the Integrity Rules. Integrity, because it helps reunite our fearful, Tiger-ridden self with our true Self. It begins to make us whole. It begins to lead us in the direction in which we truly wish to go rather than the direction that is governed by fearfulness, the need to please other people and habit.

Rule 1, the bold action, pours a bucket of cold water over a sleeping spirit, provides challenge and opportunity and leads us to the moment where commitment is possible.

So my question to you is this: what is the bold action that will wake you up, lead you to your equivalent of shaking hands with Gee Armytage and committing to working with another to make your dream become reality?

There is a consequence to not acting, a consequence to sleeping on. You get to keep it safe. You get to keep it stagnant. And, yes, this becomes as good as it gets. The human spirit needs growth. But the Tiger prevents growth. Now don't be blaming anyone else if this incredible opportunity called life seems stagnant.

Have you carried out your bold action yet?

You're going to do it tomorrow?

Really?

OK – I had better cover that briefly before we move on to Rule 2 . . .

Tomorrow . . .

Ah, so we meet the greatest lie of all: tomorrow will be different. Tomorrow I will act boldly. Tomorrow I will tame that Tiger.

Tigers are not tamed tomorrow. Bold actions are not planned for tomorrow. It is all done today. It is all done now. It is a change in how we want to handle the Tiger, not a plan. And that's why Rule 1 is Rule 1 and not Rule 10. Because tomorrow feels just like today when it arrives, and one more day has passed with the Tiger writing your story. One more dent in your self-confidence.

Today is the only day there is. There is only now, there will only ever be now. Change your relationship with yourself by changing your relationship with now. Do the thing you want to do.

Time to carry out your bold action. Enjoy it.

Over to you.

Things the Tiger wants you to forget about Rule 1:

Rule 1: Act boldly today, time is limited

The bold action is not complex to do (but it is not easy, as you have discovered!).

The difference between those with a great story in the nursing home and those with regrets is that the first lot acted.

You can do this – and it is worth doing it to write your story

Rule 1 and the bold action it asks you to complete bring you five big steps forward in your quest to write your own story and not your Tiger's:

1. It shows you that only the Tiger is stopping you
2. It interrupts your habitual patterns of Tiger appeasement and exposes them to your own gaze
3. It takes you closer to commitment
4. It often delivers a bold result and causes your story to jump forward
5. It helps you to Wake Up!

Now log in to the Campus at tamingtigers.com and watch the film entitled 'I don't want to do my bold action!'

Twitter: @jim_lawless
Web: tamingtigers.com
Facebook: facebook.com/pages/Taming-Tigers.

Case Study 1:
Chris Stevenson

I have always wanted to be able to look back on my life knowing I've been to different places and done different things. It's your life and your story, right?

In 2005 I left university and began a career in procurement. I started thinking about moving to Australia in 2007 but I always put off doing anything about it. My Rulebook (see Rule 2) told me that I didn't have enough money to make it feasible.

In the summer of 2009 I had to come to terms with the fact that I suffer from depression. At the same time a long-term relationship ended and big project at work came to an end – more routine tasks lay ahead. It was a difficult time. It seemed like I had to take a chance if I was to get some momentum into my life.

During that summer a friend recommended that I learn about *Taming Tigers*. Towards the end of November, I made my bold decision to give Australia a go. But I had no job to go to and financial security is important to me. After staring at my laptop screen for about 30 minutes one Wednesday night, I took a deep breath and pressed 'Book Now'. I had a one-way flight to Melbourne.

My Rule 1 Bold Action changed everything for me. Rule 1 showed me that, in reality, the only thing between me and my long-term dream was a credit card payment, a 24-hour flight and a big roaring Tiger. Once the flight was booked, that was it. The money was spent and I couldn't ask for it back. I am a Yorkshireman after all!

I remember walking round Melbourne on the first day after I arrived. It was raining. I was unemployed, lost, bewildered, jet-lagged and lonely. I had booked myself into a horrible hostel, which made the feelings worse. I was scared and shocked – I had never been in such a position before.

Not for the first time on this adventure, I had to start re-writing my Rulebook (Rule 2). I had simply presumed that if I was staying in a hostel, then I would meet people like me. I'd have a starting point. It didn't work out like that! I soon realized it was going to be very tough, but I had enough money to stretch to maybe three months and I had backed myself to win. I dared not think of giving up because I hated the thought of going back home. The fear of failure would not stop me trying to write my story – but it *would* stop me giving up.

I had huge self-doubt at times. I felt like I was being selfish in leaving behind people who loved me. I felt like I was doing the wrong thing: running away; assuming that the grass would be greener. I went through those emotions when I was alone for a long time too – realizing the things I had left behind were actually really good. There was a time when I thought that if all this journey did was to open my eyes, then that wouldn't be such a bad thing.

Rules 3 and 10 became very important at that difficult stage. I knew where I wanted to arrive: a great life and a great lifestyle (though I wasn't 100% sure what that looked like), a fresh start and an adventure. I didn't anticipate how tough it would be, but I gained strength from Jim's Ten Rules for Taming Tigers. I realized each day would become a little easier as things started to fall into place. Each day was a big step on a steep ladder. I know that I'm there now. Every morning I drive to work, along the beach, and I smile. I always think, "I did it – I made this happen".

When I felt most lonely or isolated, it was without a doubt Rule 10 that pulled me through. At first I thought it was just stubbornness and the fear of failure; I really didn't know how I would have coped if I'd have gone back to England, failed, with my tail between my legs. But *Taming Tigers* helped me to realise that I wasn't just stubborn. I had strength and character. That gave me a huge amount of confidence.

I had Rule 9 Disciplines and Basics. My 'Basic' was to work hard in my job. The job was key to a visa and long-term stay in the country. If I was disciplined with that, the rest I could enjoy.

My Discipline was to say 'yes' more. I'm a very sociable person with those that know me, but not always the most forthcoming with people I've just met. But I didn't turn down one invitation to any social function in my first 6 months in Australia – BBQs, speed-dating, parties, drinks after work with people I didn't really know, even a weekend in New Zealand! I have a great circle of friends in Melbourne now.

Rule 5 was also important. In early 2009, I had contacted CIPSA – the Australian branch of my professional body. I mentioned that I was thinking about coming out to live and work and attached my CV. I received no response.

The day after I resigned my job in England, I received an email from a global, iconic company in Melbourne, offering me a job interview for the role of Strategic Sourcing Manager just four days after my flight would arrive. It transpired that the then Head of Procurement had been on the board of CIPSA and had kept my CV. The Tools for Taming Tigers really are all around you.

It was exactly the position I was looking for. My career plan was to find either a management role, or a position in a much bigger company. This role gave me both. I'm still enjoying the role two years on. My boss leaves the company at the end of 2011. I will act as interim Head of Procurement and will be applying for the permanent post.

I have also developed a new Rulebook regarding my behaviours when I feel a bout of depression occurring. I can react to the initial feelings, addressing them directly and putting them in context, i.e. not letting tiredness take over my day, or removing myself from a situation which makes me irritable – both things that would have lead to downward spirals in mood. In the past this would cause me to worry, question the decisions I had made, my future, my friends: everything.

Now that I understand my Tiger better, I can see its impact on my story, particularly through my perceived constraint of a lack of money. It has also affected me in competitive situations – the fear of losing, which clouded my approach to playing sports and other confrontational situations. I think my depressive moods are linked to that too. My Tiger has stopped me being bold in relationships also.

Knowing I have tamed my Tiger gives me so much confidence. I think, 'if I can do that, I can do anything'. I feel so much pride and satisfaction when I talk to people about my journey. I'm really happy in everything I do so have little desire to change things at present. However, I understand that I am capable of a lot more – in all walks of life.

Taming my Tiger has made me feel incredibly powerful. I remember the moment it hit me that I had tamed it. I was driving by the sea in Melbourne in a convertible car I'd just bought, music playing. It was precisely the image I had in my head the years before I came: driving along, the sun shining, enjoying life and being free to do whatever I wanted.

A bold action is the catalyst for change. We are all capable of incredible feats of change but you need to put yourself in a challenging or an unfamiliar position to recognize that. Once you have done it, it becomes 'sink or swim' and that is a simple choice. After all, it's your life and your story, right?

Rule 2

Rewrite Your Rulebook – Challenge It Hourly

Why was your guide to Tiger taming so slow to take a bold action to win his bet?

I had a Rulebook and I was acting according to it. You have a Rulebook, too. My actions were being dictated by my Rulebook, just as yours are. It is a creation of the Tiger. Let us give it our full attention for a few pages.

My Rulebook, whatever my brave words to my heckler from the stage might have been, was clear. Thirty-five-year-old, overweight, smoking and drinking business consultants who went to large state schools in densely populated, urban south London and were not remotely talented at sport did not become jockeys. Little guys, probably aged around sixteen, who had been riding horses since they were six months old and who lived in the country, with family connections to racing – those were the people who became jockeys.

How has your Rulebook been guiding you these past years? What is it stopping you from doing today? What has it stopped you becoming today? Will it stop you the same way tomorrow?

The Rulebook is one of the most terrifying ways that the Tiger attacks us. Terrifying because the rules in the Rulebook appear to be real, intellectually justifiable and often, to our minds, unchangeable. For that reason, many people live their whole lives according to an unhelpful Rulebook. My Rulebook about becoming a jockey was false. But it made sense – to me, to my friends, to my family and to almost everybody in the racing game. The Rulebook nearly made me abandon the project. Only bold action overcame it by introducing me to Gee Armytage. Why? Because Gee had a different way of viewing the world – she had a different Rulebook. She had learned this through bold action. When Gee wanted to race ride, women were simply not able to. Gee, and some other brave female pioneers, changed that forever. Gee is an experienced re-writer of the Rulebook.

Our Rulebook is often reinforced by our colleagues, our superiors at work, our friends and our families. But it is a fiction designed to keep us safe; to keep the Tiger on top. Those around us have an interest in us keeping it like that as well. If we successfully challenge our Rulebook, they lose some of their faith in their own Rulebook, their own defence against the fear and discomfort of looking at themselves honestly. Let me explain.

What is our Rulebook?

Our Rulebook is how we see the world and our ability to interact with it. In other places you will see this expressed as beliefs. Beliefs are merely a subset of the Rulebook. Beliefs don't give us the full extent of what we're up against here. These are rules because they often appear to us to be set in stone, to have consequences if we disobey them. Rules, because often they have come to us from society, from our peers, from the culture of our workplaces. Rules, because they are often *actively shared and 'policed'* by the media, our family, our peers and our colleagues. This is no mere 'belief'; this is a reality. Disobedience may even have real social consequences.

Except, of course, it isn't a reality. Not at all. It's just lots of people subscribing to the same rules and keeping themselves safe. I am not speaking about the law of your land, about the rules of a religion that you may choose to adhere to, about your morals or the voice of your conscience. I'm not talking about the ways in which you have learned to behave in order to do the right thing by your family and others around you.

I'm not talking about rules that can be proven either: if I walk off the edge of a cliff, there will be a whistling sound in my ears before a long silence commences.

I am talking about the fictional rule that says: 'I have to attend meetings when requested to by my boss' (without a polite discussion about why I have to), or 'I have to present with every word written up behind me in mind-numbing bullets on PowerPoint slides', or that great leadership mantra, from C-level (job titles with the word 'Chief' in front of them – Chief Executive Officer, Chief Finance Officer and so on) to front-line team leader level: 'I have to spend so much time doing other people's work, I cannot possibly inspire and encourage people to achieve our vision' – I cannot 'lead', in other words.

Why do we each create a fictional rulebook that dampens our experience of life?

We promised ourselves that we'd be honest, didn't we? So let's face reality. The uncertainty of our fragile existence is terrifying. We have no certainty that the floods will stay away, no certainty that the company will survive, no certainly that we won't wake up tomorrow to find that somebody has eaten all the cereal before we could get to the cupboard.

We don't like this. In my family we love animals and we have a fair few. They don't mind the uncertainty so much. They live in the present. They are not aware of their mortality. They are not even aware of the effect of turmoil in the Middle East upon the price of oil and what that may mean to their house prices. Imagine that! We do mind, however. We don't like it.

Humans abhor a 'certainty vacuum'. We'll find a certainty out there and will fill the vacuum with it.

Usually, we fill the vacuum with terrible outcomes and the Tiger starts to snarl. And then we'll work hard to avoid those terrors. Any intelligent person would work to avoid terrors, wouldn't they?

We humans are generally kind to others – and we like to be needed by and to protect them – so we tell them 'how it is' and share our rules for survival. And we describe the terrors that lie in wait if they ignore the rules – not that many of us ever actually meet these terrors if we find the courage to tame our Tiger, plan carefully and act boldly.

The rulebook protects us from the wonders of life

This uncertainty is not all doom and gloom and missed cereal. The uncertainty means that it is equally possible that the quirky idea will be a huge success; that the conversation with the boss will lead to a new department for you to lead and a doubling in pay; that they will be writing a book about you in five years' time. Most people are unable to see that side of uncertainty. The Tiger rushes in before they have a chance.

You have to battle fear and discomfort to see such positive outcomes. You have to work hard to avoid the pitfalls that will surely be there if you reveal yourself and head from the grandstand out on to the track to take an active part in life. This is why the 'positive thinking' movement has earned itself a reputation for dispensing 'snake oil'. It misses out the 'fear and discomfort' part involved in being positive, lest people should shy away from buying the book or believing in the short cut. Taming your Tiger involves dealing with fear and discomfort. That is courageous and heroic work.

I should add here that, for some people, the consequences of challenging the Rulebook that they created in the past were, in that past, very real. For example if, as children, we were parented in a physically or emotionally abusive way. The survival strategy we created to appease the abuser or to cope with the situation may remain fixed in our Rulebooks and affect our relationships (and so our whole story – and very much our work story) until we fix the Rulebook and make the leap into full maturity. This often takes time and professional assistance. It can be done, though. Why does it affect our work story? Because we doubt our worth, and ourselves, we doubt our colleagues' support. We fear revealing who we really are. We see senior people within our organisation or our clients as 'authority figures'. The outdated Rulebook tells us clearly how to deal with such people in order to survive.

But imagine if we could change the Rulebook and see that our colleagues are pleased to support us, see the desire of senior people to help us (if we earn their respect as peers, whatever the professional job titles). Imagine the opportunity that presents itself if we challenge the Rulebook.

We use the Rulebook to make sense of the world. We use it to cope with uncertainty. We use it to navigate a course into the future in the absence of any other reliable map.

If we don't take control of our Rulebook, the Tiger creates a Rulebook designed to keep us away from fear and discomfort, to enable us to remain comfortable, but they merely imprison and restrict us. How long will you allow this to last?

When I first discussed my idea about setting a British free-diving record, all the members of the international freediving fraternity I spoke with – bar two – were clear about my chances of success. They had looked at their personal experience and the experience of watching other people, mixed in their rules about their own imagined limitations and created a Rulebook about how freediving works. But nobody has any idea how freediving works. Theories, yes. Science? No. We don't even know for sure whether supreme cardiovascular fitness aids or inhibits a dive.

The experts said that it could not be done. These were good and kind people. We all crave certainty. The two Italians you met earlier didn't share the same Rulebook. Thanks to the bold action that led me to Andrea and Rasta and thanks to Jon Pitts, the sports scientist who also helped me in the riding campaign, and thanks to Debbie Metcalfe, the underwater filmmaker whose company, Blue Eye FX, makes freediving films, I was able to see that the rules could be broken – and to break them.

When it came to my desire to ride under Jockey Club Rules in a televised horserace, all the racing people I spoke with – bar two – were clear about my chances of success. They had looked at their personal experience and the experience of watching other people and had created a Rulebook. They filled in the uncertainty surrounding my chances by using their Rulebook. These were good and kind people. We all crave certainty. Gee knew that the rules were false. Thanks to the bold action that led me to Michael Caulfield and then to Gee, I was able to see that the rules could be broken – and to break them.

What rules? The rules were never there in the first place! There is no Rulebook. It is all a great fiction. A fiction subscribed to by enough people that it makes us doubt ourselves. Nobody knows what you can or can't do. Nobody! By disregarding the fictions, you have a chance of winning.

On 23 November 1976 Jacques Mayol, the great freediving pioneer whose story inspired the movie *The Big Blue* set the world freediving record at 100 metres. A massive feat. Doctors told him that he would probably be crushed beneath the pressure of the sea at 100 metres – eleven times the pressure of the earth's atmosphere that is working on you at this moment as you read.

Mayol had eighteen divers in the water with him on scuba and three freedivers. His crew on the platform numbered seven. In 2010 I went to 101 metres with one diver on scuba (a camera operator operating in forty metres of water), one freediver meeting me at thirty metres on the return journey and a crew of two on the platform. The technological advances in no-limits freediving equipment have been minimal. What has advanced is the mental Rulebook. The terrors and protective fictions of the human mind.

Mayol disproved the prevailing Rulebook, however. He was a pioneer. He rewrote the Rulebook. I merely followed his path. That is what makes him great.

The rules were never there. It was all a great fiction. It still is. And if we even consider disobeying them, the Tiger roars at us and we feel fear and insecurity. That is human nature. That is the battle. This book is the latest in a long line of invitations to join the fray and live.

Rewrite your Rulebook – Wake Up!

Let's test your rulebook

You are in a bar with some friends – your gender and orientation are immaterial but let's say you are a straight man – and you see a beautiful woman on the other side of the bar. There she is in all her glory.

You think to yourself, 'Wow, look at that beautiful woman. I think I am going to have to go and speak to her. Perhaps she will speak back to me. Perhaps she and I will become friends, and who knows what may follow from that!'

(I should perhaps point out here that if you intend to put this practice to the test, most people's Rulebooks will suggest that you should be single when you do so.)

So you begin to stroll across the bar towards your beautiful woman with your thoughts full of witty lines and opening gambits; then, when you are just six strides away, out of the corner of your eye you catch sight of the toilet door. And as if by magic you find that you are in the toilet and have bypassed the beautiful woman.

What went wrong?

The Rulebook that sabotages us and saves us from danger – the uncertainty of the outcome of your encounter was filled with the terrors of rejection and not the chance of a great relationship. So, as we walk towards our beautiful person with our head full of witty comments, the Rulebook starts dictating:

'I don't think you should do that,' it warns.

'Why not?'

'Because she is a very beautiful woman.'

'I know. That's the whole idea here.'

'But you are an ugly person!'

'That bad?'

'That bad! Don't you remember what happened last time you tried this?'

'Hmmm. Do you think I could use my wit and charm?'

'Ha ha ha. For you, that was quite witty. I don't think so.'

'I think she's seen me. I'm committed here, what should I do?'

'Look over her left shoulder. There's the toilet. Go to the loo! Go to the loo!'

And somehow we end up visiting the toilet before reappearing at our original table and resuming our conversation with our friends.

And isn't life grand!

Instead of having to go through all the fear and discomfort of communicating with another human being, we have managed to fit in a trip to the toilet and plant ourselves back at the table to enjoy a drink and talk to our familiar friends about familiar things.

The failure of our mission wasn't even our responsibility. It was that beautiful woman's fault. That person who judged us as too ugly to speak to her. That person who was so shallow that she wouldn't, according to our Rulebook, want to spend time getting to see how great we are – underneath our physical exterior.

Of course, you have no idea what that person's reaction would have been. In fact, all you have done is follow your Rulebook, reinforcing it to yourself in the process.

This rule is a fiction. We know it is not a real rule. We know this because in the world there are some less than beautiful people going out with some fantastically beautiful ones.

They have all rewritten their Rulebook.

OK, it is very possible that some have also earned just a little bit of cash to help oil the wheels of life. But even in a case like that – think about it for a moment – unless they sauntered up to the beautiful person and threw their Lamborghini keys down on the bar before they opened their mouth, they too have had to battle a fear of rejection as they wandered across the bar. They must have challenged the Rulebook.

How to spot your Rulebook in action

There are some ways to test the strength of your Rulebook.

People with strong Rulebooks can often predict the future, for example. Perhaps you know people like this. Perhaps you are one of them. They know what will happen if you try X or Y. They have the ability to fast-forward the DVD of life, a DVD that nobody else has watched, and tell you the ending. The terrors that lie in wait to attack you. Or to attack the leader of the company. Or to attack the daring salesperson who has gone looking for contracts overseas. When you are predicting the future, rather than being present in the moment or being able to see the range of possible outcomes, your Rulebook is on the rampage.

Here's another thing that you can use to try to see how your rules are working to keep you safe from living your life. Write down a place that you would *really* like to get to – an ideal situation at work, for example. Take a moment to think of your ideal job. What would you be doing every day? Aim high.

Then write down all the reasons why you know that it's impossible for you to do that.

Now, carefully go through the reasons that you have written down. Which of them are real reasons? Reasons that you can prove. Reasons that you have actually tested – that you could defend in a tough TV interview with a great journalist? Reasons that, if somebody offered you a vast sum of money (or whatever turns you on) to overcome, or threatened you with harm, you wouldn't be able to overcome in a flash!

Now delete the false reasons. What are you left with? How long have you been labouring under these delusions? What have they actually protected you from? Success? Joy? Achievement? Adventure? Greater regard from your colleagues? Nicer holidays? Greater personal satisfaction?

Use the Ten Rules to get yourself there. Starting today.

Think about it. Could a big bold Rule 1 action coupled with a Rule 3 goal and plan, a bit of Rule 9 discipline and the assistance of some great allies (Rule 5) help you past all the rules that you have just written down and on towards your ideal outcome?

Are there different rules that could help you to navigate the uncertainties ahead in a more useful way?

And then what might your story be? What might your authentic story be?

Corporate Rulebooks

Collectively, we love Rulebooks. Communities thrive on them, and the workplace is a community. Collectively, we create them with wild enthusiasm, because collectively, just as individually, we long to know how it works so that we can keep the community safe. We desperately want to be able to predict the outcome. To get it right, just as we were taught we had to in the classroom all those years ago. But we can't get it right like that in the adult world. There is rarely a right answer at work, just the best answer that we can come up with. If that answer is to be a progression from the previous model, we need to break some of the rules that we used to get to that previous model. The more safe and predictable we manage to make our work community, the more predictable we make the irrelevance of our organisation over a matter of time.

The Rulebook is changing at work. If you have had contact with the idea of coaching at work (however well it was managed), or have been asked to take greater accountability and responsibility, step up to become a leader (whatever your job title), experienced vision or values programmes or worked on 'empowerment' – this Rulebook shift has touched you. It may have been executed badly, been loaded with annoying buzzwords and perhaps the programme even failed, but it is a sign of leaders struggling to adapt to the change that I am addressing here. These are all ways that leaders are trying to make the shift into the New Economy (See the Appendix for more detail on this great change at work).

What fascinates me is that within some organisations, some people – people just like you and me – take decisions and commit to actions that are creative, dynamic and are backed up by passion and pace, whereas people in other organisations continue to make the same old mistakes, but just in a slightly more desperate way.

Many of the companies that are thriving in the early twenty-first century have broken the industrial age Rulebook. In the New Economy, the biggest rules that are being broken are those concerning relationships – specifically communication, trust and accountability – both within the community of a company's staff and in how that community associates with those outside, its customers and potential customers.

The rules that were created a century ago to enable companies to thrive in the industrial economy are the concrete boots that many leaders still wear today as they wade into the uncertain waters of the New Economy.

Blind terror caused by uncertainty about what will happen if they ease their grip on the reins of control is the reason that CEOs are still proudly wearing these boots and displaying this fashion to their internal managers, who ape their bosses in turn. All people who are afraid seek to control others. Whether we fear for ourselves or for others (our children, for example). Control is not a tool at our disposal in the New Economy. It leads to outdated and dangerous rules in the corporate Rulebook. Let's explore why that is the case.

THE RULEBOOK LEGACY FROM THE INDUSTRIAL ECONOMY – CONTROL

The leader's job in any business is always to get a job done with and through others. The question is what that job is and how it can be done. Here I am more concerned with the 'how', but be aware that by limiting the 'how' we also restrict the range of 'whats' we see as possible for us.

In the industrial economy, control was important. Within a manufacturing context, it is clearly important on many levels. So the twin levers of carrot and stick were useful for ensuring that the 'thinking cogs' in the great machine – the human beings – were motivated so as to function efficiently as a part of the larger machine. These levers had been inherited from our feudal ancestors and our military cousins. They were even used in schools. They were necessary in order to get widgets made and loaded on to barges, ships and trains in a timely and profitable manner. The external forces of the carrot and the stick motivated people. They were not inspired to find their own deeper internal motivations. This was irrelevant – back in the industrial age.

There is a difference between motivation and inspiration. Think about motivation for a moment. It is a word that is merrily bandied about and thought to be 'positive' but it is rarely considered. The Roman galley slave was a highly motivated individual, wouldn't you agree? I bet he rowed just as fast as he could.

Motivated he was. Carrot and sticked he was. Inspired he was not!
Remove the stick and the rowing will stop.

If you have 1,000 people working in contact centres in touch with your customers every day, or 5,000 people working in your retail outlets, you cannot rely upon carrots and sticks. It is impossible. You cannot be present. If we rely on carrot and sticked managers to do this in our place, who applies the stick to the stick wielders?

When we motivate another person, we provide them with an external incentive to act in the way we wish them to. It is coercive. When we motivate ourselves it is not coercive. The motivation may or may not be good for us – that is a bigger philosophical debate – but at least it is ours.

This makes motivation a secondary management tool in the New Economy. I have no idea what motivates you. If I want to motivate you (and 5,000 or even 50,000 other people like you who work in the organisation) I have to reach for the most basic human needs – the areas in which we are all alike: food, shelter and clothing for you and your family and the need for appreciation and for comradeship ('don't let the team down!'). These basic needs are vital, of course. If we go back to the social conditions in the Economic Age, I would have been pretty motivated to perform for you if you could offer me security in these areas. Such security was not easy to find: there was no welfare state and debtors' prisons were not great places for bringing up children.

We no longer live or work in the industrial age. We are still highly motivated by the basic elements of human existence outlined above, but few of us have truly known life without them. Nor do we expect to. Life is economically much easier now than it was even thirty years ago.

We live in the New Economic Age. Inspiration is the leader's discipline now. Inspiring our people, inspiring our customers. Both sets of people have moved up Maslow's Pyramid of Human Motivations. (In his 1943 paper 'A theory of Human Motivation' Abraham Maslow set out a hierarchy of needs. At the base of the pyramid he places physiological and safety needs. As we succeed in meeting these needs, we can focus on love and belonging, esteem and gaining the respect of others and finally 'self actualisation' might be achieved). In our roles as consumers and as employees, we are seeking self-esteem, purpose and meaning. The key word there is 'self'. Nobody else can provide it – unlike the basic needs. We have to find it. We cannot find it if we are largely motivated from an external source – 'carrot and sticked'. This motivation comes from within. This requires a leader who can inspire us to find our own motivation at work.

INSPIRATION HAS REPLACED MOTIVATION AT WORK; COMMON DIRECTION HAS REPLACED CONTROL

When we inspire others, we are creating a careful, intelligent and very demanding framework in which the individual can find his or her own motivation. When we inspire we help individuals discover and believe that they have the potential to reach their own aspirations. When we use motivation – carrot and stick – we encourage the individual to meet our needs. In the organisation, the two sets of needs – the needs of the individual and of the company – must have common ground. This common ground is rarely as difficult to achieve as one might imagine, but it is beyond the scope of this book.

Look at 'motivational' speakers. Bribery merchants, the lot of them! But there are very few motivational speakers left. They are being replaced by the *inspirational* speaker. The motivational speaker used to appeal to the lowest common motivational factor. What else can the speaker do when faced with five hundred complete strangers? 'Who wants to have more money? C'mon, lemme hear ya – who wants more M-O-N-E-Y?' 'Stick your hands in the air if you want more success in your life – c'mon, who wants more success – all of you?'

The inspirational speaker, by contrast, provides a framework for individual listeners to see what they can achieve, encourages them to believe in themselves, the community and the project and nudges them towards finding their own, unique, motivation for achieving it. When you read the words of Martin Luther King, Gandhi, Nelson Mandela or the wartime Churchill, you are seeing inspirational speakers at work.

You may feel very motivated after a Taming Tigers presentation, but you will have done all the motivating. My responsibility was to provide a non-controlling, non-coercive, non-judgemental framework in which you can be inspired to find your motivation and act to discover and write you own story – and not the Tiger's.

This is not control. The New Economy requires new rules in the Rulebook.

Fearful leaders and managers who feel the need to control their people are often following a set of rules that no longer serves them. The Tiger is writing that organisation's or team's story.

I cannot motivate you without creating a control dynamic between two adults: what we describe as a parent–child culture, as outlined below. Both parties have to play a part in this game in order for it to work – and both parties have something to gain from it.

THE RULEBOOK LEGACY FROM THE INDUSTRIAL ECONOMY – THE 'PARENT–CHILD CULTURE'

The parent–child culture provides the basis of the corporate Rulebook in many organisations. In the past it benefited us to 'know our place'. It is now time to move on from this.

Our work at Taming Tigers, often with boards of large organisations, frequently begins with a confession that there is a problem with parent–child culture. By that I mean a culture in which 'senior' people feel a need to control and micromanage 'junior' people, and junior people accept this by not taking responsibility for their actions and complaining about management and sometimes impeding the progress of the organisation.

There is no true delegation of decision-making of what should be done, or how it should be done, to the local area where such decision-making should be taking place. This does not make for good results in the New Economy where the success of the brand relies on excellent decision-making at a local level and true alignment of purpose and values to guide these many thousands of local decisions.

The Rulebook operating here is that people need to be

controlled. That is how we get them to do what needs to be done.

The 'child' in this scenario also benefits from and goes along with the charade. Often this is accompanied by much complaining and the good old 'victim mentality' – but absolutely nothing is done by that individual or those individuals to change the situation with the superior at work or to leave the job. Why? Because it relieves people of responsibility. Responsibility is frightening. I might get it wrong. It'll be my head on the block. 'Play safe', 'play the game', 'don't raise your head above the parapet or it'll get blown off'. All good, understandable, perhaps even useful industrial economy survival strategies.

While someone follows the rule that 'this is the way it is, what can I do about it?' they are not being asked to face their Tiger, let alone tame it. There is no need to change, grow, mature or face the accompanying fear and discomfort. Nothing is my 'fault' because nothing is my responsibility. I 'cannot' act in the right way in the moment of contact with the customer to uphold brand and company values – because I am not 'allowed' to. For many people this works very well – superficially, at least: deep down there may be a high price to pay.

Changing the corporate Rulebook is one of the biggest challenges of the New Economy and your ability to see the Rulebook at work, to play your part in changing it, or, ultimately, to move away from dysfunctional organisations, will be a defining factor in you writing your story at work in the years ahead of you.

The Rulebook and 'fear of failure'

Our Rulebook is designed to keep us safe, masking the role that our own fear plays in that process. Unveiling our own fear is often unpalatable to us. But, in reality, from what does the Rulebook keep us safe? What exactly do we 'fear'?

Safe from the possibility of failure. The fear of loss of standing in our group – the ego's biggest enemy. One of the rules that we were taught so carefully at such an early age is that we will be ridiculed for 'getting it wrong'.

At this stage it is traditionally my role to say that we should not fear failure. That failure is an acceptable part of achieving our successes. What utter tripe; what entirely unhelpful nonsense! At this stage I am also traditionally supposed to tell you about how many filaments Thomas Edison burned before he managed to get one that would function within the vacuum that we call the light bulb, and how this never bothered him. I never met Mr Edison, but I bet it got right up his nose. I bet he feared failure. I bet Mrs Edison feared it quite a lot, too. I bet it made him work really hard. I wonder if his utter horror at the idea of failing *at what he had committed heart and soul to achieve* drove him to many late nights of thought and experimentation.

Perhaps we succeed because of our fear of failure?

Entrepreneurs often burn their boats on the shore. They throw their heart and soul into the project. They put their reputations on the line, along with their houses. In the darkest hour of the night, before the dawn of success breaks, do you think they wake up driven by thoughts of attaining great wealth or by thoughts of avoiding penury? When my house was on the line it was certainly the latter.

Fear of failing in the thing we have set our hearts, minds and hands to is a powerful and healthy driving force.

Contrary to the 'conventional wisdom' of the positive thinkers, let's you and I fear failure. Let's take *not* failing really seriously. That will allow us to make our mistakes. That will let us look daft in a meeting where the idea goes down badly. That will let us, as leaders, stand on a chair in the canteen every Friday and take questions from everybody instead of eating a sandwich in our office with our emails for company.

If we set out to build a new product or a new culture, we will make mistakes. A healthy fear of failing to write our true story permits us to risk making those mistakes, to endure the consequences, forgive ourselves and recover quickly before moving doggedly on.

The Rulebook is generally used to prevent us taking small steps that may lead to us making small mistakes. In turn, it protects us from failing in our grand plan, our great story. The Rulebook plays small. Do you want to play small?

The Rulebook is the very cause of us failing in our plan; failing to write our story. It is not our protector.

Earning the confidence to rewrite the rulebook

There are hokum CDs that you can buy tucked away inside hokum books that will promise to deliver you extra confidence while you sleep. But where does true confidence come from? Why, for example, do great jockeys look so confident on horses that are bucking and kicking beneath them on the way to the start of the Derby, whereas most mortals look terrified on a horse that is simply plodding gently along a country lane?

They didn't get that confidence from a CD or a book. They got it from sitting on a lot of horses. They got it from pushing their boundaries and sitting on more difficult horses. Their confidence was knocked when those more difficult horses threw them to the ground when they stretched themselves beyond their current limitations in a bid to become better. And then they built it up again when they eventually battled with themselves until they could ride that horse, and then it was time to move to a more difficult horse again.

They got it because they challenged their Rulebook, a Rulebook that would have said that they had found their limitations, but one that they refused to accept.

The real secret to building confidence lies in rewriting your Rulebook through courageous, committed action until you have earned the right to create a new Rulebook for yourself.

Now it is time to start setting your course. As we move into Rule 3, ask yourself how much time must elapse before you strike the Tiger's rules out and replace them with the ones you want or need to see there. What parts of your story are passing you by as you wait?

Never allow fear of mistakes to cause you to rewrite the story that is rightfully yours.

Pain is temporary, but failure lasts forever.

Over to you.

Things the Tiger wants you to forget about Rule 2

Rule 2: Rewrite the Rulebook, challenge it hourly

Our Rulebook is how we see the world and see our ability to interact with it. Our beliefs are rules in our Rulebook but are a subset of the overall Rulebook. Our families, companies, schools, societies and so on also have fictional rules.

We love our Rulebooks and build them enthusiastically because they protect us from uncertainty – but the uncertain outcome could also be great adventure, fulfilment and success and we are "protected" from this also.

The Rulebook at work has changed forever in the past ten years and is still changing fast. It will pay you to keep up with that change.

When you see an opportunity – and all the rules protecting you from going for it – ask which of those rules are provable and which you, or others, have made up.

You often need to earn confidence to change your Rulebook. Put in the hard work to earn it for yourself.

Mix with those who disregard the Rulebook, not with those who wish to terrify you with their small views. Be careful whom you discuss your dreams and plans with.

Twitter: @jim_lawless
Web: tamingtigers.com
Facebook: facebook.com/pages/Taming-Tigers.

Case Study 2:
Gary Hoffman

£24 billion was held on deposit with Northern Rock before the run on the bank in 2007. In just three short weeks those deposits were reduced to less than £7 billion; £29 billion had been borrowed from the taxpayer. Rebuilding the faith of those customers who had withdrawn their savings would be an immense challenge, and ensuring the government was on board with what we set out to do was an unprecedented situation for me. We were 100% owned by them!

I was Vice Chairman of Barclays Bank when the run on Northern Rock began. When the Board of Northern Rock, along with the then Chancellor of the Exchequer, Alistair Darling, invited me to become Chief Executive of Northern Rock some weeks later, I was stimulated by the challenge and also felt I had a duty to accept, despite my Tiger's roar.

Taming Tigers is dangerous, I should warn you now. You want to go back for more but you know you will never tame it completely. I had involved Jim in a leadership programme that I had run whilst Chief Executive Officer of Barclaycard. I was touched personally by the Ten Rules and how they had been proven – but most importantly, Taming Tigers made a huge impact on the business.

Given what I discovered when I arrived Northern Rock, I decided that the Ten Rules for Taming Tigers would be a useful tool to use there also. There was a worrying problem when it came to accountability. A great management chain passed issues all the way up to the board member responsible and all the way down again. Why were the board members interested in these issues? And what was everyone else doing all day if not making decisions and managing their people?

There was a second, related, cultural problem. If I agreed a way forward with my top one hundred staff at Barclays, people would go away and do it. It took a little time to realize that at Northern Rock it would take around four weeks for senior members of staff to come back and ask 'and how do we do that?' This was not down to idleness. It was a lack of historical leadership and empowerment. Those four weeks had been spent wondering what to do and worrying about telling me that they didn't know what to do. It soon became clear that this culture of fear, paralysis and buck-passing pervaded the organisation. Everybody seemed to need my permission before having the confidence to act. Great people had been asked to leave their personalities and their natural wish to 'get things done' at home, because only the senior people thought they had the answer. In fact, the higher up in an organisation you go the less you tend to be connected to customers and the real world. For me, this had a large part to play in the cause of the financial crisis.

The big boundaries in this organisation had not been set, precipitating its financial difficulties and the run on the bank. The small boundaries were set in stone and were stifling the business.

My job as leader was to re-set both boundaries. If we failed to set the larger boundaries correctly, the consequences would be catastrophic. If we didn't change the smaller, personal boundaries at a senior level, we could not empower the person dealing with our customers in the branch to deliver excellent customer service. Without that, we could not earn our customers' trust back – along with their savings. Increasing our deposits would be essential to begin to create value for the new owner of Northern Rock – the UK taxpayer.

It was urgent for me to get the senior team to understand that they knew more than they thought they did – and that it was healthy to ask for help. It was imperative that I handed over the reins into safe hands, and to persuade my leaders to hand over the reins to their people also. This was not straightforward; people here were not used to holding reins at all.

Taming Tigers was the perfect tool to help them learn to do so. It was not the only tool that I used, but it was a powerful tool that helped me, quickly, to begin a process of change by:

- exposing people to a set of relevant ideas about making the impossible possible – from way outside of their sphere of experience

- bringing in a new, empowering vocabulary

- creating inspiration, ambition and energy in people emerging from a very traumatic time, while helping people to want to take more responsibility for themselves and their teams

- convincing people that I meant it – they *could* take responsibility and take the initiative to act

- delivering 10 practical tools for moving past the fear of change and taking on personal responsibility

Rules 2 and 3 were the most important for us. Each individual had to change his Rulebook. As an organisation, we had to change our collective Rulebook. We also needed absolute clarity of destination; where we were going and what we had to do everyday to get there. Delivering this clarity of vision and the resources required to reach it was a daily task for me as leader. Moving towards it was the daily task of each of our people.

As we tamed our Tigers, we were able to get the message out to the customer facing staff: 'If you do the right thing for the customer without breaking our risk boundaries – which are in place to protect us and the customer – then you cannot go wrong.' And so the people in the wider organization began a journey towards empowerment also.

It was a complex process and sadly not everybody was willing or able to make the change and I let a large percentage of the top 100 managers that I inherited go. But the change was not optional if we were to deliver on our commitments to the British Government, and it was urgent. Many made the change, though, and I am hugely proud of them and of what was achieved by the people of Northern Rock during my time as Chief Executive.

The employees of Northern Rock faced huge change with great courage. I am extremely proud to have led them, and of what we achieved together. By the time I left Northern Rock in October 2010, we had, in a continuing economic downturn, grown our deposits from £7 billion back up to £18 billion. We had re-structured the business and met all of the targets that the Government had set us. We created a new culture within a fine British, and a great north-eastern business. And we faced and we tamed a good few Tigers along the way.

Rule 3

Head in the Direction of Where You Want to Arrive, Every Day

Fear and the Freediver

Many people say that going for a freediving record must be very scary. They are right, I was scared, but not of anything that would happen in the ocean. That, genuinely, never frightened me at all. I was scared of the responsibility and exposure that came with saying I would go for the record. Let me explain.

I made my bold action. This was to call the sports scientist, Jon Pitts and arrange to meet him urgently. Jon, coincidentally, is fascinated by the lessons that freediving brings to the rest of the sporting world in terms of mental control and controlling the sportsperson's physiology through breathing techniques. We met and I told Jon my goal. This was bolder than it seems. I knew that once I had shaken hands with Jon on it, I had made a promise that I had to keep.

He asked the obvious question – the one that I had been avoiding:

'How will you find the time to train in warm, deep water? You'll have to go overseas for stretches at a time to do that. Can you afford not to be working?'

'I was wondering if I could use the navy's deep tank.'

'How deep is it?'

'Sixty metres, I think.'

A silent gaze . . .

'OK, I know that's not deep enough.'

'Next idea?'

'Well, I wondered if I could use a divers' decompression chamber to simulate the effects of depth on my body.'

'And will that help your mind adapt to being 100 metres away from an air source?'

'You think I should be in deep water, don't you?'

'It doesn't matter what I think. What do you think it will take?'

'I think I should be in deep water.'

'How often?'

'Once a month?'

'At least, I'd say. It's technically and physically demanding to manage the pressure and it's mentally stressful to be in that environment unless you have grown accustomed to it. If you're going to commit to this properly you have to go and train at depth.'

'Once a month, then. For a week at a time. Every month from now until 27 August [the date I wanted to set the record attempt, so as to have it done before the busy September speaking season opened].'

'Can you afford that much time away from work?'

'Not really.'

'But if you don't do it, you think you'll fail. Are you going to do it or not?'

'Erm . . . Yes . . . Somehow.'

The next day I struck out the first week of every month in my diary. That was scary. Turning down speaking engagements and client projects when they began to come in really got the Tiger roaring. But it was the price of going for it as if I meant it, and I was willing to pay that price.

It struck me that it is not the big 'sexy' achievement that is beyond us – all too often it is the mundane reality of getting there that makes the Tiger roar. Getting up early in the morning. Refusing meetings that are a pointless drain on our time in order to focus on hitting our numbers instead. Working on our disciplines and basics. These are the realities that Rule 3 forces us to address. Taking personal accountability for what will be involved if we are to successfully reach the desired destination.

Rule 3: Head in the Direction of Where You Want to Arrive – Every Day

What are you getting up in the morning to do? Does it bring meaning and pleasure to you?

If you do not know what you are creating and contributing, what will give you the strength to tame Tigers in order to do it?

Viktor Frankl is best known as the founder of the Third School of Viennese Psychotherapy. He was Professor of Neurology and Psychiatry at the University of Vienna Medical School. He was also a prisoner for three years in Auschwitz, Dachau and other concentration camps during the Second World War. Along with Carl Jung and Joseph Campbell, his ideas have had the greatest influence on the development of Taming Tigers. Central to Frankl's work was a concept that Nietzsche neatly expressed and that Frankl often quoted:

'He who has a "why" to live for can bear with almost any "how".'

Frankl asks how we can find this 'why' to live for and describes three different ways that people find meaning in life. 'By creating a work or doing a deed; by experiencing something or encountering someone' (he brings this to the concept of 'love' very quickly); and 'by the attitude we take toward unavoidable suffering'.

We will not dwell on the third idea for long here. Suffice it to say that if you accept the invitation to do battle with your Tigers, there will be a degree of personal discomfort.

That is part of waking up. That also is a sign of growth and change. It brings great rewards. Life will throw us other sources of pain that we did not choose as well. An unsought source of learning and growth.

The second and third ideas are central to Taming Tigers and naturally fall into a discussion of Rule 3.

SELF-LOVE AND THE LOVE AND ACCEPTANCE OF OTHERS

Self-love and the acceptance and love of others is the central message of Taming Tigers. It underlies everything that you are reading, although this book examines it primarily in the context of your work. This is the reason why we tame the Tiger. This is our core tool for taming our Tigers. Don't be fooled into thinking that self-love or love of others is too 'soft' a message for work. It is key to success in the New Economy. It is central to leadership. It shines through as the dignity and respect that a true professional radiates towards herself and others around her within work and outside. It is evident in how we treat the customers we work with. It is a warrior's challenge, it is never-ending and it brings great strength and great rewards. This path of rediscovering and then respecting and loving your true Self involves a great deal of Tiger taming and it also involves letting go of many of the Tiger's favourite things.

It asks you to wake up – that means that the Tiger will roar!

Love of and respect for others, the ability to trust them and inspire them rather than control and manipulate them, the desire to see them grow and develop, to coach and lead with respect for boundaries and belief in the wisdom of the other – these are some of the most thrilling aspects of the shift from the industrial economy to the New Economy.

Which brings us, then, to the first of Frankl's ways of finding a 'why', to create meaning: by creating a work or doing a deed. The path that is often blocked by the Tiger's roar. The path that can lead us to great successes at work and outside.

Where Do You Want to Arrive?

Rule 3 is about setting the destination point and then plotting the course to get you there. Our starting point, then, should be our destination. Once we have decided on that, persistence rather than insistence will be the watchword. We may learn things along the way that mean we wish to change course. We may eventually find that the goal is beyond us – but that the endeavour has led us to a better place nonetheless.

Rule 3 as Taught by Professional Sportspeople

I don't know what it is like where you work, but when I worked in a large corporation the morning routine could often go something like this: arrive in the morning with a nice cup of takeaway coffee and congregate with others to have a chat about the people who had not yet arrived. Then some folk would move off to their desks and others would replace them. The conversation might then shift to those people who had just left the group. And, finally, the time would come for us to go and see what the great and merciless god Microsoft Outlook had sent us to do that day.

Sport is different – your results count. The fact that you showed up at work for eight hours does not. This is not to say that good behaviour is not also important. It is vital, but it is not enough. Results are not available every day, so you plan hard to achieve them. It is thrilling to watch and to take part in. An athlete knows the date of a big day far in advance, so the plan works back from that day. And it covers everything: nutrition, mental wellbeing, avoiding people with coughs and sneezes, sleep, fitness, strength, tactics and observing the competition and their likely approach, and, finally, rehearsing the skill that he or she will put into practice – from a tennis swing to riding a horse at top speed over five-foot fences.

What is your big day? What are you working towards and inspired by?

On Grand National day, a piece of history will be made. The events of the race and the result will be remembered and talked about in thirty years' time and beyond. Get ready today or miss your place in the history books. Simple.

That is why athletes tend not to start their days with a take-away coffee and a conversation about their colleagues. They don't start their work with a review of demands made upon them by others through their email inbox. They wake up with a driving purpose for what needs to be achieved that day if they are to arrive in the right state when the big day arrives; if they are to write the story that they want for themselves. They have a plan to achieve that and they need to execute that plan. They need to take the step today or there will be too many steps to take tomorrow. Today counts.

Does today count for you?

An athlete is not as different from you and me as you might think. Athletes have emails and phones and numerous demands on their time. They have relationships to nurture and children to care for and socks to be washed ready for the week ahead and cars to get serviced and food to be bought. Unlike most of us, they frequently have charity demands placed upon them as well, and if they are too busy to spend time with journalists they will often find that this can lead to unfortunate consequences for them. Jockeys even have riding boots that need a daily polish.

However, if athletes do not balance those obligations with moving towards the place where they want to be, they will fail to arrive there. That means they will cease to be able to pay the rent and soon cease to be professional athletes. So where they do tend to differ from many of us is that they are following Rule

3 and are guided by it. Because athletes know the destination:

- they have a clear image of where they need to get to
- they have a clear plan to get to that place
- they are committed to following that plan; and
- they face Tigers if necessary in communicating with others, or themselves, in order to prioritise that plan rather than the other stuff

Many people do not have this advantage in their daily work lives. Rule 3 is the tool used to find it.

Where do you want to arrive?

What result are you working towards? Why are you going to work today? What is the climax of this chapter of your story and which chapter are you thinking of writing next? Yes, I know I'm prodding. Are you so sensitive to the prod? And, no, it's not different just because you work in a regular job (or insert another excuse that you personally like): that is merely a victim rule from your Rulebook.

Yes, I know you probably don't want to be a sportsperson and that you may think there is little you can learn from their unhealthy levels of obsession – and especially from jockeys, for heaven's sake! But I'm not talking about big macho 'goals' here (unless that's your thing); I'm simply talking about the thing that you are working towards.

What is your big day? What is your inspired purpose? What is dictating your priorities today?

Are you motivated by running away – or by inspired purpose?

Are you heading in the direction of where you want to arrive, or

85

running in the direction opposite to where you fear to be? These are the two broad categories of things that motivate people. This is a big question and I would ask you to spend a moment really trying to understand what I mean by it. It could change many things for you.

Most people are motivated by fear. The Tiger is dominating their story. I know intelligent senior professionals who profess to have hated every working day in the past twenty years of their lives. In response to the obvious question, they reply that they would hate to lose the nice house and that the salary drop might even jeopardise their relationships. They are motivated by fear. Fear of loss. We will call this 'running away from' motivation. It often brings these people great material success but at a high personal price. It is not the success that they would truly choose for themselves. The external things they may lose, and the roar that this provokes from their Tiger, outweigh their knowledge of their true Selves so completely that they have often entirely lost sight of it.

Let us return to athletes to illustrate 'motivated towards'. Many athletes are motivated by inspired purpose. It may not inspire you to come a cropper at the first fence in the Grand National – but being a part of that historic race and taking your chances in the company of legends inspires the participants. The difference? They are running towards something they want. Of course, it is not only athletes who are motivated by inspired purpose. Many people in their professional lives are as well. They find purpose in the task or they find purpose in the way that they perform it, relate to customers and colleagues, nurture young talent, change their industry, change the world and so on.

Do you see the difference? Most of us are motivated by fear, the terrible things that might happen to us if we don't please the boss, get the promotion, have a fancy car and so on. Or motivated by avoiding the terrible risks and uncertainties that might await them if they did run towards their goals – the story that they wish to write. Perhaps they would fail. Perhaps . . . perhaps . . .

Others are motivated towards. They have a dream and they are making a difference. It is fundamental in your battle against the Tiger that you grasp this difference.

Let's work through this together. When do you set goals? For most of the Western world it is 1 January. So, after a really late night, a few weeks of over-indulgence during the festive period and, quite possibly, with the most severe hangover you will have in any twelve-month stretch, you sit down and start planning the 'new you' with the help of endless supplements and magazines. It is no real wonder that the monk-like pledges of sobriety and abstinence that we make on 1 January last about a week. They're not driven by a sense of purpose, they're driven by a sense of guilt, and guilt is not a good foundation for imagining a bright new future and exciting new adventures. We are running away from, not chasing, our inspired purpose.

So, instead of feeling guilty about all the over-indulgence that's left you many pounds overweight, a more exciting, and far more effective, way of thinking is to consider what you want to move towards – the things you'd like to do. Few of them will allow you to continue to eat badly or ignore your body's need to take exercise. By discovering a sense of purpose, it is likely that you will find yourself deciding to treat your body well. You can work this through with your professional goals in the same manner.

Be careful, though. Some people will say: 'Aha – I am motivated "towards" something: I am motivated towards a larger house and a Mercedes-Benz!' And here things become slightly ambiguous. If you find yourself giving a variation on that answer, you need to check your motivations. Why do you want these things? Will they bring you great pleasure or your family a great environment? Or will they prove something to your neighbour, colleague, parents, partner, husband, wife or even to your ex-husband or ex-wife? Proof without which you would feel 'less' – a position that many people fear and want to run away from? Can you overcome that fear, let go and instead move 'towards' something that, deep down, you actually want to achieve or contribute?

Once you are motivated 'towards' you have power. Immense power. Now you have the ability to bring your whole self – mind, body and spirit – to the activity. Now we will tame Tigers.

Now you are free. Now you are waking up!

What should I choose to move towards – how do I decide on a goal?

There are many books that claim to be able to help you to answer these questions successfully and guide you through the process. I haven't found any that deliver on their promise. I believe the reason for this is that it is not for anybody else to know, or for a universal 'process' or questionnaire to dictate. It is for you to discover. I will give some guidance below, but it is only guidance.

My reason for this cannot be better or more eloquently expressed than by repeating the words of former Harvard Professor of Psychology Gordon Allport in his Preface to Frankl's *Man's Search for Meaning*: '... *no man can tell another what his purpose is. Each must find out for himself, and must accept the responsibility that his answer prescribes.*'

I agree with this. I suspect that most of us know what our purpose is. We have long dreamed of fulfilling it. Our problem is in the last part of the deal – accepting the responsibility that our answer prescribes. Can we overcome our Tigers and dare to reach for that which we dream of and suspect we could attain – along with accepting the responsibility that our answer prescribes? We have for so long regarded the thing as impossible, because of the fear and discomfort in facing these responsibilities and the effort involved, that we have often forgotten what our purpose is.

When you think about what facing up to those responsibilities would entail – the apparently safe harbour that you would have to move out of, the responsibility of being true to yourself, despite the Tiger's interference, and of expressing yourself at work – is that not why we find so inspiring those stories of people who kept going, despite the risk of impoverishing themselves, and then eventually managed to achieve their dream? We tell our children the stories but rarely risk trying to emulate them ourselves. The examples of Mother Teresa or Martin Luther King are not complex ones to follow. They are 'merely' courageous. A lack of ability does not stop us; the Tiger does.

Let us have a look at setting our destination, then, in general terms. As you consider your destination, bear in mind that the Tiger impacts on your aspirations in three ways:

- what you aim for

- how you plan to get there

- in the day-to-day execution of your plan

As you read this, the Tiger will be getting to work on the first part – what you decide to aim for. It will want you to lower your ambition and therefore give you less risk. It will lower the boldness of your plan to arrive – increasing the chance of failure and, in the moment, as you try to execute the plan, it will try to sabotage you. The Ten Rules assist in all three stages to increase your awareness and give you the tools to combat the Tiger's interference.

Here are some pointers to finding your goal. Remember, I am not going to tell you how to find your path. I cannot do that and do not believe that anybody can, so it would be dishonest of me to promise otherwise.

Pointers to setting Tiger-free goals

1 THE PLACE YOU WANT TO ARRIVE AT NEEDN'T BE 'TRADITIONAL'

There is no safety in numbers (Rule 6). The position that you are working daily to arrive at can range from some fabulous public achievement, to the gaining of material wealth, to the creation of a new, permanent habit such as: 'I make people smile when I meet them' or 'I decline all meetings that are a waste of my time', 'I act from a position of love in the world rather than a position of self-defensiveness'. All are worthwhile climaxes to any chapter in your story, and all involve taming a Tiger and changing your world and your story for the better. All will help you wake up and discover your true purpose.

2 YOU DO NOT HAVE TO TRAVEL FAR TO MEET AND ENGAGE WITH THE TIGER AND BECOME FREE

Many people think that in order to tame a Tiger at work they have to leave their job and find a new one or start their own business. You do not have to do that. Your Tiger is not caused by your work. Your Tiger is within you. Your work circumstances – or, rather, our perception of and subsequent approach to those circumstances – merely provoke it.

Have you ever gone on holiday feeling down, hoping to cheer yourself up on a beach, only to find that you are still there, beside yourself, when you get to it? The problem has travelled with you. We need to tame the Tiger *before* we move on – not *by* moving on. The Tiger's roar will be loudest when you attempt to put right what is already around you.

Similarly, you do not need to aim to climb a high mountain at work or outside work. Start small, interrupt patterns, be heard and move into integrity. Take one hundred percent of you to work. Enjoy it!

A carefully thought through, honest and mature conversation with your boss about what is on your mind, and seeking his or her opinion about your ideas to improve things, may be a great place to start taming your Tiger.

3 Everything achieved has first been imagined

Now think for a moment about something that you have done – anything from passing a tricky exam, to riding a horse, to making the garden look nice.

You imagined it first.

You may not have sat down in a darkened room with some soothing music and painted the outcome in your mind's eye, but you created the possibility that you could pass the exam, or ride the horse or improve the garden. It did not exist, yet you thought it a possibility.

Therefore, you imagined it.

Think of an architect. When architects work, they go to a whole new level of imagining. They have clients who need to understand, planners who need to approve, builders who must have their instructions in order to execute them. So they bring their imagination into two-dimensional reality by drawing what is in their mind. Then into a three-dimensional model. And then, one day, we see the finished building and (either in horror or delight) we gasp.

For some, these imaginings became goals that they were desperate to realise. For some, they become a reality. The imagined possibility became a reality because they, personally, made it their business to bring it to life.

We should not underestimate the importance of imagination,

nor the ease with which our imagination can be squashed as we are told to 'get real' by the 'experts', or as we face up to the challenge ourselves and start to 'get real' about the size of the task.

Use your imagination. Take a long walk in the country. Take time to imagine and then decide upon the future that you will create. Enjoy it. It's your story.

4 TRUST YOUR SELF

As I wrote above, you very probably know what your goal is. Take time to contemplate this, to listen to yourself and to notice when you are motivated to 'move away from' things you fear about striving for the goal. Notice when the Tiger attacks the ideas that draw you. Ask why. Is the Rulebook telling you that it's not for people like you? Is the Rulebook running the DVD forward and showing you the 'certain' disaster that awaits you?

The battle with the Tiger has commenced.

Another important idea in trusting your Self is to be open to a little randomness. Sometimes we see a new stepping stone on our way across the water that appeals. It may not be the most direct route, but it none the less appeals. We are drawn to it. Consider trusting that stepping stone. Allow randomness to call you occasionally – even if you eventually decide not to answer.

All the adventures that have led me to growth have seemed random and 'silly' to others at first. Who spends a year working at their career with the handicap of becoming a jockey at the same time? Who takes unpaid leave to break a freediving record? Who leaves a career in law after ten years? I am not claiming that these were the best decisions I could have taken. They may not have been wise decisions as defined by 'conventional wisdom'. But they were my decisions and not my Tiger's. No regrets. If I had not taken them, I would not have written my story – I would have written the story that I, and others, expected of 'somebody like me'. They are also some of the best decisions I have taken and they led me to wake up and to grow.

Looking forward, the non-direct stepping stones may make no logical, rational sense. Looking *back*, the stepping stones may all make perfect sense. The slightly unexpected, non-linear decisions often lead somewhere truly astonishing.

We may be remaining linear and avoiding randomness because of the Tiger's roar.

'But I don't have time to try something that doesn't come with guarantees.' 'But what if it went wrong?' 'But nobody takes that path – it is frowned upon to take chances.' Yes. That is a risk. But, then again, it could all go wrong if you stand still – and the non-linear path may make you or your business a far better prospect down the line, setting you apart from all the 'me too' products designed through linear processes.

And what if it went right – and transformed you?

Trust your Self.

5 Set SMAT goals [sic]

The work done by Sir John Whitmore, executive chairman of Performance Consultants, gave us many of the principles of modern coaching. You can read this in his book *Coaching for Performance*.

There is only one area in which I depart from Whitmore's view. I don't think that goals should always be SMART. A SMART goal, as you are probably aware, is:

Specific
Measurable
Agreed
Realistic
Time-phased

In my experience we are unable to define what is realistic for ourselves and nobody is able to advise us. Understanding what 'realistic' means relies on one or a mix of three things:

- what I think is realistic
- what my friends, colleagues or advisers think is realistic
- what history suggests is realistic

I trust none of those sources to define 'realistic' for me and my story. Do you?

I am not suggesting that 'you can do anything'. Neither you nor I can do that. But almost every person with whom I shared the idea of racing or freediving told me they were impossible. If I asked a consultant whether I could build and run the Taming Tigers group the way that I have done (and still do), I am sure I would have been told that I could not. There is nothing realistic about it, in theory. Yet it was all imagined and then it was all created.

If Taming Tigers' clients' goals had always *appeared* realistic at the outset, they would have missed some extraordinary leaps forward. It turns out that they were *entirely* realistic – but nobody would have advised them so at the outset.

There is a big risk, however, when you remove the word realistic. You can end up being disappointed – or setting goals that you are not able to achieve for reasons beyond your control. Some people do not have the voices to be pop stars – it would be entirely unrealistic for them to set out on that path. To avoid that disappointment without completely ignoring your dream outcome, try aiming for the large goal but setting small, achievable, realistic steps to get to it. Set your ladder against the wall you wish to scale, but aim to climb a step at a time to test yourself. If you cannot haul yourself up onto step one, it may be necessary to re-set the ladder.

May I repeat: there is an unhealthy 'you can achieve your dreams – whatever they may be' philosophy being sold to people. This is not a part of Taming Tigers and I do not consider it to be true.

6 USE THE 'WHY NOT?' WHEEL

The favourite tool at Taming Tigers for exploring what is 'realistic' – or, rather, whether a goal has a chance of being achieved – is our 'Why Not?' wheel. You can download the 'Why Not?' wheel and watch a video guiding you through its use from the Taming Tigers Campus at tamingtigers.com.

The 'Why Not?' wheel is a diagram of a spoked wheel. You write on the outside of each spoke one thing that would need to be accomplished for you to have a chance of success in achieving the goal, or in achieving step one on the ladder. Once that is done and you have a collection of things on the outside of the wheel, you give yourself a score out of ten reflecting your current position in relation to the thing that you would need to accomplish. You mark your score on each task's spoke. Ten is the outside rim of the wheel, zero is the middle, at the hub. When this is done, draw a line joining the scoring points on the spokes. The line will go around on the inside of the wheel and will look very irregular – like a damaged spider's web.

On my jockey wheel, at the outset, I scored like this:

Task to be accomplished	Current score
Live in Lambourn	0
Be able to ride a racehorse	0
Lose three stone in weight	0
Be able to run four miles in forty minutes	2
	(I could walk it)
Understand how horseracing works	0
Get a permit to ride under Jockey Club Rules	0
Be strong enough to ride full 'races' on the equicisor*	0
Free time in the diary to ride out and get riding lessons	1

(*The equicisor is a machine on which jockeys build strength and stamina.)

Having constructed the 'Why Not?' wheel, you get to see the task ahead. You can shade in the area where you already have scores, and leave the remainder, between your scores and the 'ten' area, unshaded. This is the area that you would need to progress into – *if you decide to commit to the goal.* Remember, at this stage you are only asking yourself 'Why Not?'

Now that you can see what remains to be done – without at this stage having committed – you can take a decision. The important question is this:

Is there anything involved in increasing these scores that I do not think I can manage or am unwilling to take on?

In the case of the horseracing wheel that I built out of the scores above, I reckoned that I could move all the elements to a ten with sufficient application and discipline. Therefore I could do it if I wanted to. And I did want to. If, on the outside wheel, I had had to write 'be able to perform slam dunks', then at 5'7", I would probably have had to concede that there was a good reason 'why not'.

A goal may sound 'unrealistic' when you say it out loud – or when you try it out on colleagues in the team. Try the 'Why Not?' wheel, though, before you decide to abandon it. You might change your mind.

7 REMEMBER THAT SOMEBODY IS WRITING THE STORY THAT IS UNFOLDING

Your story to date is made up of the sum of your choices, your decisions to act or to refrain from acting. Either the pen is writing with purpose or it is doodling. If it is doodling, there is no need to face a Tiger at any stage. Why would you battle with it for no reason? That means that the Tiger is writing your story. It must be. We don't battle with the Tiger without a motivation to do so. Good luck when we meet in the nursing home, my friend – this'll be one for the grandchildren!

8 I KNOW THAT YOU DON'T HAVE TIME

Nobody does. That is the single most common response to an introduction to Tiger taming. I have had entire rooms filled with salespeople who aren't hitting their numbers call out almost as one that they 'don't have time' to create the plan or to act on it, in order to rectify the disaster that they are so 'busy' creating. Please read Rules 2, 8 and 1, in that order, if you truly believe that you 'don't have time'. If you don't truly believe it, throw away the crutch today.

Moving in your new, inspired direction – *every day*

There is a second part to Rule 3. You are asked to move in the direction of where you want to arrive *every day*. This is one big area in which most corporate change programmes start to go wrong. This is where personal goals begin to founder. The reality of the day job gets in the way. Read some of the case studies in this book, though, and read the other Ten Rules, particularly Rule 8. They will all assist you in keeping on track and achieving your purpose. It can be done. Success stories surround us, the stories of ordinary people with a powerful enough 'why' to create the strength to survive the 'what'. Are you going to add your story to that inspiring list?

Putting the plan in place

Here are some solid, practical steps to help you create a powerful plan, encourage you to tame your Tiger as it roars and that will take you, every single day, in the direction of where you want to arrive.

STEP ONE: LOOK FOR WHAT WILL BRING YOU DOWN

Look carefully, think carefully, imagine carefully. What is it that will really make this project grind to a halt? For me, with the racing plan, it would be nothing to do with horses or weight. It would be with having to spend fifty hours a week bringing home the bacon, eighteen hours a week driving to and from Lambourn to get to a racing stables, eighteen hours a week sitting on racehorses and six hours per week running. The maths didn't work. If I didn't deal with that, there would be no point starting on the project. This was a fascinating starting place for me. I was still stuck on the idea that a lack of any ability to ride a horse would be the stumbling block. My coaches, Gee Armytage and Michael Caulfield, didn't have any worries about that. They were worried that I wouldn't have enough time even to get to my lessons. *And they were right.*

So get real. Get real in this planning process and begin to look at what's going to bring you down. Is it the commute? Is it lack of support from your family? Is it how you fit it alongside your daily workload – do you need to delegate? Is it getting the boss onside or getting funding? Do you need to recruit or get training in new skills? These are not reasons to give up. They are things that you'll need to deal with early on. Get them on to the plan now before you put the 'sexy' stuff on there.

STEP TWO: USE THE RULES FOR TAMING TIGERS

You will find the answers to how to deal with the issues posed above within the covers of this book. They may not be obvious – you need to do the thinking – but they are there. You'll find them within the covers of this book either because I came up against similar issues on the way to the racetrack or in setting a British freediving record or the great Tiger tamers whose stories are told in this book came up against them on the way to achieving their goals. Everything that you read about in these pages has been written by practitioners, not by theorists or people who make their living from writing 'persuasive books'. You can depend on what is being said here, you can trust it and you can adapt it to your world.

STEP THREE: WRITE DOWN DISCIPLINES

You will need to put in place certain things that you will do every day – these will be your new basics and disciplines – to enable you to reach an exciting new place. So important did I realise this was to the racing year that it became Rule 9 – there were only eight rules when I first made the bet (Rule 10 was the second addition).

STEP FOUR: WRITE DOWN THE 'WHY'

Why are you doing this? What are you going to get out of it? When you are there, in the moment, thinking of cheating on one of your disciplines or giving up the project altogether, what's the big reason that you can look at in your mind to encourage you to stay on track? Note, this is not 'What' are you doing – that is obvious and also insufficient to sustain you. WHY are you doing it? What is the gain for you? How will your life be different?

STEP FIVE: DIARISE EVERYTHING AND PROTECT THOSE DIARY ENTRIES

Your plan is meaningless on some random piece of paper; it needs to be in your diary, and these elements of your plan need to be *the least movable entries* you make in it. Here you are writing the story of your life, writing the next chapter. Here you've seized the pen back from the Tiger. Don't let a meeting with a customer knock this bit out of your diary. Knock something else out to let that customer in – or delegate. Diarise planning and thinking time as well.

STEP SIX: DECIDE ON YOUR BOLD ACTION

The final step (if you have not already completed this after the challenge laid down in Rule 1) is to plan your bold action for today and to get the thing started.

You have to interrupt your patterns and habits and get it started.

This bold action should ideally involve somebody else, because that's where Tigers are tamed. The bold action is not to go to the bookshop. The bold action is to ring up somebody who could help you and announce or intention to them, or to sit down with your partner and tell him or her what it is you would like to achieve and what it is you plan to do to get there, and ask for their support. This will help you solidify both your plan and the resolve to stick to it.

You will know what the bold action is because it's the thing that you least want to do and yet the thing that is most likely to take you there. Do it today if possible or, if it is late in the evening now, before ten o'clock tomorrow morning.

STEP SEVEN: WORK WITH OTHERS

This cannot be done alone. Little of value can. We will return to this in detail very soon as Rule 5 is dedicated to this imperative.

STEP 8 STOP READING AND DO SOMETHING

Now!

Rule 3 and the plan to get to the racecourse

'Leave the racing part to me,' Gee instructed me as we set out.

'All you have to do is what I ask you to do this week.' So that's easy then, I thought . . .

I believe that luck can sometimes play a part in life, but I'm not going to give it credit for the fact that I had Michael Caulfield and Gee Armytage to work with me on creating a plan to get to the racetrack. That credit goes to Rules 1 and 5 of the Ten Rules for Taming Tigers and the fact that people are, generally, great. Working with Gee and Michael meant that I could put in place a plan that I could cope with.

Gee and Michael were able to break down the tasks involved. Why? Because they knew what those tasks were and I did not (see Rule 5). Now Michael is a good horseman and has worked in racing for many years, but he let Gee take the lead when it came to working on riding, diet and exercise. What else could there be, you might ask? Well, there were a variety of things that I hadn't even realised existed that would make the plan a failure from day one unless they were addressed. Not least among these was the fact that I needed to pay the mortgage and all my other outgoings, and I was about to introduce a huge new activity into my working week. Secondly, I lived in East Sheen at the time, in south-west London. The drive to Lambourn for a 6 a.m. start would prove quite difficult. Within a week I was under-performing at work by 2 p.m. each day.

The wonderful thing about having a sense of purpose, which I'd discovered when I shook hands with Gee in Lambourn that first night, is that once the steps have been decided you can act decisively to make them happen. You have clarity. So as I sat in Michael's cottage near Lambourn, we worked through the practical steps that I would need to take immediately if this project was to have any chance of succeeding. The first was to move to Lambourn. The second was to transform how I organised my work into an extremely streamlined process.

When I'm speaking onstage, I don't have time to add in all these little details, so it's always frustrating to find myself talking to people afterwards and realise that they've gained the impression that I took a year's sabbatical to do this and that; therefore, of course, life is different for them as they would not be able to take time off. That was not a luxury I had or would have wanted. I love my work.

The meeting with Michael highlighted the things that might overwhelm me and kill the project long before any falls from horses got in the way of my plan. The meeting also gave me manageable steps. Suddenly I didn't have to worry about getting to the racecourse. Gee, Michael and Tina Fletcher were experts and they thought it was worth a shot. And *they* had dictated what my first steps should be. Rules 1, 3 and 5 involved working together here, and together they were changing my Rulebook and making success seem feasible.

My plan, agreed with Gee and Michael in those early days, was:

1. Chat to Meregan and Charles Norwood about their cottage that might be available to rent.

Within two weeks I had let my property in East Sheen and moved into the cottage. Charles and Meregan made me very welcome in a strange new land and I will always be grateful to them for that.

2. Create a plan to streamline my work to create more time.

This plan is still in place today and has profoundly affected how I run my business. I used to spend around 35 per cent of my time travelling to or sitting in sales meetings. Dead time. This conversation forced me to imagine a different way of working, partnering with other companies to take care of the selling part, which is how we work to this day. I removed all speculative meetings from my diary and replaced them with productive work. My planning session with Michael allowed my working hours to decrease while my income increased.

3. Go to Candy and Billy Morris's store on Saturday morning to buy some kit.

Candy and Billy became friends and we ended up as neighbours by living in the same village, East Garston. Candy introduced me to her brother, Gary Moore, the unique Brighton trainer who gave me a ride on the racetrack in a charity race on a horse called Theatre of Life and for whom I rode out during 2007.

4. Go to watch Martin Bosley's string work on the gallops.

Former jump jockey and great racehorse trainer Martin Bosley, and his wife, the former jockey Sarah Bosley, not only became and remain good friends, but their patient nurturing and advice and encouragement played a massive role in helping me win my bet. Within three short weeks of this meeting and my first lesson with Tina, Martin let me go up the gallops 'riding' Franklin Lakes, a beautiful racehorse in full training, with Sarah behind shouting real-time advice – loudly! Frankie did all the thinking – but I was in the racing world and learning fast.

5 Go for a riding lesson with Tina Fletcher.

Tina Fletcher is one of the UK's leading international showjumpers and an Olympic-level coach. In 2011 she became the first woman in thirty-eight years to win the prestigious Hickstead Derby. How did I get a riding lesson with Tina? It wasn't talent or cash, I'm afraid. I think, having seen me try to ride a horse, Gee rang one of her oldest friends and said, 'You have got to see this!' Once Tina saw the scale of the challenge, I don't think she could resist it.

So we went on, day by day, week by week, challenge by challenge towards the place where we wanted to arrive. About a week before I thought I was ready to move ahead, Gee presented the next challenge. Each week had a goal, each day had a target. The clarity was vital, the progress was encouraging and confidence building and the sense of purpose was exhilarating. The Tiger didn't stand a chance.

You are writing the story of your life. What chapter are you going to commit to writing next?

An inspired sense of purpose – the 'why', nectar for the human soul

The greatest effect that delivering the Taming Tigers speeches and seminars around the world has had is assisting people to discover or rediscover their sense of purpose. The rules have done the same for me over the past ten years. By identifying the Tiger and how to tame it, you, too, can discover that you are free to get on with writing the story that you want to write for yourself, your family, your colleagues and your business.

You have met people with an inspired sense of purpose. Maybe you have been such a person or are one today. You know the glow that radiates from a person who has purpose. You have seen the optimism in their eyes. You have wondered at their ability to make clear decisions based on some solid core. You may have thought them 'brave' because they were willing to deal with Tigers to move forward. You have probably referred to them as 'inspirational' or 'a breath of fresh air'.

These 'inspirational' people come in all shapes and sizes. The sixty-five-year-old who suddenly decides to face the Tiger's roar and learn to drive in order to play an active part in the lives of her grandchildren. The unassuming teacher who has quietly dedicated four decades to spreading a passion for literature in the local school. The man who goes to prison in 1964 stating a willingness to die for the cause of a 'democratic and free society in which all persons live together in harmony' and repeats that same intention the moment he re-emerges into the world in 1990.

They all have a sense of purpose and we remember them for

it; we love them for it. They inspire us. They change us and they change our worlds.

A sense of purpose gives our lives new meaning and gives each dawn a new meaning. It drives our decisions and gives us a reason to be courageous and tenacious when the moment suddenly and unexpectedly challenges us and our resolve wavers.

Acting in accordance with our sense of purpose presents us with the last plank in the Integrity Rules. Acting on Rule 3 today will bring you a whole day closer to the things that you want to achieve.

Over to you.

Things the Tiger wants you to forget about Rule 3

Rule 3: Head in the direction of where you want to arrive – every day

It is wonderful, and healthy, to have an inspired sense of purpose. It enables us to face challenges and grow.

We are either motivated away from or motivated towards. The latter is a healthy, inspiring state to cultivate.

Nobody can set your goal for you – you must find it. If you are confused, start with a small goal and the experience of reaching it will increase your self-awareness and likelihood of finding your purpose.

Tips on setting your goal:

- It needn't be 'traditional'

- It's OK to start local, you do not need to have a huge life disrupting goal

- Everything achieved has first been imagined – give yourself time to reflect and imagine

- Listen to and trust yourSelf.

- Set SMAT goals

- Use the 'Why Not?' Wheel

- 'Nobody has time', apparently – yet some people still achieve. What does this tell you?

How to stay on the path to success in your goal – every day:

- Look for what will bring you down – plan for it

- Use the Ten Rules – they work

- Write your disciplines down (Rule 9)

- Know your 'why' – and remember it

- Diarise the plan and protect those entries – they are your story

- Work with others (Rule 5)

- Decide on your Bold Action and do it

Now log onto the Campus at tamingtigers.com and watch the film entitled 'The "Why Not?" Wheel'.

Twitter: @jim_lawless
Web: tamingtigers.com
Facebook: facebook.com/pages/Taming-Tigers.

Case Study 3:
Lt Dennis Narlock

Like many people I met Jim when he was speaking at a conference. In my case, it took place in London in April of 2009. It really was the universe aligning at that moment as I almost skipped his session to drift off to the pub for a pint. Instead, I sat through a session that was energising and changed my life for the better over the past two years. I grabbed a book, spoke for a few moments with Jim and embarked on a journey to tame my Tigers. I enjoyed great success employing the rules in my daily life. The most important ones to me were Rule 1 and Rule 5. In fact, taking that bold action is what led me to access many of the tools that were all around me.

In the early months of 2010 I assumed a position as the director of quality for an organisation of more than three hundred technicians performing scheduled maintenance and unscheduled repairs in support of the aviation industry. Shortly after moving into the office and meeting the team of quality inspectors that I had working with me there was an inspection to evaluate our performance with multiple regulatory programmes. We earned a less than stellar 43 per cent compliance rate. Our next inspection would be only five short months in the future.

Facing pressure from higher levels in the organisation to dramatically improve our compliance rate and emboldened by my personal success, I once again turned to Taming Tigers and the Ten Rules to improve our compliance rate. The challenge I faced was that I was not Jim; I did not have a compelling story to illustrate the Ten Rules, nor did I have the charismatic public speaking ability to energise the team. At that point I must admit that I allowed the Tigers to get the upper hand in those first weeks on the job. Then I received the first blog from the Taming Tigers website. Looking at the rules I realised that I had allowed myself to become paralysed by a fear of rejection. 'What if my team didn't support the road I was leading them down?' When I reviewed the Ten Rules I realised that I needed to take that bold action and do something that was scary.

I began by forwarding Jim's blogs out to my team and talking about the rules at morning and afternoon team briefings. This allowed me to relate our situation to the Ten Rules and to interject my personal experiences. At first very little seemed to come of these emails and discussion, but that quickly changed a week into the process when my quality manager, Joe, approached me and wanted to discuss the Ten Rules. I gave him my copy of the book and within a few days he handed it back, stating that he had ordered his own. I was no longer one against many; instead there was the core of a team, ready to lead the way forward to success.

Sharing the blogs became a good routine and as time passed I began to add my own interpretation of what Jim wrote. I was able to relate each of them to our current challenge in the quality arena. At the end of the first thirty days in the position, four of the twelve quality inspectors had read the book, all twelve routinely read and discussed the blogs that had been forwarded and we were discussing our Tigers during our morning and evening briefs. The team had come together around the Ten Rules and I felt that we were ready to begin applying them to our preparation for the upcoming inspection that was now only four months away. Joe and I spent a couple of days formulating our plan of action; the plan that, infused with the Ten Rules, would lead to our success. While all of the rules would be utilised, Rules 8, 3, 9 and 10 would form the way as we progressed toward the inspection.

'Understand and control your time to create change' (Rule 8) served as the starting point: we had a specific time frame when the inspection would take place. We had the criteria we would be evaluated on and we had our results from the previous inspection. In order to communicate where we stood and what needed to be accomplished, a chart was created that depicted the status of each programme, which inspector was responsible for the programme and the time remaining until the inspection. This visual aid was clearly displayed in the office and communicated to everyone in the organisation how much time remained to create change.

'Head in the direction of where you want to arrive – every day.' Once the whole team had a solid grasp of Rule 8 it was time to move forward, but to what end? We need to start with the end in mind and clearly establish our goal. Rather than direct what this goal would be, Joe and I asked for recommendations from each of the twelve inspectors. Their recommendations ranged from 80 to 90 per cent of the programmes being evaluated as compliant. This was great since it opened the door to an intense team discussion as to whether or not it was OK to decide that a failure of up to 20 per cent of our programmes was acceptable. The second portion of that discussion was whether or not it was acceptable to allow programmes that affected personnel or aircraft safety to be evaluated as non-compliant. The end result was that as the driving force behind quality, we could not accept any programme being evaluated as non-compliant. The direction where we chose to end up was 100 per cent programme compliance. This was expressed in a team mission statement that was proudly displayed at each person's desk throughout the office. It would remind each of us as to our purpose and the direction we were heading. It turned Rule 3 into our compass for the coming months. When Rule 3 was coupled with Rule 8 it provided us with both direction and progress.

'Create disciplines – do the basics brilliantly.' Each programme is evaluated using a comprehensive checklist with equipment, licence and personnel touch point numbered in the thousands. In order to achieve the goal that the team had established, a methodical approach was applied to evaluating each programme. It was at this point that Joe and I began to discuss the day-to-day basics with our team. Rather than exercise the standard method of directing those we lead by providing them with the basics, we utilised the tools that were all around us; we challenged the twelve team members to develop the basics that would guide our daily tasks. Three short days later the team presented their basics for approval. They were:

- be on time
- be prepared
- be proactive, not reactive
- be flexible
- be supportive
- assist your team-mates
- communicate
- accomplish your intentions
- don't hesitate to call a meeting
- obtain customers' expectations
- plan tasks ahead of time
- be open-minded
- share the workload
- don't just lead – empower

The team achieved consensus in recommending the basics; they were able to define each of them and I provided my full support to adopting them. They were added to the mission statements at each person's desk. My promise to each of them was that I would hold them to the basics. Combining the effects of these three rules empowered the team; they knew the goal, the direction and how we were going to achieve success.

'Never, never give up.' As a team we moved into the final rule that we would apply on a daily basis. We were supportive, lending strength and knowledge to each other. It was as if the entire team was a single-entity focused on achieving the goal.

This gave them the strength to overcome the Tigers from within the organisation, those other members of the organisation who worked outside the quality office. The quality team was challenged daily, by their peers on the production line, overcoming this resistance with their feet firmly rooted in the foundation created by the Ten Rules. When the week of the inspection arrived, we were cautiously confident and worked well with the team of inspectors. Five hectic days later the results were delivered. We had achieved a 95 per cent compliance rate. While we did not achieve our goal of 100 per cent, no programme affecting aircraft or personnel safety was evaluated as non-compliant. We exceeded the results of similar organisations that were evaluated that year. We had tamed many of our Tigers. In the months that followed the inspection several of our team members, including Joe and myself, were moved to other parts of the organisation. The new challenge that each of us would face was to elevate the performance of the new teams we were assigned to.

Prior to this experience I had not considered using the Ten Rules as the leader of an organisation or part of an organisation. What I have learned is that these simple rules can be used to bring a team together, establish a method for interacting and relating to the organisation as a whole and, finally, to achieve success!

Intermission - Understanding the Tiger, Understanding Our Selves

Now that you have read the Integrity Rules, you have got to know your Tiger far better. So now I can explain a little more about it to you than I could when we first met.

I'll start by increasing your awareness of fear and discomfort. I'll then try to persuade you that these things are attractive and not to be avoided. We may fall out there for a little while but I think we'll come out fine the other end. Finally, we will look at how your perception of fear and discomfort creates the roar of the Tiger and dictates the quality of the decisions you take, and so the quality of the story that you write.

'Living with ourselves'

Who are the two people involved in this statement? There are many theories. For now, let us take it as your true Self and your Tiger. The two often conflict. A balance of the two is required for us to live in harmony with ourselves and in the world. In our current age, we tend to have more Tiger than true Self active in our heads and in our decision-making. Let me explain this:

Your true Self is that part of you that takes its value from internal sources. It tells you to:

- act in accordance with your personal values

- develop and follow your personal sense of purpose

- have meaning in your life

- have real, authentic connections with others; and

- grow – a sense that you are evolving and moving forward rather than stagnating

Your Tiger seeks value more from external sources. The Tiger seeks to *guarantee* that the basics of life will be provided rather than trusting that you will be able to provide them. It seeks to protect your external 'stock', to diminish any risk to your reputation or status in the pack – what do they think of me and how can I be sure to 'save face'? Am I 'acceptable' or 'needed' or shall I compromise my values and purpose to become so to these people?

As a rule of thumb, the more we listen to the Tiger, the more we compromise our true Selves and therefore our story. I repeat: a balance of the two is required for us to write our stories. Of course we need to consider our financial security. There are, however, those who have spent their whole lives kowtowing to people they do not respect in order to do this. It has been their primary purpose and meaning in their working life to protect that security.

What of this person's true Self? This was sacrificed, seen as less important and even self-indulgent. Perhaps they never learned to see themselves as deserving of a great story, of having purpose, meaning, values, connection or growth. But the true Self doesn't go away. A resentful, angry 'victim' usually emerges to compensate for the anguish of knowing that there is another story, smothered beneath the Tiger's roar.

Pain, fear and discomfort

Human beings do not like pain, fear or discomfort. But facing fear and some minor discomfort is required in order to set ourselves free from the Tiger and to grow, to live according to our values and to write *our* story.

Pain is the vital warning sign, the motivator of personal change. When we experience pain we want to move away from it. But as a species, we have worked very hard to mask pain. This means we stay stuck! There is no motivation to move away from a sensation that we have numbed.

In the twenty-first century, there are a whole range of options for masking pain – all affordable in our current period of relative economic ease (even in the current climate, most of us have wealth our grandparents could not have imagined), to anaesthetise ourselves against the pain of knowing we are living life while asleep.

We can drink alcohol, smoke dope, visit dodgy websites, indulge in some charming but phoney people pleasing (and then enjoy whinging to others about how put upon we are), we can numb ourselves in front of the television, we can do hard drugs, we can go shopping and enjoy the heady pleasures of retail therapy, we can throw ourselves into our work, we can overeat or we can starve ourselves, we can smoke a cigarette, we can let off steam by ranting at our partner, parents, children or dog.

What do we have left after we lose all of our 'pleasures'?

Real life, real love and real adventure! 'Real' means accepting life's realities, including pain, fear and discomfort; including the Tiger.

How Do You Feel About Pain, Fear and Discomfort?

I thought so. That's how I used to feel too.

I want to let you into a very powerful secret. All growth, all adventure, everything that we strike out to achieve that is worthwhile, everything that has been achieved that is worthwhile involves or has involved some form of personal fear and discomfort in order to allow us to move away from the sensation of pain. Such sentiments are extremely unfashionable, of course in the age of the quick fix promise.

When you think about taking away the options used for masking pain as listed above, how do you feel? A little uneasy? Yet all of these addictive pastimes keep us asleep.

Wake up!

There is a whole adventure to be lived; you are capable of achieving things way beyond your current level of imagination. We all are. But there is one thing that we all need to recognise before we are allowed to embark on that journey:

Fear and discomfort are often your compass bearing. Head straight for them and away from the pain source.

As children we were constantly thrust into new, often scary situations. We generally took these in our stride. We didn't have a lot of choice. The danger kicks in when we move into adult life and take the helm of our little ships. We decide what challenges to face. We can soon forget the skill of dealing with fear and discomfort – so when they arise we will avoid them because we can. And so we are now in the 'rut' that so many people speak of – despite living in the most fascinating, peaceful, economically wealthy, liberated, healthy age that most of the world has ever known.

Wake up!

Why Do You Keep Talking About Fear *and* Discomfort?

Sometimes the only thing to fear is a little discomfort. There is nothing to spark off what we usually experience as fear. We don't go near the discomfort because of the fact that we don't want to experience it; it frightens us away.

Imagine that you want a new business qualification. You want finally to unravel the mysteries of the balance sheet. This is not hard to accomplish. It is not of itself frightening. There is little risk of harm. But there is discomfort. You will have to keep your evenings free to attend classes and carry out your exercises diligently. That's all. But this is a discomfort.

Much of my training for freediving and racing had no fear attached to it, merely discomfort. It was the discomfort that was hardest to deal with. Try getting up at 5 a.m. for a week to fit in your training and you'll see what I mean about discomfort. Is that a good reason not to race or dive, though? I had to wrangle with that question on more than one occasion I can tell you!

The thought of that discomfort will put many people off writing their story. Yet discomfort always becomes comfortable – because we grow, evolve and adapt. We change.

The Tiger will roar when we consider committing to anything that involves discomfort. That is why fear and discomfort are the dynamic duo that the Ten Rules for Taming Tigers help us accept again. Our fear of facing fear and discomfort is the main barrier to us writing our wonderful stories.

Fear Is Good for Me – It Keeps Me Safe!

A comment that often comes up during Taming Tigers workshops and presentations is: 'The Tiger is a force for good! It keeps me safe. The Tiger is the thing that stops me walking off the edge of a cliff.'

Well, I don't know about you but I don't need the Tiger's roar to keep me away from the edge of a cliff. Common sense does the job nicely for me. Few of us need to experience a pounding heart, sweaty palms, a dry mouth and a feeling that our brain has turned to sponge to protect us from that danger. However, many of us will have experienced those sensations when walking into a senior leadership meeting, sitting opposite a senior member of our client organisation or picking up the telephone to make a cold call to a potentially important new contact. As a result of the feeling of fear, we may have chosen not to pick up the phone – or to act defensively and unnaturally in the meeting room.

It is said that most working people fear speaking in public more than they fear death. Stop there and think about that for a moment!

As we go about our working day, the fear of loss of face is generally a far greater motivator than a desire to succeed and achieve, to lead, to be a role model at work and at home, to write our stories.

The Tiger does not keep you safe from walking off the edge of a cliff, your intellect does. The Tiger keeps you safe from learning how to move into new and currently intimidating areas of performance. It keeps you safe from improving, growing, learning and being more successful in your work and wider life.

Wake up!

FEAR AND THE TIGER CYCLE

The sensation of fear is the physical response created by the release of hormones from the adrenal glands when the brain perceives a threat to its wellbeing – for example, a meeting with the boss to ask for a pay rise.

The physical response triggers a further mental heightening which in turn can create a greater physical response. When this process gets out of control in a person, we observe panic. This, incidentally, is why freediving and riding racehorses are very good tests for the Taming Tigers ideas. Panic at 101 metres without air is lethal. Racehorses seem to be able to smell an adrenaline release – and reward you by bolting. You have to learn to interrupt the Tiger Cycle very quickly.

The fear response is designed to prepare our system to survive physical attack from a predator through flight, fight or freeze. It was very useful when we lived in the wild. It could be very useful now if you had to run to find help in an emergency. But it is a poor aid to facing the boss and asking for a pay rise.

The adrenals release their hormones when the brain perceives a risk. The risk may be imagined, the adrenals don't care. They'll pump away. The terrible outcome that we create in our minds about the meeting with the boss tomorrow, for example, is imagined. But the adrenals haven't evolved to distinguish that from reality – so real fear is what we experience when we imagine a distant, possible, threat.

The Tiger and your decision-making process

You remember that we write our stories by making decisions, acting and getting results? For many people, this outdated hormonal mechanism guides their decision-making. The Tiger's source, the reason we perceive the situation as a risk, is deep-rooted and complex. This hormone release, however, is the Tiger's roar that causes us to back away from opportunity. In *Taming Tigers*, we work on not letting the roar hold us back from writing our story rather than on the complex source of the roar – which often diminishes of its own accord when we see we can move past the Tiger (or may be addressed through a range of psychotherapeutic interventions).

It is important really to understand this part if you want to improve your decision-making.

If you avoid the perceived threat, the fear and the hormone release subsides. So we are motivated to avoid the threat! The roar decreases. The Tiger writes a sentence of your story.

We agreed that the biggest day-to-day threat in the modern world is fear of damage to reputation – which has a small, potential link to fear of damage to finances (I might fail and look silly and therefore not get the promotion and the pay rise). So the threats that we avoid to silence the Tiger are the innovation, the leadership stance, the sales opportunity, the bold, honest comment that could invigorate or coach a colleague, the decision to fire a poor performer with a bad attitude.

This is why Rule 3 is so vital. You need to know *why* it is necessary to face fear and discomfort rather than avoid it. Without a defined end point, nobody would face the Tiger when, in the moment, they have to decide whether to open their mouths and speak or remain silent.

Here is the magic part of being a human being and the basis of all Tiger taming:

We are not like other animals; we can become self-aware and interrupt the Tiger Cycle to make better decisions and these decisions are how we write our story and achieve successes. We can break the Tiger cycle!

BREAKING THE TIGER CYCLE

Let's look together at the Tiger cycle and how to break out of it and create growth and change. Have a look at the diagram on p. 120. A challenge of some kind hits us: 'Deliver a presentation to a group of twenty people on Monday!'

THE CHALLENGE AND THE RULEBOOK

We immediately begin assessing the risk that this challenge poses to us. We do this, of course, in the light of our Rulebook (Rule 2), the way we see the world. Let's suppose you have a rule that says: 'I am a bad presenter. I know this, because I have received feedback telling me that I am a bad presenter. In fact, now that we have 360° feedback, everybody has been telling me what a bad presenter I am.'

THE EMOTIONAL AND PHYSICAL RESPONSE – TIGER ATTACK

Information contained in the challenge interacts with this rule in our Rulebook that we have built up to keep us safe from

Breaking the Tiger Cycle.

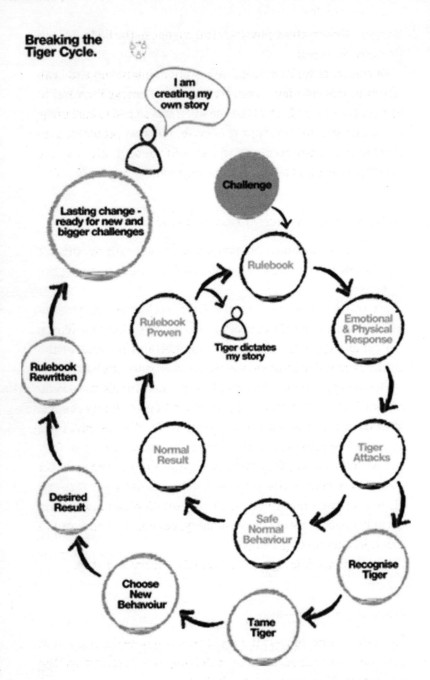

'danger'. This creates a physiological change in the body – which we perceive as fear.

Of course, as we have seen, we are not animals. You and I can interrupt this emotion – even rechannel the energy it creates to work in our favour. Each of the Ten Rules is designed to encourage and assist you to interrupt this cycle. But few people care to develop the self-awareness and the courage to do this. So the response grows and becomes more physical. Feeling tense yet?

DECISION TIME – WHICH ACTION TO TAKE?

Now you have a choice. Do you avoid the scary thing and the Tiger's roar or do you head straight into it, skilfully taming the Tiger as you go?

We could choose to tame the Tiger, seek training, prepare with the assistance of a colleague who is an excellent presenter. We could choose to rehearse in the evenings in front of the family camcorder until we feel we are doing an excellent job.

Most people do not choose to engage their intellect. They do not want to face the fear and discomfort of growth and change. They do want to avoid the Tiger's roar. So they permit their emotional response to override their desire to do a good job. They run with the crowd; they avoid engaging with the audience, let PowerPoint take centre stage and deliver what we at Taming Tigers call 'the middle-manager's presentation', a presentation entirely unencumbered by personality, passion, vision, commitment, leadership or gravitas.

They have met their Tiger and permitted it to write their story.

DECISION, ACTION – *RESULT*

The latter action delivers the usual poor response that they have become accustomed to. The Rulebook is reinforced by the experience. They are more stuck than ever.

'Poor me, why was I born without this module fitted correctly? I wish I were a natural like (insert name of person who has worked bravely on their presenting skills).' They will dread the next invitation to present. The Tiger cycle continues.

The former action brought minor discomfort in the form of preparation and brought fear into the room when the presenter courageously tried the new, exposed and engaged way of presenting to the group. It might have gone wrong, of course. So what if it did momentarily wobble? It might also have gone right – and if that happens a new result is achieved and a new rule is written into the Rulebook.

Through facing the Tiger – and some fear and discomfort – the Tiger cycle of poor results has been broken.

This cannot be achieved by mouthing affirmations in the mirror. It is not achieved by listening to a CD or reading a book.

This new, bold result is achieved through courage, bravery and heroic action. It is achieved by facing our fears and discomfort and moving through them to a new us. This new, bold result is available to you today if you decide to face your Tiger and tame it rather than flee from it. You can do this. Everybody can. The question is whether you will choose to tame your Tiger and write your story or whether you will choose to let the Tiger dictate it.

Things the Tiger wants you to forget about the Tiger and your Self

Your true Self seeks value from internal sources – who you are. Your Tiger seeks value from external sources – how 'they' see you. It will roar if you threaten that source of value. We need to balance both but tend to focus on the latter.

Pain is the stimulus to move through fear and discomfort. It is normal and it is to be listened to. Facing fear and discomfort - doing battle with the Tiger – to move away from pain can bring great rewards.

Fear begins as a result of the way our Rulebook sees a situation. It becomes a physical sensation as our body reacts to our mental processes and releases hormones to assist us cope with the "threat". The hormone release can create greater mental turmoil. Eventually we will reach panic if this cycle is not interrupted. You are in charge of your fear response.

The Tiger Cycle shows how failure to deal with the Tiger leads us repeatedly to the same result and a strengthened Rulebook. The Tiger is dealt with and the Cycle broken by the Ten Rules in this book.

If you want to begin achieving different results in life, attack the Tiger, face the fear and discomfort of trying a new approach and you will eventually create a new rule in your Rulebook. This state is called 'confidence' in dealing with the previously scary situation.

Confidence can be earned by everybody prepared to face minor fear and discomfort – everybody who is willing to tame their Tiger rather than to appease it.

Part Two

The Leadership Rules

Rule 4

It's All in the Mind

Cantering to post with myself and my 'Saboteur' in the saddle

The voice in my head, that of what I call my 'Saboteur', was intense in the run-up to my first race. In fact it crossed my mind that if I stood up in the saddle while I was in the starting stalls and reached up high, I would be able to hold on to the top of the stalls. Then, when the starter opened the gates and the horse jumped off, I could climb down and walk home safely.

Why was this voice – the Saboteur – so active? Well, a jockey's first job is to get his horse to the starting stalls, and then to stop when he gets there. This sounds like pretty basic stuff if you haven't ridden a racehorse – just apply the brakes. But there is a design fault in the thoroughbred racehorse: no brakes. Just two lengths of leather and the word: 'Whoa'.

Better jockeys than me have lost control on the way to the start. And if they can get run away with, so can I. And where better to do it than cantering to post the first time you've taken a horse on to a racecourse?

As I was being led down the chute by Caroline Grimes at Southwell Racecourse on 22 November 2004, my mount, Airgusta, was certainly on his toes and looking forward to getting his hooves on to the sand. As we got to the track, we had to turn left and canter past the grandstand before pulling up as we passed the crowd, doing a U-turn and cantering back to post. Excellent. I had two opportunities to fail to pull him up.

As I passed the grandstand, I heard the commentator pipe up:

'And here's number ten, Airgusta, ridden today by Jim Lawless. Jim is having his first ride here at Southwell Racecourse this afternoon, and, for those of you who have not read today's *Racing Post*, you may like to know that Jim has been riding horses for just twelve months. So now is not the time to visit the bar, ladies and gentlemen. Things could be about to get extremely interesting out here on the track!'

The Saboteur was getting louder.

Airgusta was an angel. We took a steady canter to the starting stalls and pulled up nicely, so the Saboteur changed tack. 'All you've done so far is ride a horse to the starting stalls.' We walked around in a circle with all the other horses, waiting for the stalls handlers to load us.

The stalls are the most dangerous place on the racetrack, so once loading begins it happens quickly and efficiently. When you're in the starting stall itself, it's an intimidating place for the novice. You're locked up in a steel, coffin-shaped cage with half a ton of really wound-up pure equine muscle beneath you. The stalls are very narrow and your feet and legs are squeezed against each side. If the horses buck or kick or try to escape beneath the gates at the front of the stalls, things can very quickly become tricky, so the stalls handlers and the starter are keen to load and release the field as quickly as they can.

As the stalls handlers load each horse in they call out 'Ten to load, nine to load, eight to load' and so on. As the last horse is loaded in the final stall, the stalls handler clears the front of the gates and signals to the starter that all the horses are loaded.

The starter calls out 'Jockeys', then drops his flag and the gates fly open. You move from nought to thirty miles an hour in around twenty-five yards. My main focus at this stage was still to be on Airgusta's back in twenty-five yards' time, and not lying on the floor of stall number one. So it was imperative that I was sitting balanced on the horse and ready for the acceleration – which I had been warned would be so much faster than anything I'd experienced in the practice stalls at the yard – as soon as the starter pressed his button. My eyes were glued to the hand holding the flag as I listened to the stalls handlers count down the horses left to load.

At this stage the Saboteur was not doing me any favours. I was battling hard to focus on not falling off Airgusta or jabbing him in the mouth with the bit by having too tight a hold as he leaped forward. But the voice got even louder when, just as they announced that there were only two horses left to load, I saw not one but two ambulances pulling up behind the starter.

I knew that one ambulance was required to be there for Health and Safety regulations at the track, but the Saboteur immediately informed me that 'the second ambulance is here because they've read that some idiot who has only been riding for a year is about to take part in the race'. This was my last thought as the gates flew open. I did exactly what I had practised doing and got off to a great start, chasing Airgusta into the position we had been told to achieve by his trainer Charlie Morlock – at the front of the field, up against the inside rail. Concentrating on the task. No Saboteur space left at all. Clear and focused.

Rule 4: It's all in the mind

Yesterday is information, tomorrow is imagination, neither is reality. There is no Tiger in 'now'.

Every advancement that humankind has created and every advancement of an individual is as a result of that greatest of battles: the battle that takes place in our head between our true Self and the Tiger.

We write our stories by making decisions, acting and getting results. The difference in the quality of our stories is in the quality of our decisions and therefore in quality of our actions.

We can create the story that we want to write only if we win the battle in our head. If we fail to win this battle, the Tiger dictates our story to us.

How we fight this battle and choose to act is ultimately how we are defined. Victory in this battle is heroic. This is the battle that creates the national and international heroes and heroines, real and fictional, who inspire us. More importantly, it is the battle that people in our families and neighbourhoods do on a less epic scale – but nonetheless heroic and inspiring to us. All the Ten Rules assist us to prepare for or fight this battle. As we turn to the first of the Leadership Rules, however, we face it head-on.

THE CHALLENGE OF WINNING THE BATTLE IN THE MIND

Why is the battle difficult? Why is heroism a hard test to pass? Because:

- it is when we either face our fears and have to accept the terrors and discomforts of uncertainty and change, letting go of our securities, habits and attachments or we turn back on our quest

- there is huge encouragement from society to cause us to be fearful of moving away from the usual 'rut', which makes it intimidating to progress and easy to turn back

- it is accepted in modern societies that we will indulge in various unhealthy activities to protect us from the frustration of being stuck – we can turn to these instead of to growth. The modern hero has to resist the socially acceptable path of self-numbing

- our emotions get involved and adrenaline and cortisol are released when we fight the battle in our heads just as powerfully as if we were to fight the battle in reality – the fear is real though the threat is imagined

- the 'voices' in our heads appear real at key moments in this battle and will talk us out of heroic action

- we are not used to looking after ourselves, coaching ourselves or bravely or authentically seeking help (rather than platitudes to excuse defeat) from others. We are not taught how to do this. Indeed, seeking such vital sources of strength are often seen as a sign of weakness in both sexes

The central questions that we are wrestling with are: what will I make of this situation? Who will I discover myself to be as I decide and act? That is never going to lead to an easy time. We only discover such a thing when the pressure is on us.

The good news is that none of the real-life trials that we encounter are nearly as intimidating as the phase in our heads when we are contemplating whether or not to take the heroic path.

The bad news is that most people never get to engage in the trials of transformation and growth, of leadership, innovation or creation at work. Most of the great battles are lost while sitting in the bedroom worrying – letting the Tiger rob us of our story during that contemplation phase. That is why *Taming Tigers* starts with 'Act Boldly Today – Time Is Limited' rather than Rule 3 – Head in the Direction of Where you Want to Arrive.

To understand more about this trial that we all face before we can change and progress, log on to the Campus at tamingtigers.com and watch the film entitled 'The Hero's Journey'.

THE VOICES

Do you hear voices in your head? I do.

If you think you don't, the voice that I'm referring to is the voice that you're now having a conversation with:

'Hmm, I wonder if I do hear voices.'

'Don't be ridiculous!'

'No, really, do we hear voices?'

'What's this "we" business?'

Let's try again. Have you ever stood up in front of a group to speak, whether at work, at home or at college? As you stood in front of that group, did you have a voice in your head saying to you:

'Wow, you are hot! They love you!'?

Or did you have a voice in your head saying:

'You are really awful. You'd better get this done as quickly as possible and sit down fast'?

Now, let's just say for a moment that this voice that sits on your shoulder and puts you off doing things, or criticises you while you are in the middle of doing things, is the Tiger's voice. It is a symptom of the heroic battle raging. How many times a day does that manifestation of the Tiger dictate a decision and then an action to you? How many times a day do fear or discomfort trump the action your true Self would like to have taken?

If this voice dictates your actions five times in one day, thirty-five times in a week, how many times is that in a year? 1,820. Multiply 1,820 by seventy years and you get to an incredible 124,400.

That's 124,400 times in your life when the Tiger has dictated the decision and the action to you over your true Self.

But it gets more alarming. This voice does not interfere with you when you are sitting with your family enjoying a nice meal after a great week at work. If it does, you need help that is way beyond my area of expertise and I wish you every success with the journey.

The voice only gets loud when we are facing opportunity and placed under pressure of some kind. Therefore it is likely that these are our 124,400 most vital decisions.

Who is writing this story of your life? You? Or the Tiger?

This is the heroic battle. The battle to discover who we are, what we are 'made of'. Are we our Tiger or are we our Selves?

IT'S YOUR VOICE

The first step in dealing with this voice is to recognise that it's you, *your* voice. It was always your voice. If it's your voice, that means you can change it to say things that will help you.

The voice in your head, the Tiger's loudest roar, will keep you in the safety zone and stunt your growth and progress. It is a normal response to fear. We can learn to deal with it, but most people prefer not to. We will explore how to deal with it in the following pages.

If you are tempted to think that the Tiger only attacks *you* in this way, think again. If you're sitting anywhere near a computer, Google the phrase 'sports psychology'. Have a look at how many pages and books are dedicated, in part, to dealing with the voice when the pressure is on. It's one thing to sink a four-metre putt on a nice flat green when you are by yourself. It's quite another thing with a rival competitor standing opposite you. It's another thing again if there's a bet of a thousand pounds riding between the two of you. And it's something else yet again when it's a putt to win the US Open being broadcast live around the world. And, as the pressure mounts, so the little voice becomes louder. This is the heroic battle that we watch, live, when we see great sport. It is, in part, why sport inspires us.

If all those sportsmen and women and, indeed, everybody else who puts themselves under pressure out there on a daily basis can deal with the voice, so can you.

Self-awareness, acceptance and the battle in the mind

Unlike most animals, we humans have the ability to observe

ourselves. Sadly, this is an activity that many people never take part in. Happily, that fact alone gives you an advantage – if you have the courage to take it.

Here's an exercise. The next time you are about to send a difficult email at work, pause over the send button and ask yourself why you have not telephoned the person instead. It's a small question that may lead to a big answer, illuminating the presence of the Tiger.

Self-awareness includes noticing our thought processes and, once noticed, smiling at them and reflecting upon them. Why do I choose to send an email instead of making a call? Why do I not speak up in meetings? Why do I choose to blame others/the government/the industry/the economy for my lack of opportunity or progress? Are these thought processes serving me? This is not the time to give the voice extra power by criticising yourself. Accept the processes. You are what you are at this moment. Smile at yourself.

Accept that your thought processes are not reality. We confuse them with reality because they take place within our heads, so we are used to them. They feel very real.

Self-awareness includes noticing your emotional response. You can think worrying thoughts now as you sit here and read this book. You can project all sorts of imagined horrors on to the uncertainty of the next few hours in your mind (standard human behaviour) or you can project fluffy loveliness or huge pressure-creating achievements (the positive-thinking approach). Neither is real and I find that neither is useful.

The alternative is the route that spiritual practices encourage us to follow. Accept that neither is real and both are imagination. Accept that you can cope perfectly well with either reality as it unfolds before you. You always have done, haven't you? You're still here, doing great and interesting things, while never having been able to predict the future. Now you still act with determination to prepare for the task, but without the pressure of being wedded to an outcome. You may still desire that outcome, but increasing the pressure to attain it is not going to assist you to succeed.

Given your acceptance of that uncertainty, you are stronger. Ready to trust yourself and your abilities rather than concerned about forcing your outcome. You have nothing to fear because you are in the present. In the present moment, there is nothing to cause you fear, is there? The fear is in your imagined future.

Let me explain that. You are not worried about the terrors that fill the uncertainty vacuum of the future as you have let these imagined disasters go. You are not worried about creating your perfect outcome – although you will strive for that – because you have accepted that there are no guarantees. There is nothing to worry about, nothing to force, nothing to fail at, *at this moment in time*. You can trust yourself to do what you have readied yourself to do.

If you do eventually fail in the endeavour, you can take comfort from Rule 10 and move forward to try again. But filling your head with that possibility in advance of the performance (we'll call that voice 'the Headmaster') or in the moment of performance (we'll call that voice 'the Saboteur') will not influence the outcome. Only your actions to date, your readiness and your current relaxed mental preparation can achieve that for you.

The wonderful, unique advantage that human beings have is the ability to become aware of these processes and, once aware of them, to work slowly to change them to processes that are helpful to us.

You will know many people who have no interest in this practice of awareness. They have no interest, in fact, in taming any Tigers or in changing their situation. They will tell you endlessly how they wish to do this but they do not. They are too fond of speaking about their fears, they are too fond of drama, they are too fond of gaining attention from other people in this way.

And you? Are you willing to become aware of your own processes and work to improve them?

Self-awareness is vital for going on to use the tools for Taming Tigers contained within this chapter. As you read about the Saboteur and the Headmaster in the following pages, your self-awareness will increase. It has been increasing since you first opened this book at page 1 and were introduced to the Tiger and the Ten Rules for taming it. Increasing your self-awareness is, in fact, the most important task of this book.

The types of voices in our heads

There are three types of voices in our heads. The Saboteur, the Headmaster and our Self. The first two will be used by the Tiger in an attempt to dictate our stories to us. The last will appear when we learn to quieten the others.

THE SABOTEUR

This voice attacks us 'in the moment' when we least need the interference. It attacks us while we are doing something, causing us either to lose focus momentarily or, worse, to pull back from giving something our best shot and give it a second-rate shot instead.

THE HEADMASTER

The second voice is the Headmaster. This is the voice which can masquerade as the voice of reason or common sense. It is the voice that says to you, 'Who the hell do you think you are to try to ride in a horserace/get a promotion/change the way your company operates/pass that exam/start your own successful small business/lead other people?'

We need to be very careful here. We need to distinguish

between the Headmaster and the wise voice of our Self. They can sound very similar and I recommend you test your thoughts with others before acting. The examples I have given above are the kinds of questions that many of us experience from the Headmaster. They are negative and often aggressive. Self-coaching questions, such as 'Am I ready to ride in a horserace/succeed in the promotion/change the way the company operates/pass that exam/start my own business/lead others/what should I be doing to ensure a greater chance of success?' – well, those are very different questions. Such questions deserve intelligent reflection and assessment and the Rule 5 assistance of others to answer well. But, unless the Headmaster is acting behind the scenes here, such questions rarely call a halt to our plans. They merely help us decide the right path to take to achieve them safely.

THE VOICE OF OUR SELF

Recognising this voice is a vital part of all spiritual practice. Discovering this voice is the purpose of meditation and retreats and, for me, my purpose in writing, speaking, riding, freediving and the practice of Kundalini Yoga.

You have been hearing from this voice as you have been reading *Taming Tigers*. You've been working to distinguish between this voice and the Tiger as you have read each of the Ten Rules. That process will continue throughout this book.

Honesty caveat: at the beginning of this book, I promised to be honest with you. These pages will give you some introductory knowledge from a book – but this is not enough. There is no book, CD, DVD or two-day training course that can assist you to turn that knowledge into wisdom. That will come from experience. And that experience will come from action and risk – facing fears and discomforts. It will come from using the tools below to go out there and intentionally face the Tiger (see also Rule 7).

I would guess that 80 per cent of the readers of this book will never want to do any such thing. They will want to be treated to the traditional 'feel good' thoughts. But this is not the path to growth or change or learning to defeat the Tiger. It's your decision.

Do you want to be in the 80 per cent or do you want to be in the 20 per cent?

Dealing with the saboteur

TOOL ONE: EVIDENCE

You will know by now that we are not into 'short cuts'. This is because short cuts rarely work unless you are physically travelling from A to B. If you have solid evidence in your head to suggest that what you are about to do is going to go horribly wrong, you will have fear in your mind – the Saboteur will go crazy. It is very important to realise that this is not a fictional Tiger giving you a hard time; it is common sense telling you that you are not ready to take on the challenge you are about to face.

If somebody handed me the keys to a shiny new Boeing 747 and said that they would pay me £10 million to fly it from London Heathrow to JFK, and I agreed, the Saboteur would be kicking off with all the noise of a football crowd as I took my seat in the cockpit.

Seek out evidence that you can perform the thing well – earn that evidence. If you don't know what you are doing, get training. Ask for advice. Read. Get mentoring. Do the rehearsal. Have dry runs. Do whatever it takes to ensure that when your time comes you can do the thing well. List all these things that you have done on a piece of paper and look at them and marvel at yourself and take all that evidence with you into battle.

Do not expect any of this evidence to stop the Saboteur's

attack when you enter the fray. What it will do for you is two things. Firstly, it will reduce the ferocity of your Saboteur's attack as you stand before your real challenge. Secondly, as you stand there and the Saboteur begins to take hold, you can fight back. You can recognise that this is the Tiger in disguise. You can recognise that it is your natural instinct kicking in to force you towards mediocrity and away from a wonderful result – a result that you were always capable of achieving, but that you have now put in the work to deserve to achieve. If you seek out opportunities to face the Saboteur (with evidence that you can perform gathered in advance), you will learn to stop the Saboteur in its tracks.

TOOL TWO: BUILD SELF-CONFIDENCE

Now you could buy those CDs that profess to give you instant confidence as you listen to them in your sleep. But this confuses me. Give you instant confidence in what? Your ability to hold a conversation with a beautiful stranger? Your ability to ride a horse at speed or fly a 747?

Think for a moment of the areas in which you would be willing to say that you are 'confident'. Has that confidence arisen as a result of reprogramming your mind subliminally? Or has it come about as a result of your willingness to put in the work? Has it arisen through your willingness to challenge the Rulebook (the route to all personal development) until you have the right (as bestowed by you, yourself) to create a new Rulebook that you can believe in (and let's call the possession of that new Rulebook 'confidence')? Has your confidence arisen because you didn't give up when the going got tough? Has your confidence arisen because you went out day after day and practised the thing? If you're a parent, were you more confident on week fifty-two after the birth of your child than you were on week one? How did that arise? Could you have achieved this in week 1 with a CD? Was it reprogramming? Or was it practice, dedication, love and persistence that brought you self-confidence?

We become confident in ourselves through facing fear and discomfort and winning. Repeatedly. We will meet this idea again in Rule 7.

The more confident you are as you approach a challenge, the less the Tiger dares to release the Saboteur into your head and the more you are able to defeat it.

Is there a flaw here, though? How can you be confident the *first* time you do this thing under 'live' conditions? The answer is that you won't be. This is the time to rely upon tool one, building up evidence to do battle with the Saboteur before you go into the trial – all that training, all those dry runs. Building enough evidence to begin to feel as though you have some right to be 'confident' of getting through. This was my challenge on the day of my first race. I had to go in without any evidence that I could cope on the racetrack – I had never been there before. But what a disaster it would be if the Saboteur prevented us from doing new things. This also is the time to learn tool three to combat the Saboteur.

Tool three: The task in hand

When we focus on the task in hand rather than on how well we may or may not be performing that task, the Saboteur disappears and we start to perform far better.

Let's go through that again, and let's use the presentation room again as it is a common place for fear to be felt and for the Saboteur to make himself heard.

When you stand in front of your friends and tell them a funny story, the Saboteur doesn't appear in your head. You are lost in the task in hand. You have no little critique in your head undermining your confidence in real time as you stand in front of them. What did you do with your hands? How did you use your voice? You will never know and you will never care. You were absorbed in the task and not in such irrelevances. All that matters is that your friends enjoyed the story and laughed, and the evening went on merrily.

When we present to the board, when we talk to a group of strangers, we begin to ask ourselves irrelevant questions. We begin to ask ourselves, 'How am I doing? Do they like how I look? Can they see that I'm nervous? Am I speaking in a boring voice? Will I forget my : . . Doh!' The Saboteur is as work.

And then we are sunk.

If the Saboteur gets a proper hold of a jockey midway through a race, the horse will sense the fear and doubt and begin to share it. A horse sensing and then feeling fear and doubt is not one you want to sit on as it approaches a big jump at speed. Jockeys talk about being so preoccupied with the task in hand that they 'throw their heart over the fence and the horse will follow'. Their minds are occupied with nursing the horse over the jump in the right stride, at the right pace, with the right distribution of weight so that they can move off quickly as they land on the other side. There's little time for self-criticism and there is no place for it – until the race is over.

If you let the Saboteur in during a freedive, you will start to worry and that will cause a release of adrenaline. That in turn will kill you if you are at depth. You cannot panic at 101 metres and expect the oxygen in your system to keep you alive until you reach the surface. You will burn up all your fuel.

When we are absorbed in the task, we do not have time to worry about the consequences of failure – and therefore add pressure – and we do not have time to worry about mistakes we made in the past and have stored up as evidence in our Rulebook that we are poor at this skill. We just get on with it – and the Saboteur is sidelined.

Yesterday is information, tomorrow is imagination, neither is reality. There is no Tiger in 'now'.

The next time the Saboteur is giving you a hard time and you have worked on creating the evidence as to why you have the right to carry out this task successfully, and you have worked on building your confidence, stop being so self-indulgent! Get on with the job you have trained for and the thing will take care of itself.

Get out of your own way and let yourself shine.

Tool four: Mental rehearsal

Mental rehearsal was vital to me in preparing for my first race. I used it to help me get through those starting stalls. Perhaps it is the reason why I didn't cling on to the top of the stalls and let the horse run on without me.

Here's how it works. You run through the event, as you want it to occur, in your mind's eye and with as much detail attached as possible. You work on it going well, you work on the detail of what you are doing that makes it go well, you work on being lost in the task itself and you work on enjoying the sensation, watching the result unfold and enjoying the success.

Find a quiet place, close your eyes, run the thing through your head in as much detail as you can and work on the points above.

Let me tell you why this was so important to me in the run-up to my first race. I was concerned about two things as the race approached. Sometimes I would lie in bed rehearsing them going wrong in my mind and becoming more anxious as I saw all the many and varied possibilities for me failing. Very helpful.

The two things that I was concerned about were sitting in/jumping out from the stalls and the horse bolting as a result of him sensing my nerves as we began to canter down towards the start. I was working on finding the evidence, I was working on building confidence, I was hoping that I would be able to concentrate on the task in hand. Despite this, I was concerned that the Saboteur could still get the better of me.

So I went to speak to Michael Caulfield, whom we met earlier and who, by now, had moved full-time into his new profession of sports psychologist and was already achieving some great results. It was Michael who persuaded me to use mental rehearsal. Not as a short cut, I must stress – mentally rehearsing that flight in the 747 is not going to help me (or my passengers) – but as an additional tool. Now I had been through the starting stalls at home, of course, many times in preparation. I had been through the starting stalls at the British Racing School in Newmarket under expert guidance. But I had not been through the starting stalls on a racetrack with thirteen other horses.

Michael advised me to go racing as many times as I could over the coming weeks, and to go to the start of every single race. He advised me to listen to what the stalls handlers shouted, to look at how they moved, to look at the order in which they loaded the horses according to the draw, to listen to what the starter said, to watch how tight the jockeys and horses were in the stalls and how little room there was for manoeuvre, and to watch the runners jockeying for positions as they belted off having left the stalls.

So I did this and, armed with all the new colours that this gave me, my imagination was able to rehearse going through the stalls on a racetrack.

Of course, I went there without true confidence – you can't have very much confidence in your ability to do something that you've never done before – but I did go there with lots of evidence to say that I should be able to perform the task. And I did go there having been successfully through the stalls many tens of times in my mind's eye. We jumped out nicely and I managed to get the position that Charlie had instructed me to get. Confidence rising. Saboteur almost silenced.

Dealing with the headmaster

TOOL ONE: COACHING OURSELVES

When you are sitting in an aeroplane and the person giving the safety briefing instructs you to put your own mask on, in the case of a depressurisation, before assisting those around you – even your children – do you feel uncomfortable or do you think 'of course!'?

A human being's first duty is to take good care of him or herself. Many of us are brought up to put others first, so this concept feels very uncomfortable. But think about it. What use are you to other people if you are hungry? What use are you to other people if you are distressed because you have nowhere to live? Well, let's move up the pyramid of needs. How effective will you be in interacting with others to assist them if your personal self-esteem is dragging along the floor behind you? Not only might you be of little assistance to them but, if you are actually looking for assistance in boosting your own needs as you 'help' them, you might even be a significant hindrance.

Most of us have learned through life to give ourselves a hard time. We have learned to criticise ourselves harshly, to see our faults and shortcomings. We need to give ourselves a break. There is always room for growth, but we are far more talented, have achieved far more wonderful things, are more loved and respected and worthwhile than we would ever give ourselves credit for.

Because we have not learned to coach ourselves, to look after ourselves mentally and spiritually (I use this word in reference to your human spirit not in any religious context), we generally do it poorly. But when we are locked in battle with the Tiger in Rule 4, deciding whether to run with the idea, deciding whether to take it to the board, losing faith in ourselves on the dark days, we need this skill or the Headmaster may talk us out of moving our idea forward.

The Ten Rules for Taming Tigers is an excellent but complex coaching tool. The rules can be used by a coach, or by you when you coach other people. They can also be used as a self-coaching tool. Everything that we have been doing in this book together is a form of self-coaching. Yes, I wrote the words, but I'm not with you. I cannot hear your answers. I am not coaching you. You are coaching yourself.

How has this been happening?

You have been asking yourself questions. I have asked some of the key questions to start you off on the thought processes, but you have been having a lot of thoughts, haven't you? These aren't all to do with my questions. You have added many of your own. The key to coaching yourself is found in these questions. All these tools require self-awareness but this, above all, asks you to practise the skill of being aware of yourself.

The questions you have been asking, guided and provoked by the book, have very probably been following the two fundamental tenets of coaching:

- You have been owning the 'problem' and the opportunities – thinking what *you* could do rather than what others should or should not do.

- Your self-awareness has been increasing (yes, I suppose I could . . . after all, perhaps it is only the Tiger stopping me – I can see that now!).

Tools like the 'Why Not?' wheel are excellent at increasing self-awareness. That is their purpose.

When you self-coach, follow these tenets. Don't blame others, and then you can see what you could do to solve the problem or get to your desired result. You may find this a powerful tool against the Headmaster's voice of doom. See yourself as the good person that you are, trying your best to see the way through – not as an 'idiot'. Try to remove such vocabulary from your self-talk. You would not expect to hear it from your coach, would you? Try to remove it from your real speech as well. We do not need to call ourselves derogatory names when we speak to ourselves or of ourselves.

The next time you find yourself frustrated by the action you have taken or by the fact that you did not take action, pause. Instead of criticising yourself, take a deep breath. Ask yourself gently how you might have acted if you were in the body of your role model, a role model at work or in the wider global sphere.

Ask yourself why you would not act in that way in the future. Are there good reasons? Is there a 'what if it went wrong?' question to deal with? Often this needs to be met head-on and considered. I'll return to these at the end of the chapter. Seen in broad daylight and with honesty, the 'what if?' consequence is rarely so very terrible – especially when compared with the consequence of not trying at all.

Then ask which of the Ten Rules, listed together on pages 25–6, would have helped you most. Ask which of the Ten Rules you least want to work with (the Tiger's roar is generally a good indication that you have found the very rule that you *should* work with). What is the Rule 2 Rulebook challenge that you may need to make here – about yourself or about others or about 'the way the world works'? Ask if you are afraid of a certain thing, or of discomfort that you should put yourself through to win.

You will probably find that there are clear reasons why it went wrong and how you could have acted differently. There is little point berating yourself over this – prepare differently next time!

And, finally, ask: 'Who can help me?'

TOOL TWO: GET SUPPORT – FOLLOW RULE 5

The battle in our head is, ultimately, ours to win or lose alone. But nobody said we couldn't get support and advice to help fight it. I will cover this in Rule 5.

'But what if . . .?'

We often lose the mental battle because of unaddressed 'but

what if . . .?' questions. This is where merely 'thinking positively' does not serve us well.

If we do not address the 'but what if . . .?' questions that trouble us, for fear that they will frighten us or that it is 'negative thinking', we leave room for legitimate fear and a Saboteur attack. The uncertainy vacuum is likely to be filled with imagined terrors and the Tiger will provide the answer to the question while we pretend to ignore it.

What if those things did happen? What if? Would it be so bad? Would anything really change?

We can list the 'but what ifs?' and decide if, really, they are so unacceptable to us to prevent action.

Sometimes the downside will be unacceptable – and then we should not act unless or until we can bring them to an acceptable level.

Usually, 'the what ifs?' are quite acceptable if we stare them in the eye and ask what the problem would really be if that outcome came to pass. And, importantly, what the likely consequences are for our story if we fail to act.

Breath-holding training in Egypt – a conversation with the saboteur

There are many elements to a successful freedive: the technical elements of the dive itself; dealing with the effects of extreme pressure on the human body; keeping the mind serene and clear at extreme depths and, holding the breath for long enough to complete the dive and to return safely.

In February 2010 I was in Sharm el Sheikh, beginning my training with Andrea. One morning I arrived at the Only One Apnea Centre to be told that we were staying dry that day – we were going to be doing breath-holding training. Not my favourite.

After we had done two hours of yoga together, Andrea attached a sensor to my little finger and I prepared to hold my breath for as long as I could. As you begin breath holding (please don't try this without supervision and coaching) the world feels very calm. After a while it becomes a little dreamy. Over time this relaxed period can be extended. In the early days it doesn't last very long. I always found that after a couple of minutes I returned vividly into my body and began to do mental battle with the urge to breath. That day was no different. I went through the frustratingly familiar, urgent conversation with the Saboteur:

'I want to breathe.'

'You don't need to breathe yet.'

'That's OK for you to say, you're not in here. It feels pretty urgent – it is natural after all.'

'Take it easy, of course I am in here, too, and, yes, sure it's natural but people have held their breath for four times this length of time – you're fine. Chill out and go with it.'

'I'm going to breathe!'

'Not just yet – you can breathe in thirty seconds – not just yet.'

'I'm going to breathe now!'

'OK, you can breathe in ten seconds. Can you manage ten more seconds?'

'Shuddup – I am counting.'

'Could you make it to twenty?'

'Four . . . three . . . We had a deal at ten! Two . . . One . . .'
I opened my eyes to see Andrea crying in silent laughter.

'What's so funny?'

'Your face! If you spent a little less energy at war with yourself in there, you'd hold your breath for a much longer time.'

Andrea took the monitor off my finger.

'Your oxygen saturation is 99.8 per cent. Did you really have to breathe?'

I resisted the temptation to unleash some British sarcasm.

'Yes.'

'Well, nothing in your body needed to breathe. Your mind needed to breathe.'

'How long did I do?'

'Two minutes thirty-two seconds.'

Not good. I'd complete the dive in less than two minutes and thirty-two seconds. That wasn't the point. If I couldn't keep my Saboteur at bay to hold my breath for four minutes lying still on the surface it would be unlikely I could hold it for two minutes thirty for a dive to 101 metres in the ocean.

I needed to use the tools of Rule 4: acceptance, confidence building and evidence gaining. There was no point seeing this as a failure. I was where I was but I needed to move on from there. I needed to practise this skill every day – until I could operate well within my maximum breath-holding time on record-attempt day. Then I could bank the evidence against the Saboteur.

Five months later I was back in Sharm. I had worked on the mental battle every morning. I had pushed myself beyond my comfort zone (my initial, desired giving-up point) when I was writing, running, working, when I was doing Kundalini Yoga exercises. I had learned to extend myself far beyond the point where my mind wanted me to stop.

But as I extended myself I learned something far more important than merely doing battle. I had learned to trust myself more and, when it got really unpleasant, I just stopped before the brutal element of fight began.

Was I giving up? No. The only thing I had given up on when I was holding my breath was fighting myself. I learned that if I kept my mind still and avoided the battle for longer and longer the battle to breathe came later and later. When it came, I breathed. If I needed to go as far as the battle stage to secure the record, I knew that I'd still have at least a minute of breath-holding time left (I knew I could fight for a minute) beyond my time on dry land.

I also made another breakthrough discovery. I have two channels of thought, it seems, but no room for any more. If I can occupy one channel by being completely engrossed in the technical task that needs to be accomplished in the moment and play a musical backing track on the other, I allow no room for the Saboteur in my mind. In the past, in both riding racehorses and freediving, I have found that if anything distracts me from the technical, especially an imagined problem, this unoccupied channel of my mind could start to play a disaster movie that would rival *The Towering Inferno*.

This has taken practice. I have taken the same piece of music to every yoga session, on every run, on every riding outing and on every dive. You can listen to it, too, in the Taming Tigers Campus online. Of course, I have to be able to play the music in my imagination.

So there I was, five months later, diving 'free immersion'. This meant that I pulled down the rope to begin the dive, attain neutral buoyancy and sink – at first slowly, then increasing in speed. When I reached the planned depth, I turned around and came back up the line, hand over hand. This was a warm-up dive before taking the sled to ninety metres for the first time.

Andrea suggested going to thirty metres. I'd no idea what depth I was at now, though. The water was rippling past my body as I concentrated one channel of my mind on relaxing my muscles, scanning myself for tension, checking my position in the water. The music was playing loudly, beautifully, and I didn't want the dive to end – I had no desire to look at my computer and see how deep I was. But I was moving very fast – the rate of descent alone meant that I must be well past thirty metres. Time to turn.

I began the ascent, hand over hand. As I had no idea how far I had descended, I had no idea how far I had to ascend. I'd been enjoying myself and chosen to make a schoolboy error. But becoming concerned about the error could not help me.

I was looking forward to breathing, but there was no fear or tension. Why would there be? What purpose could it possibly serve me?

On the surface I opened my eyes and my D4 computer read fifty-two metres and a dive time of two minutes and forty seconds.

Andrea smiled. 'Ready for ninety metres?'

'Ready.'

124,400 decisions

We are writing the story of our lives. Are we choosing the words, though, or is our Tiger dictating them? If the voices temper our actions five times a day, we calculated around 124,400 decisions and then actions that are dictated by the Tiger.

Who do you want to write the story of your life – you or the Tiger?

Over to you.

Things the Tiger wants you to forget about Rule 4

Rule 4: It's all in the mind

The battle in the mind is the heroic human battle. It is why we watch sport, read literature and go to the movies.

You have three voices in your head:

The voice of your Self that you have been listening to increasingly throughout this book

The Saboteur - criticises you in the moment of performance, live and in public

The Headmaster – criticises you and your plans as you contemplate them in advance of action

Tools to deal with the Saboteur:

- Build evidence

- Build self-confidence

- Focus on performing the task in hand brilliantly

- Use mental rehearsal

Tools to deal with the Headmaster:

- Coach yourself

- Get support – follow Rule 5

- Deal with the 'what ifs' head on and intelligently

Now log on to the Campus at tamingtigers.com and watch the film entitled 'The Hero's Journey'.

Twitter: @jim_lawless
Web: tamingtigers.com
Facebook: facebook.com/pages/Taming-Tigers.

Case study 4:
Murray Elliot

Before I went to see Jim speak, I was a club archer. I had even represented Scotland a couple of times, but hadn't really pushed myself to take it that step further. For a few years I had been talking to people about the disabled Olympics, or Paralympics squad. People had suggested that with my physical disabilities I might qualify, but I had never done anything much about it.

There was a point in Jim's Taming Tigers presentation when he spoke about how limited time is and how if you want to do something you need to move towards it today, and also about making sure you stand on your own two feet and speak to the people you need to speak to in order to progress. I thought, 'He's right.' There were lots of things he said that tied together almost as a philosophy for life and it had a significant impact on me.

After the talk I took some steps and got in touch with people about the Paralympics squad. I had started this process before and had written applications only to not really follow them up, but this time I thought, 'I'm actually going to do this, or I am always going to wonder about it.' This time I wasn't going to drop it.

Within two or three months I was invited to a talent identification weekend, where I was told that I was absolutely appropriate for the Paralympics squad and in fact I would be one of the guys to challenge their existing athletes. I then contacted various people with the aim of finding appropriate coaching facilities and getting someone to coach me. I stuck my neck on the line a bit and told people what I was doing and through that I managed to get free training facilities. Following that, I was delighted to be offered a place on the Paralympics team development squad and I was invited to join the British Paralympic Association's fast track, which offers additional training with a view to getting to the Paralympics. This meant that I was looking at getting to London 2012. Going from being a club archer to imagining I might be in the running for London was a huge leap!

Once I had heard that news, I did some more asking around and managed to get myself into the Eastern Scotland Institute for Sport, which helps athletes to receive additional training, including psychology, lifestyle and fitness. Before now, nobody had been doing these things for me but, thinking back to Jim's talk, I realised I needed to go and speak to the right people and drive this forward on my own behalf. The Eastern Scotland Institute for Sport offered me membership and gave me the additional training I needed for free, which was extremely valuable.

Everything that happened has really turned my life inside out. I find I'm taking more charge of lots of things in my life as a result, such as work and financial commitments, because you have to make a plan to deliver yourself into a high-performance environment. I've had to change my diet, too.

The whole experience has brought about a fundamental change which has been scary but exciting, too. The way I look at my sport and also the way I see my work life has really changed. The amount of time and effort I have put in to me as an individual has also increased but, fortunately, I've got a wife who is supportive; she is competitive in archery, too, so she understands what I'm trying to do, which is absolutely vital.

I went into Jim's speech with an open mind as I hadn't really seen any motivational speakers before. You hear about people going to see them and they come away talking about it and it all sounds great but nothing actually changes. I thought Jim's speech would be a bit of light entertainment in the middle of a long conference – I wasn't expecting to make any life-changing decisions. Since then I've seen two other speakers. One was quite entertaining but didn't really tell me anything, and the other I found interesting but I didn't take much away with me in terms of things to apply to my life.

I think my main Tiger is my lack of self-confidence and self-belief. It's that little voice that keeps saying, 'You're not good enough'. There's a bit in Jim's speech where he talks about the guy going up to the beautiful woman to chat her up and the little voice is saying, 'You're not good enough. Get back in your box.' Since going through this process, my self-belief has expanded enormously. My friends and family were supportive, which is important, but, even more so, people in the sport who didn't know me were giving me the affirmation that they thought I was good enough.

I've certainly had a few setbacks along the way. This year I've had a lot of coaching from people who didn't really know me, or understand me as a person, and as a result my performance has actually dipped in the last season. There have been times when I've felt that old Tiger coming back. At my first international event, my first time in the British team shirt, I shot so badly I burst into tears afterwards. I knew I was more than capable of beating the people on that field but I was shooting so badly. It was a really massive downer for me after all the training but in the end I thought, 'I can do this! I do want to get to London 2012 and whatever the issues, I'll cope and resolve them.'

I'm now making a plan to recover technically and emotionally and get rid of the performance anxiety. In the end, even the difficulties have been a positive experience because I've learned a lot of valuable lessons about myself and the way I perform, and after all, they are just Tigers I need to tame.

The Tools for Taming Tigers Are All Around You

How do you hold a racehorse?

Early in 2004 this was a burning question for me. If I didn't start getting better at it, I was going to fail in my quest. Or, worse, cause a horse or a person an injury. Let me explain.

Holding a racehorse refers to how you stop it from bolting. When you are standing in your stirrups on half a ton of bolting thoroughbred muscle, there is little you can do. It is like standing on the seat of a motorbike as it accelerates along a motorway of its own accord, weaving through the other traffic (there are always horses ahead to dodge) while you try to steer it with two bits of string attached to the handle bars and slow it by saying 'Whoa'.

It is deeply unpleasant and it is extremely dangerous to the horse, to other riders and their mounts and to you, the jockey. There is no Health and Safety measure to protect you. You cannot press Control/Alt/Delete to make it stop. You cannot wait for somebody else to rescue you. It is not a video game. It's not a carefully shot stunt scene in a movie where the viewer trusts that it will all turn out well. You are out of control at nearly forty miles per hour at 7 a.m. in the pouring rain. It is very real.

Shortly after Gee introduced me to the Bosleys, she also

introduced me to their neighbour, Charlie Morlock, who kindly agreed to give me a hand as well. Every day I would do two lots (taking a group of race horses out to exercise) for the Bosleys, or two for Charlie, or carefully time a dash from one yard to the other to do one for each.

Initially, Charlie's team weren't too impressed with the new 'jockey'. They had reason not to be. I was making things a little more lively than they ought to have been. I had also made no secret of my plan to ride on the track and I think they saw this Londoner who couldn't ride as just a bit cocky. A fair point.

During one of my first mornings at Charlie's, I was told to jump off (start cantering) at the back of the string of horses and stay there. We were exercising the horses on the Blowing Stone gallop in Kingston Lisle, which bends through almost ninety degrees about a third of the way up. The horses always try to speed up coming off the bend and that day was no exception. As we rounded the bend, my mount put his head down and went. I didn't hold him and we steamed through the string and past all the others until I found myself trying to tuck him in behind the lead horse ridden by 'Magic Hands' Leon. If I failed to hold him in behind Leon, nothing stood between me and a long white-knuckle gallop across the Berkshire countryside.

The problem was that Leon, a very talented work rider in his late sixties, was sitting on one of the most difficult rides in the yard. As I tried to hold my horse in behind his, it looked as though I would cause them to clip heels (touch each other's hooves), bringing us all to the floor in a very dangerous accident that could easily kill a horse or a jockey. I didn't like the risk, so I gave up, pulled him out from behind Leon and – when the horse saw the open gallop ahead – finally lost control and went into a full bolt. Leon's mount tried every trick in the book to escape him and follow us, but he was kept at a steady canter by the maestro. My horse decided to come to a halt at the top of the hill. I clearly had a lot to learn.

We walked back to the yard and untacked the horses. I was doing two lots that day so there was breakfast in between and I wasn't really looking forward to it after my performance on the gallop. I got into the kitchen at Raceyard Cottages and, not having ever met Leon before, put my hand out to introduce myself. He shook my hand and said: 'I think we've already met once this morning.' Leon and I went on to become friends and he helped me a great deal, but it was not a great start.

Shortly after that I was invited by Gee's then fiancé (now her husband), Mark Bradburne, to visit Henry Daly's yard in Ludlow where he was stable jockey. As we approached the gallop, Mark told me to stay eight lengths from him and to come no closer. There were only a couple behind me and the string of around fifteen horses was disappearing into the mist up the hill ahead. The sight was breathtaking. I felt great as we set off up the gallop.

I kept the mare eight lengths off Mark and was beginning to relax and enjoy the ride when I heard a shout of 'Coming through!' – it's the cry of a rider who is being run away with and it is warning you that they are about to set your horse alight as they pass. Off went my mare like a flash. I was then upsides Mark himself, calling, 'What do I do?' But I didn't hear his answer as we disappeared into the mist ahead of us. We weaved through the string until, in the mist, I began to make out a dreadful sight – seven or eight of Mr Daly's finest chasers taking a turn at the top of the gallop. And an even worse sight – Henry Daly himself in peaked cap and wellies standing beside his four-wheel-drive, watching the adventure unfold with wide eyes and an open mouth.

We were not slowing up. What would happen next?

I decided to take action and steer the mare off the gallop. We headed off into the mist on the field. Now gallops usually end at the tops of hills and Mr Daly's was no exception. And if you gallop off the top of a hill, you start to go down it. And that means you pick up speed.

And now we were off – in a full bolt – downhill.

Just the noise of hooves and a horse breathing in the still, misty Shropshire morning. Until, that is, we were joined by a third presence: a fast-approaching hedge. A huge hedge that I didn't think she could clear even if I had any idea how to jump over a hedge on a horse.

I decided to bail out. Sit on the saddle, both feet out of the irons, swing off, crunch.

When I looked up, the horse was leaving the field at a calm trot, reins flapping and irons dangling, through an open gate. I was relieved to discover that I could stand up. Apart from where my goggles had been, I was covered in mud. Otherwise, I was fine.

I got back to the yard ten minutes later and the horse had already been hosed down and was in her box. I decided to make my peace with Mr Daly. At first he didn't look like he was ready to smoke a peace pipe with me. After a while he relented. Thank you, Mr Daly. Sorry about that, Mark.

Enough. Time for Rule 5, The Tools for Taming Tigers Are All Around You.

I did not want to ride out the next day. I didn't feel safe. It wasn't about not 'getting back on the horse', it was about damaging a person or hurting an animal. So I didn't. I simply didn't know how to do it and everybody told me it was 'feel'. Well, I didn't seem to have much 'feel' and I didn't have a lot of time to get any either. I rang Gee and told her the problem. That night, Gee, Mark and I made a plan.

We would borrow a racehorse that had not been out exercising that day. We'd take it to a gallop after all the other horses had gone home. And I would pull it up. And pull it up and pull it up until I could pull it up every time.

Mark came along, Gee came along and Charlie – who had lent us a racehorse – came along, too. Charlie was at the start of the gallop to help me start off steady and not get into a battle, Gee part-way along to call advice about my position in the saddle and Mark varied his position beyond Gee to make different stopping points. We were not to pull up at the end of the gallop where the horse knew that pulling up was expected, but at *exactly* the point where Mark stood along the way.

I had Charlie, a former jockey and talented trainer, Gee, a former Champion Lady Jockey, and Mark, a top-flight jump jockey who had just come second in the Grand National standing in a field teaching me to hold a horse. How did that happen?

Rule 5. People are great.

After half an hour of intensive coaching, I was good. Not great. But I had a whole different approach and I was getting stronger in my technique. I also had some confidence back. We were back on track and I would ride out again the next day. Rule 5 had worked its magic again.

Rule 5: The tools for taming tigers are all around you

Whoever it is that could most help you to do the thing you want to do at this moment in time is waiting for your call.

Ah, are you thinking, 'They may be waiting for your call, Jim; after all, you have written a book and you have a website. But I don't think they are waiting for my call'?

This is the most common response to an introduction to Rule 5. Isn't it exquisite? The Rule 2 Rulebook kicks in and provides you with the perfect intellectual argument to protect you from facing the fear and discomfort of doing something mildly scary: making a phone call. At what cost to your story?

As we go into this rule together, you will stop believing me. We will have a little blip in our relationship of trust. We have probably already had it with the opening statement of this section. I will try to win you back and then, finally, I will ask you a killer question. I'm hoping that by the time I do that, you will have come back to me, you and I will have dispelled the doubt and we'll be flying again.

If I succeed, and you do decide to use this rule to help you tame your Tiger and write the next chapter of your story, extraordinary results will follow. So, here goes.

THE PROBLEM WITH ASKING FOR HELP

We have huge cultural problems about asking for help. Many of us were taught at school that it was a weakness to ask for help. Many of us carry that belief and the consequent Tiger-tickling fear of seeking help into the workplace: asking for help will be viewed as a sign of incompetence, of imperfection.

Imperfection, however, is not a barrier to our success and it is not a barrier to asking for help. We waste valuable time trying to become perfect before seeking the assistance of others. Since perfection is impossible, we are also more likely to give up. Imperfection is not the barrier. Seeking perfection is the barrier.

Seeking or attempting to feign perfection is also a barrier to interdependence. Something with a smooth surface finds it difficult to gain any traction with another surface. It is difficult to gain traction with perfect people because they are unreal; they are hiding from us. Rule 5 does not work well for the non-authentic person. That is why it takes its place as rule number 5. Rules 1 to 3, the Integrity Rules, must come first. Then the processes of the mind must be understood (Rule 4). This is a Leadership Rule.

DEPENDENCE

We start life as dependent creatures. We cannot survive without another caring enough to feed us, clothe us and even deal with our bodily waste. As I grew to the stage where I could deal with the latter but was still reliant on my parents to feed and clothe me, I began to get pretty impatient about getting to the next phase: 'Independence'.

When would I be out there on my own?

INDEPENDENCE

The thrill of it! The freedom to come home at a time of your choosing, to a place whose front-door key you own, perhaps to another person who is, amazingly, actually attracted to you.

As a young lawyer, the word 'independence' was particularly important to me and my colleagues. We were in a rush to prove that we didn't need other lawyers watching over us. By my mid-twenties I had finally achieved some level of independence at work and outside of work. I felt free.

But I was not free. I had found a new prison. A prison surrounded by Tigers. A prison called me. A freedom of ambition defined merely by my independent imagination. A freedom to act defined merely by my independent level of courage. A pace of execution defined merely by my independent ability to get things done. In retrospect, independence had its limitations.

I had no idea that life had another level on this particular growth adventure. I had not given any thought to the tremendous thrill, responsibility, joy and terror of genuinely throwing my lot in with that of others.

I was a late developer in this area, for sure. The reality dawned on me during one of my regular trips to Gee's office at AP McCoy's house to tell her how things were going at the yard. We chatted and she had a Diet Coke and some Minstrels, my very favourite sweets. I had water and pinched one of the champ's Jaffa Cakes. We went over how I was doing on the gallops.

Just as I was about to head off to London for a meeting, Gee commented on how surprised she was that I was never scared by what she was asking me to do or the situations that our pace of progress was forcing me into. I remember pausing and thinking in detail about whether I should follow my gut instinct and give a bland answer or whether I should tell the truth. I told the truth.

'I'm scared quite a lot of the time.'

'What? You have to tell me if you are scared. I have to know!' She was almost angry. I had never seen her like this. I was astonished.

'Why?' I asked, regretting my honesty.

'How can I possibly help you if I don't know what I need to help you with?'

This was when I began to appreciate that Gee was operating on a different level from me. Until then I had thought that she was skilled in her area and was passing that skill on to me. Now I realised that there was much more going on, that she knew things that I hadn't discovered.

She was telling me that if I was not willing to be vulnerable enough to be honest with her about my weaknesses, she could not work with me as fast as she otherwise could. I was frustrating the project with my pride. But I had never told anybody about these things – my worries and fears, complete with cold sweats and everything. Surely she'd bail out on me if she knew how pathetic I really was?

I was being what I had been so proud of becoming: 'Independent'. I had kept my true cards close to my chest. I needed to understand the next step: 'Interdependence'. I needed to show Gee my hand – the twos and threes, as well as the aces. I had to face a lot of Tigers about that. But I tried to do it. And she helped me get to grips with things that worried me. And she didn't bail out on me. Ever.

INTERDEPENDENCE

Accepting the value of interdependence – and being willing to strive for that – is the starting point for earning the right to use the power of Rule 5. It is partly about the power of teams and teamwork, but there is much more – how do we move that team, and ourselves, to interdependence? By becoming vulnerable; imperfect. Becoming part of, and building, a truly great team with members' strengths recognised and cherished and weaknesses accepted and covered by other team members.

When we are acting outside a team, can we be authentic with others in our approaches for help and support?

A beginner's guide to rule 5

Rule 5: The tools for Taming Tigers are all around you. Whatever it is that you would like to start writing into your next chapter, the tools to assist you in doing that are all around you. Why don't you list them? I have no idea what they are for you. Maybe it is the brand that you have on your business card – have you ever thought of the power that that brings you? Maybe it is the people you know at work, the experience that is sitting all around you but that the Tiger prevents you from displaying vulnerability to and seeking assistance from. Maybe it is a friend of a friend whom you have yet to meet.

Maybe the tool for you is your creativity, your ingenuity, your communication skills, your education, your mum, the meeting you have with somebody this afternoon to which you could add a new element.

Whatever it is you want to write in the next chapter, the tools for taming that Tiger and getting it done are all around you. Maybe you are reading the tool right now. I don't know. But I promise you that *you* do.

Think!

During the course of this book you have been thinking about the things that you haven't done – opportunities that are no longer there and that the Tiger has stolen from you. But the tools were always there to help you. Don't repeat the error.

During the course of this book, you have also been thinking about the things that you should be getting on with now. What you will write into the next chapter of your story.

During the course of this book, you have decided to do things and the Tiger has *already* stopped you from doing them, hasn't it? Don't let the Tiger waste another sentence of your story!

Use Rule 5 to find the tools to write the next chapter of your story.

Let's just work with people as the 'tool' for a moment. Think of the person that you need to help you – the most outrageous, powerful, apparently unattainable person who could help you to get done what you want to get done, or at least get started. Yes, we are back to the statement we started Rule 5 with:

Whoever it is that could most help you to do the thing you want to do at this moment in time is waiting for your call

Now call them up. If they refuse, call the next on your list. The one who could most help you is waiting.

I promised that at some stage we would fall out during this chapter, that I would stretch your confidence and lose you. This is that stage. If your confidence is not being stretched, then I guess you are already on the phone. If you are unsure, then think about it for a moment before you skip this chapter.

People are the most thrilling 'tool' to help you to get things done. They are more wonderful than you can imagine. Look at the bold action that I chose to start the racing project off. Michael was waiting for my call. Gee was waiting for my call. Neither of them knew that they were waiting for my call, of course. They had no idea that I existed any more than I had any clue that they existed, but that is not the point here – although the Tiger will tell you that it is. Six days after she heard my name, I was being given a horse riding lesson – from Gee Armytage!

Turn this around for a moment. If somebody rang you up and announced that you were the person who could most help them, that you had the experience and wisdom to give them some advice and that they were prepared to travel across the country to visit you for some advice at a time of your choosing – would *you* tell them to get lost?

So what's stopping you from calling? The Tiger?

You can't find the number? Try harder. They say that there are only six degrees of separation, after all. Get on to your email list, your social networking site, their website. Use your imagination and your creativity to work out how to get to them.

Have I got you back yet or are you still unconvinced? Stay with me a little longer. We have to reach that killer question.

Earning the Right to the Power of Rule 5

This is a very potent rule; it sits at the centre of the Ten Rules because it is a pivotal step. Such powers and such movement do not come for free. You have certain responsibilities to fulfil and to maintain in order to earn the full power of Rule 5.

RESPONSIBILITY 1: AVOIDING *X FACTOR* THINKING

You need to have established integrity, moved towards self-sovereignty (Rules 1–3) and be in control of yourself in pressure situations (Rule 4) before you'll make a real success of Rule 5. The only exception to this is if you are stuck on finding integrity and need assistance to use Rules 1–3.

Let me explain with a story of something that happened in March 2008.

I was challenged hard on this rule during a presentation after a gala dinner in Leeds by a woman who worked for a British governmental body.

'Hold on,' she heckled, 'are you telling me that if I rang up Lord Andrew Lloyd Webber and asked him for a part in one of his musicals that he would give me one?'

'She's one hell of an amateur actress,' her neighbour added.

'I don't know,' I busked, 'but I reckon that if you call his office politely, tell him all the work you have done to become a musical theatre actress, say that you are prepared to carry on working hard to be a performer, then ask him very nicely for five minutes of guidance, he'd probably give you it.'

She didn't accept the challenge. I guess she wasn't prepared to do anything at all. I think she wanted to publicly knock Rule 5 because it just might work – and that would require her to confront the fact that she would never face up to the Tiger and pick up the telephone or work with the tough Integrity Rules 1–3. Time to examine the *X Factor* problem.

Rule 5 is one of the Leadership Rules. The Leadership Rules

enable you to take control of or 'lead' your story and to work with others to write it. Their foundations are the Integrity Rules, the courage to take bold actions, the willingness to question the Rulebook (all of that received wisdom that imprisons us), the courage to build a plan and every day, whatever happens, to put one foot in front of the other to hit our self-imposed deadlines.

People who think that Rule 5 can work without Rules 1–4 are suffering from the *X Factor* problem – the belief that it can be possible without the graft, but just with some luck and a leg-up. A belief backed up in our culture of instant fame and fortune and by claims from self-help gurus that their book can provide us with success/happiness/weight loss. Interestingly, the instant stardom an *X Factor* triumph brings is usually awarded to a person who has worked long and hard, in obscurity, on their singing.

Rule 5 says: get yourself on to *The X Factor* if you want to perform. Use any possible legal and ethical route you like to reach your goal. But do not go on *The X Factor* unless you have put in the graft to justify being there. Use it as a Rule 5 tool by all means, but not as a substitute for graft – unless you want to be mocked on prime-time television, of course.

RESPONSIBILITY 2: SUPPORTING OTHERS

It would be unreasonable to expect others to support you while you were too busy to support others in turn. Nobody keeps a tally of this, of course, and don't ask me how the mysteries of the universe operate in this regard, but operate they generally do. As you make your journey towards interdependence, you will open yourself up to approaches from others seeking access to your wisdom, your experience. Be solid for them. Enjoy and relish the opportunity.

RESPONSIBILITY 3: RESPECT YOUR WORDS

It is common to hear people criticising others. It is rare that we see those same people demonstrate authenticity and courage by having an open conversation to resolve their differences with the other person. It has become normal, even at the highest level within corporations, to have factions emerge – united in a bond against an individual who has no idea what he or she has done to find themselves in such a situation. This dysfunctionality and dishonesty damages the power of Rule 5 for us as individuals, and it has an impact many times more powerful than we might suspect upon the performance of the team or overall organisation.

All of us are human, so all of us will speak harshly about others on occasions. Here's a suggestion you might like to consider to help you to keep on track and to benefit from the full power of Rule 5. Whenever you find yourself speaking about another person, imagine that they are listening to the conversation. Are you sure you would be happy for them to hear everything that you are saying? It's a simple enough test to check that you are in integrity, being who you want to be, and not elevating yourself at another's expense.

Many of us underestimate our own powers. We certainly underestimate the power of our words. Our words are immensely powerful. You impact on others with your words far more than you may think. Enjoy this power positively; enjoy your words. Put energy and thought into them. Your words are a unique fingerprint upon the world, upon your colleagues, upon your business, upon your clients. When we leave a fingerprint of which we are not proud, it is generally because our Tiger is at work creating and feeding our fears and insecurities.

The killer question

Of course, by now you know the question and have probably been hoping that I would not ask it.

Why have you not put the book down and called the one person in the world who could most help you to write the next chapter? Surely it's not the Tiger stopping you?

Over to you.

Things the Tiger wants you to forget about Rule 5

Rule 5: The tools for taming Tigers are all around you

Whoever it is that could most help you to do the thing that you want to do at this moment in time is waiting for your call.

We have a cultural problem with asking for help – when was the last time you did this? Would you like it if somebody else asked for help?

We waste time becoming perfect (getting all the exams or whatever it may be) before we try the thing or even ask for help with the thing. Be imperfect, accept it and get started!

Interdependence is more rewarding, more fun and provides a greater level of adventure and chance of success than independence.

You have to earn the right to the power of Rule 1 with certain responsibilities. These are:

- Avoid *X Factor* Thinking – do the hard work of Rules 1-3 before you expect anyone else to carry your load

- Support others

- Respect your words

Now log onto the Campus at tamingtigers.com and watch the film entitled 'Seven Billion People'.

Twitter: @jim_lawless
Web: tamingtigers.com
Facebook: facebook.com/pages/Taming-Tigers.

Case study 5:
Peter Winters

I had worked in pharmaceutical market research for fifteen years. In the last few years I had started to think increasingly about the challenge of climate change and in my spare time I started reading up on it and thinking, 'What can we do about it?' I thought about what I could do but was struggling to see a commercial opportunity in that area.

I attended a talk by Jim Lawless in Malta last year. I had no real preconceptions when going to see him but I heard that he had a good reception with the group at the previous event and thought, as he had been recommended, it might be worth going along. I found Jim's talk both entertaining and motivating – he makes you feel like you can do anything – and I took a leaflet home afterwards. What struck me about Jim is that he had the balls to take up a challenge himself. Something he said that really hit home for me was that nobody wanted to be old and sitting in a nursing home reminiscing and feeling like they'd missed their chance. It's a powerful idea.

I started thinking again about what I might be able to do with climate change. After the talk I spoke to someone else who had attended. She had come especially to see Jim's talk and was very encouraging, too. I said to her, 'I do have this idea and I need to do something about it.' It was a combination of Jim's talk and speaking to her that got me started.

A couple of things then happened in my personal life. My wife is French Canadian, and had decided she wanted to move back to Montreal. That was the trigger to take the plunge, give up pharmaceuticals and see what I could do with climate change. I came up with the idea of setting up a research agency, carrying out a syndicated survey on the market and climate change, and then selling the data.

The challenge for me was the leap into the unknown. The first step was moving to Canada as it gave me the opportunity to make a change. I had to leave my job but I had some savings, and as Canada is a lower-cost environment than the UK, there were good conditions for setting up a business.

I began looking in detail at the challenges of climate change. I did a lot of research and then put together a fifty-page document containing a plan to help clients understand what's going on with climate change. I think it's important to be pointing in the right direction and know where you're going. Without having a plan, I think you can lose direction. I started sending it out and got a lot of nice comments on it, lots of people were interested in the document and in potentially buying the data. Three or four people who read it said they wanted to work with me and I was able to form a management team of four or five people.

Jim is very can-do and brave. That's what comes through more than anything else. It makes you challenge yourself and say, 'Are you brave?' Part of my business plan was to sell my house in the UK which, with the state of the housing market, was a risk, but it was worthwhile in order to be able to start the business.

I think trying to do something scary every day is a good motto. Sometimes I do, sometimes I don't. But I think that once you have committed yourself to doing something, you have to do it and you'd look a fool if you didn't. The situation you put yourself in when you commit to something makes things scary every day anyway.

Work does get wrapped up in my personal life. I'm married with two small children and moving to Canada, finding a new house, all took a lot of time. There's a bit of juggling going on but if I still worked for a big company, I wouldn't have the freedom to do that.

I haven't hit any obstacles that made me want to give up but

I find you have to be alert for potential problems in the future. Yesterday, someone who was going to do something quite important for the business realised that it wasn't going to work for him. It could have been a problem but I had a back-up arrangement. You don't always know what's going to work in business planning, so it's always a good idea to have an alternative plan.

Overall, the project has worked really well so far and I have had lots of support from people who would like to join the team.

There is No Safety in Numbers

If you want to find the most brilliant jockeys in the world, go to the bar at any racecourse.

In that bar you will find the person who *really* understands race tactics, who *really* knows how to judge a gap between two animals travelling at forty miles per hour, who *really* knows how to read a race unfolding around him, and who knows *exactly* how a particular animal will respond to an instruction from the rider.

He is five stone or more too heavy to race. He's never even sat on a riding school pony – 'You must be joking. Those things can do you a right mischief!' – never mind a racehorse in training at 6 a.m. on the roads of Lambourn or Newmarket. Early mornings and the risk of a fall are not his cup of tea. He's nursing his third beer of the day at three in the afternoon and he's watching the racing on the bar's television because it's cold out there by the track – and it looks like rain.

He hasn't worked for years on his riding, race tactics, weight or fitness. He hasn't spent years trying to maintain his integrity so that he will be trusted, when the big day comes, to sit on the favourite.

But if a jockey who has done all that work makes a 'mistake' in the view of our expert, based on the expert's television-eye view of the race (very different from the jockey's view of the race, I discovered), our expert will make his way down to the unsaddling enclosure to tell the jockey what the jockey did wrong.

Meanwhile, in the press room, salaried wordsmiths make or break careers based on their assessment of what has unfolded on the track. Only a select few have actually sat on a horse. Fewer still have ridden in races – and those who have are always worth reading.

Where on your metaphorical racecourse do you wish to live your life, my friend? In the bar? In the press room?

Or on the track?

Surely your heroes – whoever they may be, from Mandela to you mother – are your heroes because they were on the track. They set their compass on a worthwhile purpose and they tried to make it happen whatever the naysayers had to say from the bar and in the papers. Not that they ignored the advice of others; they knew better than to be arrogant because there was too much at stake for that. But they made their own decisions, stuck to their ideals, dared to dream that they could make it happen.

The people we admire have spent their lives avoiding the temptation to sit for too long in the grandstand. They all preferred to be on the track. They knew that that was where they would *have* to place themselves in order to write their own story to their own satisfaction.

While the others watched and passed judgement, our heroes became accustomed to how exposed they felt as they cantered past the grandstand to post on their big day. That's a lot of people over there, and a lot of cameras. There is nowhere to hide from judgement out on the track.

Leaving the stalls, they're concentrating on perfect balance and finding the perfect position for their horse rather than on the danger that they are suddenly launched into. It happens fast out there. Decisions are called for at breakneck pace. But they concentrate on keeping steady breathing; trying to perform everything that they have planned under the intense pressure of race conditions.

They enter the home straight to see the grandstand and the

winning post ahead. They hit the noise of the commentator barking out on to the track as they get lower in the saddle and begin to work hard with their horse to produce one last surge – maybe three, maybe four horses in a row now – horses eyeball to eyeball – jockeys clanking stirrups at nearly forty miles per hour, horses barging. Gaps opening – and closing – and all the time the finishing line approaches. Time's running out.

They meet the wall of sound – the roar of the crowd – and as soon as they meet it it's gone. Distant and behind them as they calm the horse and bring it to a gentle canter, then a trot. Then turn to leave the track. Elated? Ecstatic? Years of commitment finally bringing the prize?

Or disappointment? A feeling of having let great supporters down, of having missed a moment that, with hindsight, was theirs for the taking. A decision that was taken in the rush of competition that may have been the wrong call. The video watching. The analysing. The slow recovery. The vow to learn and to improve.

Our friends in the warmth of the grandstand know little of this process, but they'd be quick to pass judgement if they lost a few pounds on the race.

All our heroes were on the track, making things happen.

You cannot write your story or tame your Tiger from the grandstand. For you, sir or madam, this may be old news. You have been out there trying your best, exposed, for years and you know the feeling well. They have criticised you and you have withstood the barbs. Perhaps you have pushed through that phase and perhaps they have eaten their words now.

But maybe that is not you. Maybe you, in company with most people, prefer the crowd. The grandstand. Spectating others' adventures. Judging the performance of others. Watching as they write the story of their lives. As they make things happen.

Rule 6: There Is no safety in numbers

Our media tell us that there is. Our families often tell us that there is. Our schools almost always tell us that there is (while we are there and also in their advice to us about the great adventure that awaits us once we leave). Often we even persuade ourselves that there is. It is so much more appealing than facing the Tiger's attempts to scare us away from the all-exposing track.

So why, when it is clear even to a child that the real adventures are not to be had while we run like a wildebeest with the herd, do we persist in sticking with the crowd?

The Tiger tells us to.

Let me make an important distinction here. No aspect of Tiger taming requires us to run against the crowd for the sake of it. This is not about being rebellious or ignoring good solutions that others have already created when we could (ethically) borrow or build upon their work. Rule 6 is not about arrogantly ignoring the advice or feedback of others whose assistance we would be wise to accept.

Rule 6 is about not fearing to stand up and be counted when the time comes – even if that means they'll be talking about you in the stands, wherever the stands are in your world. Rule 6 is about not fearing to be judged by others, to be thought foolish or 'above oneself' when the time comes to make your move, to take your own decision, to make things happen. On the track, we have to cash the cheques that our mouths write. On the track, there is nowhere to hide and there are no excuses.

Spotting oneself in the grandstand

Whenever you find yourself passing judgement on others, in your head or in company, take a pause. Are you becoming a 'grandstand jockey'? It is fun, for sure. It spreads negativity and fear around our societies, for sure. It inhibits innovation and crushes youth, for sure. But, above all, it makes us feel good.

A reassuring feeling of belonging to a group. A group that knows best. Although almost certainly none of the group has ever been on the track.

When I first began to meet professional sportspeople, I noticed how little 'grandstand jockeying' they did. How impressed and pleased they were by achievement in any field, perhaps because they knew the cost of achievement. How generous they were in their congratulations. How they tended to empathise with somebody who had made a bad decision, because they know the self-criticism and anguish that comes from a bad call made with only the very best of intentions.

Professional sportspeople share a humility that prevents them from judging and that perhaps can only come from realising how close one is, personally, at any moment, to the humiliation that comes from putting oneself to the test, way outside the safety zone, in a public forum.

So any Tiger tamer needs to develop an awareness of when they are straying into the grandstand to join the easy life of the crowd. Finding oneself in the grandstand is a sure sign that you are not on the track. It is hard to be in two places at once. To learn more about the excitement of walking out onto the track and being the leader of your story, log on to the Campus at tamingtigers.com and watch the film entitled 'The short walk to the better view'.

THE GRANDSTAND JOCKEY IN THE WORKPLACE

In the twenty-first-century workplace the grandstand jockey is more damaging than ever before. He or she damages not only themselves but also their team and has a negative impact on the success of the organisation. The change is happening. The grandstand jockey merely delays his organisation. In doing so he jeopardises not only his own future, but that of all his colleagues.

We can all take a seat in the grandstand from time to time, so it's worth bearing in mind the consequences of this when we are tempted to join the seductive court of King Cynical, which is being held in the bar after work or at the espresso machine.

THE GRANDSTAND JOCKEY AND 'SAFE' INNOVATION

Innovation requires courage on the part of the individual or team bringing forth ideas which may be ridiculed, and it requires courage on the part of the organisation to bring these ideas to life in internal process and external product. It is possible only within a very fragile framework of trust – which the grandstand jockey can bring crashing down with the raising of an all-knowing eyebrow.

When working with a senior team on the subject of innovation, it is easy to spot the grandstand jockey. As the conversation begins to move every member of the team out on to the track, he struggles and squirms and desperately tries to go back up the chute to find his spectator position again. Not all the team will recognise this, of course. But his fear is infectious. The difference between this fear and candid, vital criticism of the idea is the honesty with which it is conveyed. Honest critics are on the track, not in the grandstand. Watching this team work is like watching a ship sail with an anchor down or a drag car trying to accelerate with its parachute open behind it.

By definition, innovation requires a departure from the crowd. It requires a challenge to personal, team and organisational rules – the collective corporate Rulebook that we encountered in Rule 2. But our grandstand jockey always has certainty. That certainty is unavailable in innovation.

So what will happen?

There are three options. The team can persuade the grandstand jockey to gently dip his toes in the water of change. This is often very threatening to him and surprisingly difficult, often leading to very highly charged conversations.

The team can reject the grandstand jockey and move forward without him – this is exceptionally rare as often the team don't see the importance of what is unfolding for them in the context of their overall long-term story.

The final and most appealing option is to keep everybody's Tiger at bay. This is done by reaching a stalemate in the guise of an anaemic 'committee-led' version of innovation. Somebody out there, however, is not afraid to leave the safety of the pack to make a dash for victory. Somewhere, the competition is setting out to write this team's story.

When you consider all the great innovating businesses, you can see how they have been fearless in leaving the grandstand and getting out on to the track, despite judgement from others and often contrary to conventional wisdom. In some older cases, such as that of First Direct Bank, a division of the HSBC banking group, a team was set up in a brand new location in order to reduce influence from colleagues when defining how the new bank would operate. The same is happening now, also in finance, with the mobile phone operator O_2 and you can read the experiences of the MD of O_2 Money, James Le Brocq, in his case study (see page 246). Both teams were given broad parameters and had little interference from HQ. They were free to embark on radical thinking and to create radical values and a radical approach to customer service. The First Direct result has been an extraordinary success and has spawned many imitators. But can you see? Even the method of establishing this team was to dismantle the grandstand around them in order that they could dismantle the grandstand of banking for themselves.

Other companies that have made hugely innovative steps by not seeking safety in numbers include: EasyJet, Google, Amazon, Apple, John Lewis Group, RyanAir, Innocent Drinks, Virgin Group, Toyota, Swiftcover.com, Dell Computers and Direct Line.

Spend a moment thinking about your favourite 'stand out' brand. How do you think it really felt for those people to commit to shifting away from the pack – long before they knew it would become the success that you now admire?

It is very important to remember when thinking about a 'company' or 'corporation' that these are not faceless entities. Men and women with Tigers like yours took these decisions, persuaded others and then – vitally – executed the plan. They faced fear and discomfort while doing this and pushed past the Tiger's roar. You are part of such a group of men and women. Whether you are junior or senior, you play a vital part in shaping what that group will be tomorrow.

The Grandstand Jockey and 'Safe' Vision, Values and Branding

The 'me too' nature of most corporate 'vision and values' exercises is a wasted opportunity to move onto the track. All over the world on weekends we human beings display our desire to be part of a tribe. We love it. We wear the football scarves, the baseball caps and the shirts and we play our part in roaring our team on to success. The failure to recognise and to work with this human trait is one of the biggest tragedies in the old way of running a corporation. A tragedy not only because it stunts the successful growth of the organisation but, far more, because it denies the people within it one of the main tools for finding meaning and purpose in their work. A meaningless vision with 'me too' values, defined in isolation by the board and dictated by a cascading communication exercise will not inspire loyalty to the cause.

How does Rule 6 help overcome this? By giving the members of the organisation permission to contemplate producing the products and offering the services that they truly want to bring to market. When the board is nervous of stepping away from well-trodden paths, both in internal leadership and in market-facing products – the 'me too' vision is inevitable. Because the vision is bland (and frequently meaningless) the actual products and services that follow often are as well. If the leaders of the corporation were prepared to leave the grandstand and get on to the track, to move away from the 'me too' language and processes of most vision and values exercises and walk out on to fresh snow . . .

Well, how would I know what might happen in your organisation? But you might well do.

Is that worth getting out onto the track and having a conversation with somebody today? Is the Tiger roaring? Is it going to write this sentence of your story? Your decision, your action, your result.

Leaving the Grandstand

There comes a point in the Taming Tigers coaching process when the coached decides that he or she has reached clarity and wishes to step on to the track, perhaps for the first time. This is a very exciting moment for both the coach and the coached. The Tiger is identified and tamed and it will never again be able to roar so loudly.

When we reach the point at which we can see the world and the Rulebook that society wants us to live by for what it is – rather than from the inside looking out – then we can choose to go on to the track and look back at all the faces in the grandstand.

For anybody who is out on the track, loneliness comes and loneliness goes. Self-criticism comes with the turf. But if you take the decision not to run with the pack, you will meet other Tiger tamers. You will run with a new crowd. You will gain new supporters and admirers. These are people who will take your call late at night when you are smarting, because they have been stung, too.

You will be writing your story.

Rule 6: The final leadership rule

Rule 6 is the final leadership rule. It's the final one because it's the most difficult of the three to work on. It is a major shift towards self-sovereignty. If you desire to write your own story, to lead your life, to influence, impact upon, be a role model for and leader of others, you will need to let the grandstand seat flip up from underneath you as you stand, put down the plastic glass of beer and the hot dog and walk down towards the track. Hop over the railings and you'll feel the springy turf beneath your feet.

The Tiger will roar with every step you take but the liberation, the freedom brought about by defeating that roar and being your own person is a truly great reward. A heroic reward for a heroic action.

And then there is the thrill when you get it right. When you know you took the decision and backed it with your reputation and lost sleep about it and cared deeply.

And you made it happen.

And you won.

Things the Tiger wants you to forget about Rule 6

Rule 6: There is no safety in numbers

You find the most brilliant jockeys in the world at the racecourse – in the bar or the pressroom. From where, on your metaphorical racecourse, do you want to write your story?

All of your heroes were on the track, trying their best to do the thing that mattered to them, ignoring the barbed comments from the spectators – think carefully and decide whether you agree with that statement

The grandstand jockey at work stifles innovation, progress and change.

The 'me too' grandstand jockey vision and values statements that are cascaded on posters keep the company from engaging with its people and writing its own great story.

To write your story you have to be out on the track, exposed. The Tiger will roar and you will need courage. The rewards will be great.

Now log on to the Campus at tamingtigers.com and watch the film entitled 'The short walk to the better view'.

Twitter: @jim_lawless
Web: tamingtigers.com
Facebook: facebook.com/pages/Taming-Tigers.

Case study 6:
Isobel Ryder

My story really starts when I was two and taken into care. A couple of children's homes followed before I was fostered by a very nice family at the age of eleven until I was fifteen, when I returned to live with my mum – this had a catastrophic affect on my education. I joined the army at eighteen with the grand total of three GCSEs. Various jobs followed, including a spell with a private defence company and a well-known confectionery company. On a personal front, I got married and had my daughter who has given me the opportunity to understand and give to her the mother–daughter relationship perhaps I should have had.

From September 2002 to February 2004 I completed an HNC in Business, getting distinctions in most of my assignments. I was working full time; I loved my job and my life. It was always my intention to go on and get a degree to enhance my employment prospects and prove something to myself.

I then had to put my education on hold while the ensuing dramas unfolded around me. In March 2004, my mum was diagnosed with a terminal illness and my husband ended our marriage, all in the space of forty-eight hours. I continued to work full time, had sole care of my daughter and tried to ensure my mum and I covered every unsaid misunderstanding in the time she had left. It was a particularly difficult year as I would have turned to my mum for support over my marriage and to my husband for support regarding my mum. But I found, of course, that I could not turn to either of them. I still sorely miss my mum and on the night she died, on her instructions, my sister-in-law gave me a picture of my mum getting her degree at fifty-six years old.

I moved into my own home with my daughter and in March

2006 I was made redundant – every life-changing event that could happen seemed to have happened to me in the space of two years.

However, in the preceding August, my employer had run a 'Careers Workshop' day which had got me thinking once again about my education with a view to picking up where I had left off. Initially I thought I had lost the opportunity to further my education but on reflection the choice was mine. I went on holiday to Australia to visit my foster parents and decided to enrol on the Masters in Personnel and Development on my return using the redundancy money. I undertook a part-time, fixed-term contract post to help with living costs.

The next two years were a rollercoaster of temporary employment, emotional and intellectual challenges but it was towards the end of the course that Taming Tigers entered my life. I had always suffered from self-doubt and insecurity – I'm sure psychologists would put this down to the lack of parental support and encouragement during my early development years. I was trying to complete my dissertation. I had never done anything like this before, let alone at this level and on this scale. I was scared, feeling out of my depth and convincing myself that I had taken on too much – no one would blame me for opting out, surely. I was looking for excuses to drop out or delay completion for a year despite the support and encouragement from my programme manager and close friends – but what did they know? I obviously wasn't going to pass, I had no A levels or first degree. Who was I kidding?

At a local careers conference, I listened to Jim Lawless give his talk on Taming Tigers; these voices telling me I was not going to make it, I was doomed to fail, had bitten off more than I could chew, etc. I was particularly impressed by the comment that the Grand National doesn't change its date just because a particular jockey may not feel up to it that day – tough! Prepare and be ready or miss the opportunity; you may not win the race but taking part means you tried and can be proud the hard work was not wasted.

My mum's photograph has been on the wall behind me as I studied during the programme. I truly believe she knew what she was doing when she requested I had this picture – she was telling me to go for it. So I got those Tigers off my back. Because my dissertation was driven by two deadlines, the school year and the date for submission, I got focused. I decided I had nothing to lose by trying but everything – financially, my self-esteem and pride – to lose by quitting. I ultimately had three people to do it for: my mum, my daughter and myself.

More recently I have acquired a new, full-time, higher level (and pay) post and my life is progressing in leaps and bounds – I am heading in the direction I wanted to go.

As I look back over my life, I realise I am a fighter and a survivor and have been dealing with Tigers all my life – I just didn't know that's what they were called. I also believe in fate. Jim's talk on Taming Tigers came into my life at that point for a reason. It turned me around, stopped me feeling sorry for myself. I graduated in December 2008, and I know my mum was watching.

Part Three

The Change Rules

Do Something Scary Every Day

Rule 7 at the races – a tiger tamer well outside his safety zone

23 December 2003, my thirty-sixth birthday. It's 5.45 a.m., pitch black and the frost on the verges is sparkling in my headlights. I have driven down from London to the backstreets of Upper Lambourn and I am hopelessly lost.

My lateness and the fact that I'm visiting Jamie Osborne's famous yard for the first time, won't know anybody when I get there and will have to sit on a horse in front of all those experienced riders is making me nervous. I have been riding for one month and one day.

I turn a corner and my headlights pick out a new sight – a string of fifteen racehorses coming down the road towards me in the dark. I'll never forget the first time I heard that mass clacking of hooves on tarmac. It is still a sound that gives me goosebumps when I hear it. I get some muffled directions from the riders and it turns out that I'm pretty close to Osborne's yard. I ease to a halt in the car park at 6.05 a.m. Five minutes late. This is a bad introduction. Racing yards don't do late.

I'm now lost in a massive yard, trying to find the only person who is expecting me, Jamie's assistant trainer, Roddy Griffiths. In about half of the boxes there is a light on and somebody working away. Ominously, there is also a fully tacked-up horse in each box ready to go as soon as the cry 'pull out' goes up. I haven't even found my bridle. I eventually find Roddy, though, who doesn't look impressed that I'm late but is good enough to put me at ease with a smile and a handshake.

'You're riding Jamie's cob, Victor, today.'

'Great, thanks.'

'He's easier than a racehorse, but he's a bit of a stubborn so-and-so with an attitude. Do you reckon you can handle that?'

Oh, Gee! What have you set me up for here? Am I ready for an animal with 'attitude' after only a month of riding? Roddy's looking as if he's also wondering what Gee has set him up for.

'Pull out!'

Riders are being legged up and the string starts to move towards the covered trotting track to warm the horses up. Roddy and I approach Victor's box. Roddy's carrying the tack and, thankfully, sets about tacking Victor up rather than expecting me to.

He leads Victor out of the box, legs me up and tells me to check my girth. Check my girth? While I'm actually sitting on the horse? Little do I know that it's perfectly normal for work riders to be tightening and loosening their girth at different stages of the morning while they are in the saddle. I look at Roddy in alarm. He looks back at me, slightly more alarmed.

He tightens the girth for me and tells me to join the others in the trotting school. He jogs on ahead to get into the school and starts giving the riders their instructions.

We go through the dark, frosty morning towards the well-lit trotting area in the distance. I can see horses being warmed up inside it. It's like a sandy running track – but with a high fence at either side of the track and a roof over it.

I can see around twenty-five racehorses moving at a brisk trot. It's the first time I've seen anything like this. I am struck by how casual they all seem, and how relaxed they are. I thought this was meant to be dangerous! Maybe it's all going to be OK. Some are standing up in their saddles, other rising in their trot; some are speaking to each other and others are riding around on their own or talking to their horses. All are so wrapped up in balaclavas, scarves, gloves and numerous layers underneath their jackets that they look like little footballs sitting on top of their horses.

Victor steps on to the sand and I ask for a trot. He doesn't trot. Unknown to me he has understood, from the moment I entered the box, that I know nothing about how to deal with the wily character he prides himself on being. Victor moves from walk to canter in a blink, and we're off, weaving our way between the work riders who yell their disapproval back at me as I set their horses alight by carving through them.

Except that I'm not the one carving through them, I'm not steering this thing at all. Victor is in charge. I ease back to start pulling against his mouth and realise that my reins are far too long – I hadn't been ready for the canter – so I quickly change my hands to shorten up the reins. Now this, I will learn in the weeks to come, is a sign for thoroughbreds to speed up. If you watch jockeys approaching the finishing line at a race, you'll always see them shortening their reins and changing hands. It's like pressing down on the throttle of a racehorse.

You might think it wouldn't be the same for a cob, but it turns out that Victor's been hanging around racehorses for far too long and he takes a change of hands as a very clear signal to speed up. Up until now I merely felt total embarrassment. These experienced riders seem to be able to sit on their jumpy three- and four-year-olds, even with Victor and me cantering steadily through them, so I'm not too afraid at this stage. But the burst of speed that this little cob gives me as I change my hands, ups the stakes considerably. Now we're galloping and now I'm worried.

I suddenly start to notice how loud the wind is going past my ears. There's really not much else that I can notice up here. I can't stop this horse, and the view that I'm getting is a little bit like the view you get in a computer game, sitting in a car that's dodging and weaving its way past other cars at a rate of knots on the track, leaving havoc in its wake. I am awake, having a nightmare.

I'm on my third lap now. I've lapped most of the horses in here at least twice and, as I come round, Roddy decides that action needs to be taken. He's standing in the middle of the school with his arms outstretched – is he mad?

Roddy stares Victor straight in the eye. Victor stares back at him. And I stare from one to the other and wonder what's going to happen to us all next.

Victor is clearly a sports fan. Not only has he been hanging out with racehorses, but he knows how to sell a dummy. He jinks left, but Roddy's no fool and he leaps over to the outside of the track in front of Victor. Victor picks up speed and, as he gets to Roddy, he jinks right. He's beaten that last defender and there's nothing between him and the line. His ears prick and he enjoys his victory.

Victor can't think of any more fun to have. He's outrun every racehorse exercising in the first lot and his cocky, pricked ears are asking the trotting thoroughbreds 'Who's the daddy?' But, better, he's put in a sidestep that would have made Phil Bennett proud. He pulls himself up to a trot, sticks in a great victory buck, dumps me on the ground and trots round to where Roddy is waiting to pick him up. I walk back around the track to meet up with Roddy and the enemy.

Sometimes it's the little things in Tiger taming that seem hard, like having a whole string of riders look at you in utter disgust. One girl smiled at me on that walk to Roddy. Thanks, Sam.

Roddy's a complete gent and tries really hard to smile as well and tells me not to worry about it. As we walk back to the box while the rest of the string meanders to the all-weather gallop for their morning canter, Roddy asks if I wouldn't mind being on time tomorrow morning.

Oh, God. Only twenty-three hours left until I have to do this 'scary thing' again. And again. Can I do it for a year?

Until eventually it is 23 October 2004 and there is just under a month to go until we race. I jump into the car at my new home in East Garston and drive the fifteen minutes to Charlie Morlock's. It's a crisp day and it's exciting. There's another 'scary thing' to do today. I'm doing my first piece of work on Airgusta, whom I'll be riding in my race. I've exercised him before but not worked him.

We pulled out into Kingston Lisle. The Blowing Stone gallop is ahead, winding up the hill into the mist. But we're not going there. We're working on a flat all-weather gallop where they can really get some speed up.

We jump off and take a long, steady canter from one end of the gallop to the other. And with this and the trot, Charlie is happy that the horses are ready to do their fast work. We walk back to the start.

'Work' in a racing yard means riding the horses 'upsides' or next to each other at a fast gallop. I've ridden work for Charlie and for Martin Bosley and I've worked at it at the British Racing School in Newmarket, but I still have to think things through beforehand so that I don't miss anything. The first time you ride work is breathtaking. The speed you reach is, because it is on a horse and not a machine, like nothing that you have experienced before and you ride so close to each other, touching irons, that at first you can't believe it'll work out.

Charlie gives me and Leon our instructions. Leon is to jump off first, I am to be tight behind, go on a good clip before joining at the second bush and letting them gallop hard, upsides for the rest of the gallop. OK. Goggles down, girth rechecked. The horses are on their toes – they know exactly what's coming and they couldn't be more excited.

Leon jumps off and I am tight in behind. Airgusta shakes his head at me and pulls to go and race but he comes back to me and quickly settles. We're belting along now, trees blurring to the right, grass to the left and the noise of hooves and wind. He's giving me a great feel – well-oiled movement and nicely balanced – it'll be great to go racing with him. He's also facing a lot of kickback here – sand being thrown up by the hooves of the horse in front. He'll have to deal with the same at Southwell and he doesn't seem to even notice it's there.

First bush. I pull him out from behind Leon, trying to anticipate the tug that will come as he takes our move to be a signal to speed up. He's a racehorse and he knows his job. I want the speed, but only enough to join Leon at the second bush – then we'll go on together. If he gets too much speed on now, we'll fly past Leon and the work will be totally wrecked. He comes back to me again but only just. I'm swinging off the back of him now as we get to Leon. I need to be toe to toe with Leon, boots touching, before we accelerate together. Then we stay together. Working to the weaker horse – nobody 'wins' this piece of work.

Leon grins as my iron clanks against his precisely as we arrive at the second bush – he's helped so much to get me here.

'Ready?' he yells above the thunder.

'Ready!'

A gentle easing forward of weight, a centimetre more rein and he flies! We're stride for stride for a furlong until he feels like he's about to weaken. Click in the back of my mouth, change hands, drop lower in the saddle and he's back.

We flash past Charlie and I just manage to glimpse that he's grinning. Airgusta is doing really well.

'OK!' Leon calls. We both lengthen the reins and stand up in the saddles a little with a 'Whoa!' and they slow up and trot into the turning circle at the end.

'That'll do. Take 'em home,' Charlie yells to us. And Leon and I start the journey back through Kingston Lisle to Raceyard Cottage.

Whoever would have thought when I wrote 'Do something scary every day' into the Ten Rules that it would lead me to this?

Rule 7: Do something scary every day

'Hey, friend! Can you tell me how to get to Carnegie Hall?'

'Sure – practise!'

Dealing with fear and discomfort is a learned skill that requires practice. Unless you practise that skill, you will be unprepared when life throws you an opportunity – complete with some fear and discomfort – and invites you to take a bold decision and a bold action – and secure a bold result for your story. Those who avoid that practice are likely to be intimidated by the Tiger's roar when opportunity knocks. The Tiger is dictating their story.

Dealing with fear and discomfort is a learned skill.

Think about it for a moment – it is vital that you don't skim over this.

Dealing with fear and discomfort is a learned skill.

Fear and discomfort are extremely unfashionable words, however. That is why Rule 7 is embedded in the Ten Rules: Do Something Scary Every Day.

Rule 7 is the first of the Change Rules because addressing our attitude towards fear and discomfort is the long-term change that we need to make before all other long-term changes can follow.

Practising Fear and Discomfort? Are You for Real?

Oh, yes. Are you for real about wanting to tame your Tiger? Nothing worthwhile comes for free, does it?

I let you into a very powerful secret a little bit earlier. Let me remind you of it. All growth, all adventure, everything that we strike out to achieve that is worthwhile, everything that has been achieved that is worthwhile, involves or has involved facing up to fear and discomfort.

The Tiger roars at us when we move in the direction of fear and discomfort. But of course there isn't really a Tiger, is there? However real and noisy the Tiger may appear to be, he isn't really there. There's just us, trying our best to get it right out there and battling with our outdated fight or flight system shoving a dose of hormones into the process to make it more entertaining.

The decisions that you take during a working day are, when you add them up, how you have written the story of your career so far. You weigh up the desired outcome versus the risk of action. 'I want to speak with that stranger in this networking session but I fear they may think that I am dull and I find small talk uncomfortable.' Or 'I want to study to learn new skills but I also like watching television.'

A vital part of Taming Tigers and core to our 'No-Limits' coaching process is to underscore the risk and consequence of *inaction* – to consider what we are sacrificing by avoiding the Tiger. We can use that as motivation to tackle the Tiger head-on and move forward. Are you going to act on this?

Remember, as we saw in Rule 3 we are either motivated away from or motivated towards something. Most people spend their entire working lives moving away from things they fear rather than dealing with that fear as they move towards the things that they wish to achieve. In the twenty-first century this is no longer an option. The rate of change in the workplace is too great for us to indulge in this luxury and expect to survive at our current level, let alone move forwards.

Now we have to be able to deal with our Tiger when it roars unexpectedly at us or when opportunity briefly emerges and fear tries to prevent us grasping it. It is becoming a required work skill. We have to keep up.

Wake up if you want to keep up!

Don't allow yourself to read these words numbly and nod wisely. Wake up! If we are dealing with the sum of our decisions when considering our story and those decisions are influenced heavily by our attitude to fear and discomfort – then learning to deal with fear and discomfort will play a huge part in the result we get in our lives and so the story we choose to write.

How Do I Use Rule 7?

Rule 7 is not about thrill-seeking, although you could use thrills to help you become more comfortable with risk and dealing with your mental and physical response if you wish to. Rule 7 is not about acting irrationally, recklessly, negligently or without regard for others.

Rule 7 is about becoming a little more comfortable with risk and fear every day in a controlled environment of your choosing and in a considered fashion. Try making the person who sells you a newspaper or who sells you fuel for your car laugh tomorrow. It is low risk, because you will not face major loss of face if you fail. But, unless you are a natural joker, you will experience the entire Tiger cycle shown in the figure on page 120 – including the temptation to take that inner road and not try – to avoid the Tiger altogether once the adrenals get to work on you and produce fear as you advance in the queue towards the person you intend to amuse.

You can go further if you wish. Take a class that 'scares' you. Get moving on challenges that you have put off for years because they come with a slight feeling of intimidation attached. It could be along the lines of a sport. It could be getting involved in amateur dramatics or local politics. Whatever your personal bag is, stretch yourself and use that stretching to practise fear and discomfort.

Rule 7 and personal change – the advantages of practice

What advantages will regular Rule 7 practice bring you?

Rule 7 keeps you aware of the Tiger. You can't let it lurk around the perimeters of your activities any more, quietly encouraging you to stay within your current limits. We conjure him up every day when we do a scary thing, and every day we realise that he has no teeth. You lived!

Rule 7 takes you through the Tiger cycle (see page 120) every day. You feel the emotions that are created when the adrenal glands start to respond to the challenge hitting your Rulebook. You will experience the physical changes, experience the Headmaster and the Saboteur attacking your story. You will be interrupting this instinctive 'animal' response to this outdated warning system (designed for an attack from a real, living Tiger) and creating a different reaction every day. The more you do this, the faster you learn the skill of dealing with fear and discomfort.

Rule 7 generates new energy and excitement about doing something different every day; it causes you to overcome an emotional and mental resistance to change. It builds your confidence and helps you to move away from the crowd and build your own career, your own story.

Rule 7 builds practice, learning, progress and advancement into every day. When we take a risk, we learn something. Always. If you are disciplined in doing that in a controlled and careful way then you are on an impressive personal growth trajectory.

Rule 7 becomes fun. You will meet new people as you practise your spontaneous conversations or tackle some previously intimidating challenges – and get into some new situations!

Learn the skill of dealing with fear and discomfort

Rule 7 changes us. It teaches us how to deal with fear and discomfort – that they are actually acceptable. This continued growth effect through being just a little outside the safety zone, every day, was the most important factor in enabling me to get to a British freedive record and to get to the racetrack within a year. It remains a principle that I use in my daily activities running Taming Tigers.

Gee, my racing mentor, managed this brilliantly. She always presented a new challenge for me about a month sooner than I might have believed I could do it. Andrea, my freediving coach, always greeted me with a cheery 'Ciao' as I arrived for training – and then announced what he was stretching me to achieve that day with that same confident and reassuring smile.

I wasn't always smiling at the thought of the challenge. But I was always smiling when I looked back at it three hours, three weeks or three months later. And as I practised dealing with fear and discomfort, each challenge became easier to face.

Things the Tiger wants you to forget about Rule 7

Rule 7: Do something scary every day

Dealing with fear and discomfort is merely a learned skill – practise it.

We are motivated away from things we fear or towards things we desire - Do you want to write a story based on avoiding fear and discomfort or on the learned skill of passing through it to the things you wish to achieve and contribute?

You can use adrenaline filled adventures as part of Rule 7 but this is not necessary. Try a more scary test of communicating with somebody in an authentic way, for example.

Rule 7 brings you the huge advantages of:

- Increasing your awareness of the Tiger's impact and of ways to overcome it.

- Helping you understand and interrupt the Tiger cycle (page 120).

- Generating energy and excitement and building confidence.

- Building practise of this vital skill into every day.

- Being, ultimately, enjoyable and spicing things up

Now log on to the Campus at tamingtigers.com and watch the film 'How do you get to Carnegie Hall?'.

Twitter: @jim_lawless
Web: tamingtigers.com
Facebook: facebook.com/pages/Taming-Tigers.

Case study 7:
Chris Pierce

I saw Jim speak at the itSMF (IT Service Management Forum) conference for IT service management professionals in Birmingham in November 2006. I enjoy conference presentations but, in the past, I've been frustrated by speakers who don't use plain language or give practical tips. With Jim I was impressed by what I saw straight away, in particular his idea about doing something scary every day. In fact I was so inspired that I decided there and then to speak at the following year's conference. I mentioned it to the colleague who was with me and she didn't believe that I would see it through. I assured her that I would – even though it would be the scariest thing I'd ever done – and that she was my witness!

I have worked in IT for a major police service for nearly thirty years and, if I'm honest, I had become used to being in my comfort zone, so this was a big thing to put myself forward for. The first step was submitting a synopsis for my presentation. I called my talk 'Think of it like this . . .! (The power of analogies and doughnuts in getting your message across)'. I was determined it would be interesting and it wouldn't be 'death by PowerPoint'. At this stage, I wasn't looking forward to presenting and was wondering why I had put myself forward for it – the Tiger I had set out to tame was biting back. Once I had heard that my application had been accepted, I knew I had to go through with it. I was to speak at the November 2007 conference in Brighton.

When it came to the conference, I wasn't sure how much interest there would be in my presentation but there turned out to be a full house – there were even people standing lining the sides of the room! I started by saying that this was one of the biggest days of my life, and that I wouldn't have been there without Jim, and several people in the room, who had also seen Jim speak, nodded.

The talk itself went fantastically well and there were laughs and cheers in all the right places. In the conference feedback statistics I received afterwards, 95 per cent of those who attended said that the presentation was very good or excellent and 100 per cent said they would recommend me as a speaker for future events.

I would go so far as to say that Jim has changed my life, as if it hadn't been for his keynote presentation I would never have gone on to present myself. I've carried on presenting and I'm now on the itSMF list of speakers. I recently wrote an editorial for *Computer Weekly* magazine, too. I now have a different outlook and I, too, want to inspire others to do the same. I carry the card with the Ten Rules for Taming Tigers in my pocket and when I come across difficult situations in my work (such as a recent job interview) I often ask myself, 'What would Jim do?'

For me the most powerful thing Jim said was definitely 'Do something scary every day'. Even if it's doing a regular journey in a different way, even if it's one step each day, it's a good principle and I still try to do it, even if it's something quite small. It's not just my professional life where things have changed, I've started doing things I'd been putting off in other areas of my life and my wife says (to her great delight) that I've become far more impulsive (such as booking holidays at short notice) and now just 'go for it'. Once you've cured your fears, you feel like there's nothing you can't do.

My outlook now is to make a decision, stand by it and tell others what you are going to do, then you are committed and have to see things through.

If last year's challenge was the presentation, this year it's learning Japanese. I collect retro video games and import many of them from Japan and therefore got interested in the language and culture through that, so now I'm learning to speak it. It will certainly help with reading the instruction manuals. We'll have to see what next year's challenge will be.

Understand and Control Your Time to Create Change

You are writing the story of your life. Your actions are the pen. Time is the paper. What you decide to do with your time creates your story.

You have only one truly scarce resource. There is only one thing that you will run out of and are utterly powerless to replenish. Whether you are a prince or a pauper, a CEO or a schoolchild, there is only one resource that you are depleting every moment of every day.

Your only truly scarce resource is your time here on earth.

A Tiger tamer denies the possibility of 'spending' time doing this or that because 'spent' time cannot come back to affect us. 'Spent' time is gone. Your use of time always brings a return, there is always a consequence for your story. So, you are 'investing' it in doing things, not 'spending' it. But is it you or the Tiger that dictates your investment decisions?

Rule 8: Understand and control your time to create change

If you gain control of your time you have a huge amount of it to invest, and a planet filled with extraordinary things and people to invest it in and with.

Your story is the sum of those investment decisions. The position that you find yourself in today is the sum of how you have chosen to invest your time. Even the children you have created or may create in the future are the living result of whom you chose to invest time with on that second date as opposed to the ones you chose not to invest time with after date one! Decision, action, result.

Rule 8 for Taming Tigers is not about time management. It is about creating a fundamental shift in your relationship with time and then looking at the Tiger that roars when you attempt to control your time. Rule 8 is a powerful tool for change. Rule 8 is the second of the Change Rules and it will prove vital to really understand your relationship with time if you wish to create lasting change for yourself. To look at this idea further, visit the Campus and watch the film 'Hickory Dickory Dock'.

Economists use the idea of 'opportunity cost' – the missed opportunities that must be taken into account when an investment decision regarding a scarce resource is to be made. So your decision (and it is always your decision in the world of Taming Tigers – no victims permitted) to attend a meaningless meeting that requires a day's travel has an opportunity cost of not getting your new business case written, or not getting an appointment set to present it to the board, or giving your clients some extra attention, or developing your team and so on. We'll need these concepts of allocation of scarce resources and opportunity cost for this chapter.

TIME AND THE VICTIM

'But we don't control our time', he or she will contribute enthusiastically to a group discussion after a Taming Tigers presentation, desperate to get other heads to nod in agreement. 'If I had control over my time then I could . . . but I don't, so I can't! The speaker runs his own company; he doesn't understand what it's like for us.'

Oh how I wince, because it's me. Or, rather, it was me, at my desk in Slough watching the coffins go by. I move to the next table in silence. Let's see if the group can turn itself around without me butting in.

This was my own favourite reason for not creating a change in the days before I got to recognise the Tiger. I was far too busy to squeeze it in and my time was certainly 'not my own', so what could I do? I was powerless, forced by 'the system' to stay in an oh-so-cosy rut. The Tiger, having created the wonderful 'power-less victim' delusion, wanders back to his forest victorious and all can return to normal.

So, back at the conference table, our victim of the system – a system he ironically condones by his very presence in the room – is using his considerable communication talents to convince a table of eight to twelve typically healthy and affluent members of one of the world's richest nations that they are powerless victims. They work in an economic environment hungry for and willing to reward innovation and commitment. They have been brought together by their company to create new ideas and ways of progressing. That company has invested in an entire after-noon of Tiger taming to demonstrate their commitment to their people to move forward, to give control to them, to ask for energy and excitement. But their Rulebook still tells them that they are 'powerless' to alter their position.

Despite all evidence to the contrary, 'we don't have time and there's nothing we can do to change that' is the comment that I hear most often in all Taming Tigers corporate sessions, whether it is at a high-level board strategy session or in a big conference room. Most people are engaged in a passionate, desperate, wild and utterly vital love affair with the idea that they are too busy to do anything interesting or exciting and that time is not their own to invest. But you and I have Rule 6 up our sleeves. We don't seek safety in numbers. We know the cost of failing to take a risk with Rule 2 and change this popular mantra.

The discussion in the conference room doesn't end there. One of two things will now happen. Either the group will begin to moan collectively about their situation, or the tide will turn against our victim and somebody will point out that he is labouring under a Rule 2 Rulebook delusion.

The excitement in the session comes not from seeing the shift in the relationship with time. That is a fleeting moment, a stepping stone across the river to the new pasture. The excitement comes with what people decide to do for their families and societies, colleagues and companies as a result. It's the fusion of Rule 8 and the individual's creativity, emerging through Rule 3, and giving rise to their drive to use Rules 5, 6, 7, 9 and 10 that is the thrill. Realising that they are free – their true Selves can decide what to do with their 'paper'.

The Tiger and Our Relationship with Time

How is the Tiger getting involved here? To answer that question, let's look at those Integrity Rules again. We'll start with Rule 2. The Rulebook – the source of so many problems and solutions.

The Rulebook, unless challenged hourly with intelligent self-awareness, is generally under the control of the Tiger. It keeps us safe, you will remember, and makes it all 'not our fault'. Well, by this stage in our trip, you can recognise that for yourself in the example I have given above. If you are investing your most scarce resource based on an invalid set of rules then you risk getting a tragically disappointing return on that investment.

If you upped the stakes, if you had to find the time to do the thing 'or else' (you can insert some dire consequence for yourself here), how would the Rulebook immediately alter about time? How would your relationship with time, and how you choose to invest it, shift?

Are we creating a Rulebook that enables us to achieve self-sovereignty, to be who we truly are and who we want to become (for our impact on others and our world as well as for ourselves)? Or a Rulebook that protects us from fear and discomfort, from the realities of acting with integrity, from growth, from heroism?

With the Rulebook shifted, we can turn to Rule 3. Part of the Rule 3 planning process is the very act of making the time to do the things necessary to reach the goal. It is amazing how resourceful you can be at this once you have the goal in place. But this is all 'long-term, high-risk' work, and we live in a 'short-term, low-risk' world, so most of us never allocate the time to do the planning (we'll explore these concepts together in a moment). The Tiger, as we have seen, prevents most people from seeking out their inspired purpose. So how time is invested is of less value to them.

They mosey off to work and mosey home again because that's what life seems to require of them. But what of our requremnts of life?.

With a Rule 3 plan in place, you can go back to Rule 1. Act boldly today, because time is limited. Not only is the 'T' word in there deliberately, but all of Rule 1 is designed to shatter further your Rulebook (Rule 2) and expose the Tiger at work. It is also about wrestling your time back to yourself by using it to create a bold forward step *today* – proving to yourself that you could have done it years ago and you can do it again tomorrow.

Investment strategies for time

Do you see time as something to be 'managed' or something that has come about as the result of the miraculous coincidence of you having been given life? A life that can be invested in creating all sorts of incredible things, from bringing energy and enthusiasm to team-mates and colleagues to reshaping how your business or industry operates to nurturing your children or supporting a partner in his or her own quests? That's before you visit the Pyramids or run your marathon for charity. Do you see your time as the paper on which you are writing your story? Do you know how much paper you have? Me neither.

Tick tock . . .

We'll not get an overdraft on this resource – no credit available – so it is well worth considering for a little while.

Here are four main ways that we can invest our time. Each of the four main investment routes delivers a different level of return. Every individual will invest in each area – it's part of being human. The challenge is in choosing and balancing your investment portfolio rather than having the Tiger dictate the investment and the return. That return is the quality of story that you are writing rather than permitting the Tiger to dictate to you.

'Risk' in the time investment types that follow refers to the level of risk to you of not having written the story that you wish to look back on from the nursing home. A high- risk investment, when you are dealing with your most precious resource, is an investment that will benefit your story greatly; the risk of not pursuing it is therefore great. When an investment is high risk, there is pressure – so the Tiger will roar. The voices of the Headmaster and the Saboteur will appear in your head.

Short-term, high-risk investment decisions

These particular short-term concerns are *high risk* to you because they matter.

You can spot a *short-term* decision because it has a deadline attached to it. The moment will pass.

They are high risk because, if you were to fail here, you would feel the consequences and they would be significant to your story. You want to get this right. You may have to tame your Tiger in order to invest correctly in this area. Perhaps the Tiger will have to be faced in dealing with others differently to create the time to do this thing right; perhaps the Tiger will be tamed by how you change to perform the action itself.

Fear and discomfort may exist here which is why people may try to wriggle out of opportunities like this or perform them poorly – even though there are great rewards from high performance in this area.

The meeting at which you wish to perform very well requires a short-term, high-risk investment of your time. Short term because it is in the diary, and high risk to your story and your (and others') perception of yourself if you fail to act as you hope. It is a career opportunity. It counts. You may also have to prioritise brutally and face the Tiger of saying 'no' to others in order to invest in your preparation for this event.

It is similar to the situation where a member of your team is in need of a confidence boost just before a sales meeting. It is now that you invest that time – now or never. It may matter to you for a variety of reasons that you find the time to invest here, despite the opportunity cost of not investing that time where you had already planned to invest it.

We usually make the correct short-term, high-risk investment decisions. They have an immediate and tangible impact on you and your story so they are hard to ignore. They also have a deadline, making them very noticeable.

SHORT-TERM, LOW-RISK INVESTMENT DECISIONS

Here we have it. The great, gloopy, forgettable morass of dross activity that takes the majority of our most precious and scarce resource.

These are short-term concerns because they have a deadline attached and they are low risk to you because they do not matter to your story. Nothing is at stake for your true Self. It is easy to invest here, it often helps our external 'stock', our reputation to be seen investing busily here, but we receive little real return. This is the stuff that we will have forgotten about by next week, let alone by the nursing home. There is no fear or real discomfort. Some people actively seek to fill their diaries with this stuff. It can make us feel important. It excuses us from facing challenge and growth.

In the second part of this chapter we will begin to create practical strategies for controlling your time, creating more paper for your real story. For now, however, recognise what these activities are. It is the email inbox, it is the mobile phone and it is the meeting with no meaningful output; it is the time spent micromanaging your team instead of trusting, training or bravely replacing them; it is the preparation of a report that nobody reads; it is the time spent doing a job for your boss's boss that your boss, herself didn't check was actually required – her Tiger ran rampant and you are dealing with the consequence.

Yes, I am well aware that some of it has to be done, but the question for you is how much? Which parts? What should you be delegating to others? Does the Tiger let you discriminate truthfully to yourself or does it dictate your decisions? Does the Tiger and the lack of a Rule 3 purpose prevent you from saying 'no'?

If you want to look at your short-term, low-risk investment level in high relief, try this:

- Step one: imagine that you have no salary (that'll not be too hard for the self-employed reader who will be ahead of the game on this one. Have you ever seen a plumber sitting bored in a three-hour meeting, fiddling with his BlackBerry?). From now on you are only paid for the tangible benefits that you deliver for your organisation. And you are only paid what they are worth to the organisation. This means that if you increase the quantity and quality of your results *you will get paid much more*. But if you like driving around the country to attend meetings that don't bring you results, you will struggle to put food on the table. And did I mention the good bit? You do not have to go to any set location at any set time other than the place of your choice in order to achieve your result.

Part of 'your' result is also measured on the team's result, so cooperating with your colleagues and working as a part of the team is still in the deal, but now you need the team to get a result, or your family will soon be going hungry. You'll have to take real decisions about which team activities to support with your time and when to face the Tiger and have a difficult conversation with an under-performing colleague who is reducing your income.

- Step two: now write down in black what it was that you did last week that was of tangible benefit to the organisation. Next, add in the activities that directly accounted for delivering team results.

- Step three: write in red all the stuff that you did last week that did not deliver or build towards a tangible result.

  By the end of this step you should have a full schedule for last week, Monday to Friday. If you cannot even remember what went into the gaps you have left then there really is work to be done on this!

- Step four: cross out all the stuff in red that nobody in the world would miss. The 'agenda-free-Monday-coffee-morning-to-take-the-sting-out-of-Mondays meeting' might be in there, for example. The sales meeting where ancient potential sales opportunities are listed each week to make things sound better than they really are. That trip of three hours each way in the car to attend a meeting that you could have attended for twenty minutes by phone if you'd only tamed the Tiger and rang that senior person and suggested that option. Strike through them all.

- Step five: cross out all the stuff in red that, although necessary, if you passed it on to others, would leave you free to achieve more through your particular talent for the team. This will, of course, involve confronting your 'delegation Tiger' or, if there is nobody to delegate to, meeting your 'hire (or fire) someone so that I can get better results for the team' Tiger head-on.

- Step six: here's the exciting bit. How long would it take you to do what you did last week? What would you, in a quiet moment of private honesty, pay yourself for the tangible result you produced? Half your salary? Twice your salary? If you are reading this and you are self-employed, given the real results that you delivered for customers or clients last week, are you amazed they paid you what they did or do you now want to value yourself at a higher rate? Or cut down on unpaid meetings somehow?

What you have done is to take out all of your short-term, low-risk investments. You are left with your short-term, high-risk investments and you have room for some long-term, higher risk Tiger-taming activities to go in there also.

It's human nature, of course, to do plenty of enjoyable, relaxed activities with a low-risk attached. So why don't we do those things outside work and be productive during the hours we are paid to be productive?

What is the opportunity cost of this lack of discipline? What parts of your story are not being written?

The Tiger roars when you begin to change your attitude to the short-term, low-risk investments of your precious resource because you have to push back at work. But there is a big prize for moving past this Tiger snarl: greater success in your career, more time with loved ones and the opportunity to use recovered time to create and pursue new and more meaningful goals, both at work and at home.

LONG-TERM INVESTMENT DECISIONS

If you do not have a long-term strategy to guide you, it is very hard to focus those short-term investments and take wise and perhaps bold decisions regarding the allocation of your precious, scarce resource tomorrow morning. That long-term strategy deserves some time and thought under Rule 8. It flows, however, from your work on Rules 2, 3, 4, 5, 6, 7 and 9. Check that you agree with that statement by looking at the Ten Rules listed together on page 22.

LONG-TERM, LOW-RISK INVESTMENT DECISIONS

We'll define long term as anything that does not have a deadline attached to it. And low risk, remember, means that it has little impact on your story. There is no fear or discomfort in engaging in this activity. No danger of procrastination here.

Now we are into the realms of time invested staring at the television every evening. This is not about our leisure time: that's vital and we generally do not plan it well. No, this is the time that we would immediately cut into if we had a sense of purpose. It's the time spent with a bottle of wine, because we couldn't think of anything better to do. Not the time spent with a bottle of wine and a good friend. This is time spent at the water cooler whingeing about the management instead of discussing our position paper with those very bosses. This is time spent critiquing the behaviour of celebrities as described in glossy magazines rather than critiquing our own behaviour.

You may think that daydreaming counts as a long-term, low-risk investment decision. Perhaps. But letting the mind wander to far-off places in the sure knowledge that, if we have an idea that excites us, we will act is no longer daydreaming. We're concerned in this section with the dreams that will never be acted upon. The dreams the Tiger will put quietly back to sleep. But what could they be without the Tiger? Let's find out.

LONG-TERM, HIGH-RISK INVESTMENT DECISIONS

You have no forced deadline attached to taking these decisions. Often, there is no short-term gain from taking a decision to invest here – the satisfaction is deferred. These are the decisions to care for our health, build relationships with our children, learn new and vital skills for our careers, build and maintain relationships and networks at work, attend to our finances. No deadlines attached to these.

Once one of these decisions is taken and a deadline applied by you, however, now you have the beginnings of commitment. Now you have a risk of failure. Now you have a desire to act boldly, find the tools that are all around you, challenge the Rulebook – you have a desire to win! Now the Tiger will snarl and encourage you to give up or at least play small.

Now the battle for your story is on.

Now you're waking up!

Don't you want to play here?

For me personally this is where all the big changes or achievements in my life have come from. I, too, have noisy, insistent deadlines to pay bills and do routine tasks. I have no deadline to grow my business or become a jockey or freedive to 101 metres in the ocean unless I create it. Few of us have a deadline to become a leader of others, to make an impact upon the business, to acquire the skills that hold us back from the next career move or that continually thwart our attempt to make our numbers. Few of us have a deadline to contemplate and decide upon our goals – which is why few of us have a committed inspired purpose encouraging us to walk past the Tiger's guttural growls.

Unless you create those deadlines, these things will not happen without a big helping hand from Lady Luck.

Even committing to booking the holiday and taking vital rest time, investing time with your friends or families, has some risk attached. You will need to take time out of the diary when you have no idea what your priorities will be out there in the future. You'll have to take some money out of the bank account and, worst of all, maybe find a half-day now in order to research and book it. But what an excellent investment of time it will be. Perhaps one of the weeks of this year that will be a truly memorable part of your story.

We're in Tiger-taming territory now. Now you are in danger of adventure and excitement, of fear and discomfort, of growth and development. Now you know that your daydreams may be acted out. Before you let the Tiger snarl at you and scale back your plans to a more pedestrian, mediocre, manageable level, keep on daydreaming! Maybe it's time to dream with a notepad in front of you and start putting down some of the small steps that might take you there.

Already finding reasons not to do this? Then maybe it is time to daydream with Rule 2 for Taming Tigers in front of you along with the Rule 3 'Why Not?' wheel.

It is through the long-term, high-risk time investment decision that you decide to do heroic battle with the voices in the head (Rule 4) and look for the tools for Taming Tigers to help you to get there (Rule 5). It is here that we find the strength to leave the safety of numbers and plough our own unique path (Rule 6). Now we are willing to work to understand and deal with our fear (Rule 7). This investment will encourage us to create and follow new disciplines (Rule 9). This is worthwhile and we will not give up (Rule 10).

The long-term, high-risk investment decision will also guide you in your short-term decisions. That will involve facing the Tiger and having some unusual conversations. Fear and discomfort will emerge even before the euphoria of the big decision has died down. But don't worry: there are some more tools available to help you get started on your new adventure.

Let's examine those now.

Controlling your time to create change

Rule 8 comes in two halves. The first half is a careful look at your relationship with time in order to 'understand' it. The second is practical guidance on how then to start to 'control' your time. Both parts are necessary to create change.

Now what do you think would possess a young jockey who is not particularly wealthy, but who is desperate to succeed in his career, to engage a full-time driver and reduce his take-home pay to the breadline? Kudos? I don't think so. Jockeys are masters and mistresses of investing their time. Let me explain why.

A jockey's day starts at around 5 a.m. He's not eating much and it may be the middle of winter, but off he goes to ride out a couple of jumpy horses in the rain or the fog. He then drives to the races, which may be three or four hours away. While in the car, he will be making calls to trainers – he is his own most effective salesperson – and taking calls from his agent. He will be calling other jockeys who have ridden horses that he will ride today to understand how best to ride them, and he might call his friends and family. Then he gets to sit in a sauna for a couple of hours to dehydrate his body to the required weight.

Then it's six races back-to-back, maybe hitting the deck in excess of thirty miles per hour from ten or more feet off the ground. Between rides, he will also want to make time to catch up with any owners or trainers who are at the racecourse and with whom he needs to maintain good relations. Then it's the three- or four-hour journey back, possibly without any more than a banana to eat.

When he gets home, he may have to burn off some calories or he may have to sweat in the bath and, of course, some time with his family would be nice. Then it is time to polish his riding-out boots for the morning and take himself off to bed. And the next day he does it all again. And so on . . .

Now we can begin to see why the determined jockey will invest in a driver as soon as he is able to. He only has twenty-four hours to invest each day in writing his story and he wants to write a bestseller. There is a lot of driving to be done, the only job that can be delegated. He either does that driving himself, with the physical and mental strain it places on him and the time that it consumes, or he climbs into the back of the car, makes his calls and gets some sleep.

Hiring a driver is a very bold decision about controlling your time. Would you do it to help you in your career? You can't afford it? Most jockeys aren't rich. They may well be earning less than you, but it is important enough to some of them that they will tame their Tiger and invest their time as they believe they need to perform.

How is the Tiger impeding your decisions about how to control your time? What is the cost of that to you, your career your family life and your story? I want to introduce you to practical ways to help you to regain control of your time.

TOOL ONE: THE DIARY

Your position now = the sum of your choices to date

> Your choices = your actions and inactions

> Your actions and inactions = where time is or is not invested and effort applied

Where time is invested and effort applied, or not = your diary

Therefore,

Your diary today = your position tomorrow.

Read that again and then open your diary. Do you agree that your diary and what you choose to keep in or out of it – and, perhaps more fascinatingly, who is choosing what goes into or stays out of it – is an accurate description of where you are choosing to apply your time, energy and talent?

Do you agree that your actions (and inactions) are what have put you in the position you are in now? Open this wide up; you don't need just to look at your work diary when considering the answer to this. If you diarised all the activities that you do out of work, would you see high-risk investments of time, long and short term, in there?

Then ask yourself: do the activities in there truly contribute to the story that my true Self wishes to write with my short time on earth? Or has my Tiger put them in there?

Here's how to use this tool. Diarise everything for a fortnight. Pay close attention to how things arrive in there. Pay close attention to whether there is any time being allocated for the long-term, high-risk activities that we agreed were so vital in writing your story. Once that has been done, you can decide whether this is a discipline that you want to continue until it has become second nature to take diary decisions based on your story, not the Tiger's roar. Who is writing your story – you or the Tiger?

Tick tock . . .

TOOL TWO: TAME THE 'NO' TIGER

Saying no can be extremely difficult. Saying no to senior people or aggressive people in the workplace can be exceptionally difficult. Negotiating with the family can sometimes be a minefield through which we don't particularly want to tread. However, saying no is probably the single most important Tiger to tame in terms of time control. And the Ten Rules for Taming Tigers will help you to say no to people.

Why? When you have a clear sense of purpose and have become emboldened by that sense of purpose (Rule 3), when you have a plan in place to get there and are looking all around you for the tools (Rules 3 and 5), when you have rewritten elements of your Rulebook (Rule 2) and have dealt with the mental battle, the Headmaster and the Saboteur (Rule 4), and when you stop seeking safety in numbers and following the habits of the crowd (Rule 6) you'll be just fine saying no. The Integrity and Leadership Rules will have given you that strength.

You have then become that inspirational person with the light shining in their eyes.

Now you are a force to be reckoned with. Trust me. People with inspired purpose do not need an 'assertiveness course'. Also, and very importantly, you will know *why* you are saying no and you will be able to articulate to those you are speaking to precisely and very politely why you are doing so. And if that 'why' has been arrived at with honesty and integrity and is being followed courageously, they will only push back at you if there is an extremely good reason. In that case, it is probably a very good idea to stop and listen up.

For those who have spent their lives enjoying and hanging on desperately to their difficulty in saying no and the desire to please everybody around them, here is a suggestion: harsh as it may sound, you are not pleasing others, you are pleasing yourself. It is very possible that you are also actively, and subtly, holding it against those others. You are doing exactly what you are choosing to do. You can choose to change the situation.

It will never become easier to stand up and be counted. So try saying no the next time you feel it is right. Try it politely, try it with a smile and with a rational explanation as to why it has been said. It could be a very, very exciting moment when the person you are speaking to simply nods, agrees and finds somebody else to help him. You might be very surprised by the response you receive – and the time you win back to invest as you choose.

Tick tock . . .

TOOL THREE: TAME THE 'TIME BANDIT' TIGER

You know the sort of people I mean: they do not have a sense of purpose, and sometimes they seem to have little sense of right or wrong as they accept a pay cheque for all their hard work in disrupting the people around them. You'll rarely find a self-employed time bandit, by the way.

If you've got this far in the book and you're creating a new sense of purpose for yourself, you won't need any help from me in taming the Tiger or dealing with the time bandit. All I will do is offer you a few words of encouragement. Yes, you are doing the right thing. Get away from them. Avoid them at lunchtime and, if necessary, move your desk to another part of the country to get out of the way of their vacuous noise. And, yes, we have all been caught in the error of thinking that it was our human duty to listen to them, as if we were performing the role of some kind of unpaid therapist. The thing is, the patient never gets better. The more you listen, the worse the disease gets!

Give yourself permission to get them out of your way. Excellent. Let's move on.

Tick tock . . .

TOOL FOUR: TAME THE GADGET TIGER

Nothing distracts me from my work quite so much as the gentle alarm of an email arriving. Can you resist taking a look? Then isn't it tempting to respond? And what happened to that sense of purpose? What happened to that deep thread of thought, that carefully allocated and diarised investment of short-term, high-risk time that you were making? It just got buried by a short-term, low-risk activity!

Turn your emails off. Turn your mobile off. Throw your smart phone in a drawer (can there be any excuse for checking emails or Facebook in a meeting with colleagues or over dinner with friends or family?). Turn them all back on at the appointed time in your diary for dealing with communication. It's the only chance you will have in the modern world of ring tones and wireless broadband to engage your brain for any period of time and drive your world forward on your terms.

Surely *your* badge of honour at work is not availability and speed of response? *Your* badge of honour is great results. At work, the former only matters as a genuine facilitator of the latter – other than the speed required by common courtesy. Common courtesy, though, also dictates that we should not expect a response from people holidaying with their children for a fortnight – or writing an important document that requires thought, designing the next generation of tablet computers or spending valuable time nurturing and supporting the young talent around them.

And if you're ever in a meeting that's so unimportant that people are tapping on laptops and checking phones rather than attending to the subject matter, the meeting is a waste of your time and of the associated travel investment. Tame your Tiger straight away. Leave.

Tick tock . . .

TOOL FIVE: USE DEADLINES

The key to the successful return from a short-term time investment is the externally forced deadline. The definition of the long-term investment is that it has no deadline – until you create one. There is nobody requiring you to plan your next career move or your holiday. Until you set a deadline, it remains a daydream or a mere doodle on a notepad.

Make the deadline public, share it with your fans and also with that cynical colleague who will remind you of it with a smirk every day. Put something real at stake against it; make it necessary that you hit the deadline. The greatest threat to successful time investment is that irrelevant activities with noisy deadlines eat into the time that should have been allocated to the important activities such as reading fairy tales to your children or planning how to grow your business or department. These had no deadline put against them publicly. But they all had a very real deadline against them in terms of the story of your life.

Tick tock . . .

TOOL SIX: PUT REGULAR PLANNING TIME ASIDE

This was addressed above when we examined how to understand time differently, but it's vital to list it as a tool for controlling your time. Once you remember to put dreaming and planning times – along with associated deadlines – into your diary (you can disguise it as walking the dog or taking a bath if you wish), you begin to create and become excited by change in your life. And as soon as you start acting on that path, it's different for you. Do you have your dreams and plans written down with actions and deadlines against them? What are you waiting for?

Tick tock . . .

TOOL SEVEN: DELEGATE

My team and I at Taming Tigers rarely work with a board without hearing about their exciting plans – and that they 'don't have the time' to implement them. The members of the board always recognise that statement as a Rule 2 fiction by the end of our time together. They simply have to change their habits. We never 'sell' this idea to them. They realise it.

Once the board realise that they need to create time for long-term, high-risk activities, such as leading and communicating the strategy and talent management (inevitably – it's the leader's day job if you stop to think about it), they begin to look at their diaries to see where the slack is. There isn't any. Instead there is a whole range of vital activities. Vital activities that all belong in other people's job descriptions.

I hope this is inspiring to hear. Even the boards of large companies are often poor delegators. It's because they care – passionately – about getting it right. Just like you do. However, once they take the time out to examine the long-term opportunity cost in terms of lost growth and ambition for the company, they begin to question these short-term, high-risk activities. Something has to give. 'Aren't we employing great talent that can do these things?' they ask. 'Are you stifling that talent by holding on to everything?' we ask in return. The breakthroughs are often enormous and long lasting.

Leaders become free to lead. Talent is permitted to perform.

Delegation has another difficulty attached to it: it involves trusting another with your reputation and (to some extent) your financial security. Trusting is an activity that gives the Tiger raging toothache. But you are neither manager nor leader if you cannot trust others to perform and manage their performance. The performance of this skill will alter your working life, get you home to your family on time, make you fit to be the leader that you wish to be and deliver long-term results for you and those whom you lead.

Tick tock . . .

TOOL EIGHT: TRY THE NURSING HOME TEST, MONTHLY

We acknowledged at the beginning of our time together that we would like to be happy old people, living in the nursing home. Many years away, for sure, but nonetheless better that, I presume, than any alternative. So maybe now, as we consider how to invest the time that will pass between this point in our lives and the time when we will get to master our dominos skills, we should turn our thoughts once again to the nursing home.

Travel to that nursing home now. What does the man or the woman there wish that the man or woman who is reading this book at this particular moment was doing differently in the way they invested in time? What can they see as the possibilities, the immense opportunities that are hidden by the Tiger as you sit here today?

What does the 'old you' reply when you tell them of your woes and why you cannot take advantage of the opportunity all around you? What are you waiting for?

Tick tock ...

There is only one scarce resource for humans

If we do not understand our relationship with time and use the tools above to control it, we will in all probability find that our new project has to yield to noisier requirements of our time before it really starts. This is where our dreams often falter and are quietly buried – only to be unearthed again in the nursing home. But that is a choice – and only the Tiger stands in the way of making the right decision.

There is only one scarce resource. That truly scarce resource is your time here on earth.

You are investing it now.

Be sure that you are deciding the investment strategy yourself and that you like the look of the return.

Have you got that diary handy?

Tick tock ...

Things that the Tiger wants you to forget about Rule 8

Rule 8: Understand and control your time to create change

Understanding your time

You are writing the story of your life. Your actions are the pen.

Your time is the paper. What you decide to do with your time creates your story. You only have one truly scarce resource: your time on earth

The Tiger likes us to take the easy path. The easy path is to believe that others control your time and that you are powerless. Some people enjoy playing the victim in this regard immensely.

There are four ways of investing your time:

- Short-term (with a deadline), high risk (it matters to your story)

- Short-term (with a deadline), low risk (it matters little to your story)

- Long-term (no deadline), low risk (it matters little to your story)

- Long-term (no deadline), high risk (it matters to your story)

Life is changed by making significant investments in long-term, high risk activities.

Control your time

Tool 1	The Diary
Tool 2	Tame the 'no' Tiger
Tool 3	Tame the 'time bandit' Tiger
Tool 4	Tame the gadget Tiger
Tool 5	Use deadlines
Tool 6	Put regular planning time aside
Tool 7	Delegate
Tool 8	Take the nursing home test monthly

Now log on to the Campus at tamingtigers.com and watch the film entitled 'Hickory Dickory Dock'.

Twitter: @jim_lawless

Web: tamingtigers.com

Facebook: facebook.com/pages/Taming-Tigers.

Case study 8:
Steve Holliday

I work with a number of books and coaching models and only recently heard Jim speak but I have been looking at his Ten Rules and there are several I can relate to in terms of the journey I've been going on over the past few years.

I was in the pharmaceuticals and medical devices business until about eighteen months ago. About three or four years ago, I was selected to go on a business coaching programme and for the first time I started to career manage. I learned ways of thinking and behaving to produce different results. I realised I was capable of more and started to manage my career. Most importantly, I learned the difference between management and leadership. I started reading books by people such as Steven Covey and, more recently, I have been working with a personal coach who is a psychologist.

I now work as head of Health and Safety for the power station division at e.on. I started out in Operations, but I have been a Health and Safety professional now for twelve years. I only became chartered three years ago but, because of Jim and others I have been speaking to recently, I decided to change back to Operations. The power of Jim's advice is once your direction is clear this can be a powerful magnet, so I'm setting myself in a new direction.

In my personal life, I've had an experience similar to Jim's jockeying; it happened after an old friend had skin cancer. He recovered, but our group of friends decided to do something for the hospital that had looked after him. We decided to do a coast-to-coast bike race in three days to raise money. Initially I made excuses. I thought it wouldn't be possible and I wouldn't have time as I hadn't been on a bike in years. What motivated me was that we trained as a group of friends; it was about doing something together. The first year we did the ride in three days; two years later we managed it in two days. It comes back to Jim's principle: if you even think that you would like to do it, you can do it. But the Tigers are quick to come and say, 'You can't do that'. That point struck home for me and I've been thinking about it. Last night I was with my friends and we got talking; now we're thinking about doing John O'Groats to Land's End next year, and I haven't been on a bike since the last trip, but, having achieved what we have already, it is possible.

The rules I identify with most are numbers 1, 3, 4, 5, 7, 8 and 10. Of these, rules 1, 3 and 7 are most important to me. For me, 'act boldly today' is about recognising time as one of your most valuable assets. I've realised that you can't do everything in a senior job; what you can do is a small number of big things. Do three or four key things that will have a knock-on effect and you'll make better use of time. I have the work–life challenge, too, as I want to be a good husband and father and friend.

Jim talks about how there are voices in your head. As you start coaching, you become more aware of these voices saying, 'I'm not sure I can do that, maybe it's too big a stretch'. If you don't get your mind round that first Tiger – is it possible or not? – and do things that are uncomfortable, you will never find out. I'm different now because I have a better understanding of my personal development. It isn't always easy. I think you need to plan for feeling challenged and be prepared for it.

Rule 3 is about moving towards the goal you want to achieve. I was doing some coaching this morning with a friend who is having problems at work. He knew what to do and what outcome he wanted but couldn't say so to his line manager. I gave him Jim's card with the ten rules. I suggested that he identify the top three companies he wanted to work for and talk to them. He thought I was joking, but I meant it. You need to be clear on what defines success in life, work and personal relationships and move towards it. It's like Jim and the jockeying. He clearly got over the Tiger and went every day in that direction. For me making sure people are clear on their goals and the direction they are moving is the biggest challenge for any organisation.

Rule 7 is about doing something bold every day, but it doesn't always have to be big things. Sometimes doing something quite small can be bold, and change can be incremental, as long as it's moving in the right direction every day.

Jim's Rule 5 is about finding the tools that will help. For me it was the coaching. One thing I've learned is that it's important to learn the individual characteristics and ways of working with your colleagues. Everyone has different models they find helpful.

Number 10, 'never, never give up', is something I agree with, but it is difficult at times.

Having learned so much through coaching myself, I've become interested in enlightening others. Going through extensive coaching makes you think you could be good at it yourself and so you want to try it, and to help with coaching programmes and leadership days. I have not used Jim's rules explicitly in my coaching yet as I only recently learned about them, but I have told a number of people, given a couple of them the cards and suggested they look out for the book when it is published.

Rule 9

Create Disciplines – Do the Basics Brilliantly

There is a very famous jockey called Frankie Dettori. He is probably the most famous jockey in the world today. He is certainly one of the most successful in the history of horseracing. At the beginning of June 2007 (Frankie's twenty-first year as a professional jockey) he had not won the most coveted race in the world, the English Derby at Epsom. He had tried fourteen times and failed. The pressure was on.

On 2 June 2007, Frankie Dettori and a little colt named Authorized were loaded into the starting stalls for the one mile, four furlong and ten metre classic of classics.

As the field jumped out, Frankie kept his mount towards the rear and switched the talented little colt off, allowing him to bowl along, letting the lead horses do all the hard work over the undulating Epsom track. But by the time they reached the famous Tattenham Corner and began to turn for home, Frankie had asked Authorized to show to the watching millions just how talented he was. Slowly at first, the colt gathered up the galloping field until, by the time he reached the beginning of the grandstands, Authorized and Frankie were in an unassailable position for the Italian to claim his first English Derby. The man who had made history by winning all seven races on a single race card at Ascot in 1996 added the single remaining prize he most wanted to complete an enviable collection of the world's most valuable classic trophies on his mantelpiece.

Lucky Frankie Dettori.

The whip was waved at the Epsom crowd and the viewing millions as he passed the finishing line. The famous smile beamed and the famous flying dismount was delivered to loud cheers in the Winners' Enclosure. Then Frankie, finally, accepted the Derby Trophy from Her Majesty Queen Elizabeth II of England.

Lucky Frankie Dettori!

What did our lucky hero do to celebrate? He flew to France to pair up the next day with another talented colt, Lawman, to win the Prix du Jockey Club (the French equivalent of the English Derby).

Lucky Frankie Dettori!

That's two Derbies in two days at two racecourses on two horses in two countries in one weekend for one man. What would you call that in terms of sporting achievement?

I call it plain greedy!

I got to play at lucky Frankie's jockey disciplines for a year. I stress the word 'play'. I had a back-up plan, a fully fledged, successful career. Frankie's not playing – he's at work, a professional. Having tried it, I'm not sure it's about 'luck'.

It goes like this: you are up at 5 a.m. and at work for 6 a.m. Racing doesn't do 'late' and it doesn't do 'sick'. But it does do a seven-day week seeing as there are animals to be cared for and because the betting public likes to have seven days of racing, fifty-two weeks of the year.

On a fine morning, nothing beats galloping a beautiful race-horse at dawn over a stunning landscape. In England, however, the mornings are not always fine. You can be leaving the house in horizontal rain or chipping the ice from the windscreen at 5.30. Breakfast is a banana and a coffee (black, no sugar). After three or four hours of riding out you're ready for some more to eat so another banana slips down a treat.

Why bananas? Well, if I tell you what is off the menu it might begin to make sense. I was given help on this by sports scientist Jon Pitts and here is what we cut out from my diet: all dairy products, white pasta, bread, red meat (not a problem as I am a vegetarian), oils and most sauces, alcohol, muesli and nuts, all sweets and chocolate and biscuits and cakes. Chips and curries were sorely missed. Dried fruit (unsweetened) was an occasional and indulgent treat on long car journeys to deliver speeches.

So you are looking forward to lunch and, having ridden for much of the morning, lunchtime is nearly here. A small baked potato and lots of fresh salad. Obviously without the butter, beans, cheese, salad dressing and so on that might have been there in the old days. It is now that you begin to wonder how you never discovered the delights of a squeeze of lemon before! Why did you not pay more attention to the pepper pot and its little flakes of flavour? And where has mustard been hiding all these years?

You keep to the diet. It's the job. At the racecourse, the Clerk of the Scales does not say 'look out, son, those silk breeches are getting a bit tight, time to lay off the pies for a bit!' No, he sits you on the scales and if you weigh too much he calls up his good friend Mr Commentator, who announces to the crowd that a particular jockey is overweight as he rides past them all with his backside in the air for all to judge.

Your afternoon snack is an apple. Dinner has to be eaten by 7.30 p.m. as you need to have as little as possible in your system by bedtime. No carbohydrates at dinner though, you had your quota with that potato at lunchtime. Then on go the running shoes to work off the day's intake and keep your fitness up – often in the dark and the rain. I've missed out the gym work for fear of discouraging any potential jockeys out there.

Then you get up the next morning and do it all again.

Of course, for the real jockeys, every afternoon, after riding out and while sticking to the diet, is spent travelling and racing.

My day outside riding out, diet and exercise was spent working for my business.

Lucky Frankie Dettori?

I played at that diet and that schedule for one year. Frankie and the others don't play at it. Frankie has worked at it for well over twenty-five years with consistent effort and discipline.

I promised to be honest with you, so let me make it clear that I have not tried to tell you how to win a Derby. I have no idea how to do that. I have told you how to apply for an assessment at the British Racing School in Newmarket. There, assuming you can handle a racehorse well in a variety of exercises, pass the fitness tests and explain the Rules of Racing, you may be awarded your permit to ride under Rules.

Lucky Frankie Dettori?

It is all too easy when all we see is our hero acknowledging the roar of the crowd, or the business person enjoying his or her rewards, to confuse decades of disciplined hard work, and personal, private, heroic victories over the temptation to give up, with luck. Something far more manageable – but less appealing to the Tiger – is at play here: discipline and the practice of basic skills and behaviours.

Rule 9: Create disciplines and do the basics brilliantly

What are 'disciplines' and 'basics'? If you take the analogy of playing the piano, one of the the basics is your scales. The disciplines include practicing those scales (and everything else that you have decided to work on), daily for a minimum amount of time – and never letting yourself down on that promise.

Now discipline is a very unfashionable word in the twenty-first century. And who wants to do the basics when there are more fun things to do? If you think you can tame your Tiger in any meaningful sense without Rule 9, however, you're wrong.

I'll go further: from my experience of getting to the racetrack and becoming the UK's deepest freediver, from working with elite athletes and elite business performers, I am convinced that total clarity of vision and total clarity of the plan, combined with tremendous self-discipline around performance of the 'basics', is as near to the 'secret of success' as you'll get (Rules 3 and 9).

Mundane personal tasks deliver the moment of triumph

Would you like to have founded a successful business and attained financial independence? Would you like to have won an Olympic medal? Of course. Would you like to put your house on the line and risk all? Would you like to get up every day, rain or shine, and pound the streets? Of course not.

Nobody would – but they learn to love it and their great results and inspired purpose motivate them to get started and to push through the bad days.

Is it any easier for those we see at the top of their games, in any field – business, sport, parenting, academia – to stick to the daily disciplines that underpin their success than it is for us 'mere mortals'? Of course not.

The achievers, the writers of stories and the inspirers of others have taken a choice, decided what their disciplines will be to support that choice, and set about incorporating them into their daily lives. That decision each morning to retain discipline that day is heroic. They are 'mere mortals' also.

As the saying goes, 'there are no extraordinary people, just ordinary people doing extraordinary things'. They have all met and tamed their Tiger and continue to do so.

The major Rule 9 basics and disciplines for me in riding and diving were mundane. Going to bed on time, getting out of bed on time, showing up at the yard, showing up at the gym or on the streets, practising yoga, putting different things into the supermarket trolley and always preparing fresh food in the evening are examples. The major Rule 9 discipline in writing this book is to sit down and write it today, tomorrow and the next day - after a day at work. There is nothing sexy or exciting about any of these things. But they pay us back in spades.

Be in no doubt that behind every moment of glory and triumph that you witness in any field there are many thousands of heroic decisions made to defer gratification, refusals to take the easier path. Decisions to stick to the plan. Decisions to be disciplined and to work on the basic foundations that will deliver victory. These decisions are taken in the face of the Tiger's roar. That is why we are inspired by our heroes' stories. But are you willing to learn from their stories? Are you willing to change habits, to act differently to force the minor discomfort of disciplines and basics?

Decisions, actions, results.

When you look at those top performers, in whatever field, and wonder if you, too, could work on those disciplines, the Tiger will attack and give you good reasons not to try. The Tiger attacked our heroes as well, so you are on the right path. Let's explore some popular Tiger strategies to let us off the hook of discipline.

'It's easy for *them* – if I were playing for those high stakes, I could be disciplined, too!'

Catch-22. You will never get to play for those high stakes unless you are disciplined. The rewards were not always high for them. Once upon a time, every famous sportsperson was a highly disciplined unknown, trying to get opportunities. They had people telling them to forget about their dreams. They were determined. They put great discipline in place even to reach the rank of unknown, when they were getting very little reward or recognition for working daily at this discipline. At this stage it is also very hard to sustain discipline – especially for the teenage jockey when friends are off to the pub for dinner and drinks with girlfriends and boyfriends and they have both calories and a 5 a.m. start to consider.

This strategy doesn't cut it, does it? Take a look at Rule 3, imagine, commit and then create with discipline.

'OBVIOUSLY, DISCIPLINE AND BASICS ARE IMPORTANT FOR A TOP SPORTSPERSON, BUT THEY MAKE NO DIFFERENCE TO ME'

Well, that Rule 2 rule in your Rulebook should keep you very safe from your fear of grafting and the associated discomfort. The results of discipline are obvious and high profile in some cases and less obvious and less high profile in others. The consequences of adopting Rule 9 are nonetheless there for all of us to see and to benefit from. Look around.

The people who put disciplines in place around their finances five, ten, fifteen, thirty years ago reap the reward of that discipline, don't they? The people who apply discipline to the time they spend working to be great parents (rather than relying on the TV or a nanny to do the parenting) reap untold rewards from those loving relationships and those settled children, don't they? The people who work on their integrity, their coaching skills, their courage to set a vision and to move away from seeking safety in numbers, they become the respected and wealthy leaders and innovators of tomorrow's businesses, don't they?

The super-salespeople that I meet are rarely maverick, macho, naturally gifted communication geniuses. They do the basics. They do them every day. They have great integrity – they are honest and they keep their promises. They look after their customers. They are hungry for (and humble enough to listen to) training and ideas that will help them perform more effectively. They live in huge houses. They have time for their children. They plan an early retirement.

'I don't have time for basics and disciplines'

Disciplines and basics generally save you time.

On the general topic of time, please reread Rule 8. Are you really still using that old chestnut in your Rulebook to excuse your surrender to the Tiger?

Trusting the basics and disciplines under (deep-sea) pressure

I am dripping wet. I glance at my watch: 7.30 in the morning, 27 August 2010.

Record day.

Time to get up. To keep my sinuses in good condition I have to sleep without air conditioning. In Sharm el Sheikh in high summer, with temperatures reaching 35°C/95°F, that doesn't make for a comfortable lie-in once the sun has begun to climb above the horizon. I look over at Anita, fast asleep, her hair beginning to stick to her forehead as the temperature rises. I take a shower and, with a cup of mint tea in hand, climb the steps on to the flat roof of the house.

I've been looking forward to this moment of calm and solitude. At one o'clock today I'll leave the house of my good friend and underwater filmmaker Debbie Metcalfe, where I've been staying during my training in Egypt, and head off to the sea to make my first attempt on the UK's No-Limits Freediving Record and, in the process, to become the first British free-diver to pass 100 metres and to become the deepest British freediver ever. The day is planned from nine o'clock onwards. For the moment, this is my own time.

Debbie is the owner of Blue Eye FX, the international underwater film company. Her team will start to arrive at her house at around nine to begin their preparations to film the dive.

I have been hoping for peace as I watch the sun rise and the jagged Sinai mountains turn through pink to their gritty daytime beige, but the Tiger has other plans and the Headmaster starts to make himself heard.

Who the hell am I to make an attempt on the British record? Will the sea know that I am a relative newcomer? Have I been 'good' enough to deserve a break from the planet and be helped down through the ocean and back up again? Shouldn't I have worked even harder before this day?

I practise Kundalini Yoga for two hours with my favourite yoga music, the album 'Into Silence' by Deva Premal, with its familiar rhythms and harmonies somewhere in the distance behind me. I move off into another world. Moving through the warm-up, I begin to feel the usual sense of strength in my body, my mind and my spirit. The Tiger starts to dissolve.

There is a buzz in the air at the Only One Apnea Centre. It is record day. Andrea and Rasta greet me with great big smiles and I head off to suit up.

It is impossible to get into a freediving wet suit, a special and highly flexible form of open-cell neoprene, without first covering the inside of it with soap. I head off to the showers to lather up and slide into my second skin.

I insert one Suunto D4 dive computer into my hood. This will sound close to my ear when I hit forty metres. At that depth, and at a rate of descent of around 1.6 metres per second, I have ten metres to squeeze air out of my lungs and into my cheeks during the dive before my lungs seal up and trap any remaining air in there. I will need all the air in my cheeks that I can find. It is not for breathing, it is to use to equalise my ear spaces. If I don't have enough air to do that, the pressure from the ocean as I descend will increase, causing indescribable pain. If I don't terminate the descent quickly, my eardrums will burst in seconds. I strap my other D4 computer on to my wrist, attach my weight belt, gather my mask and fins and head out alone to the sea.

The sea! I have forgotten in all the preparations that this is all about being with the sea. I remember this as I reach the top of the cliff and notice the sea for the first time today. It is sapphire-blue but a thousand diamonds dance on its surface under the glare of the Egyptian sun. The pontoon stretches out over the reef from the sandy shore and the platform sits one hundred metres out to sea. The platform is positioned in a bay. The bay opens to the wider ocean and the sea travels to the horizon. My heart jumps. I know this shoreline well. I began scuba diving here in 1998. I always feel like I'm coming home when I get into the water here. The familiar creatures will be there to welcome me back. Clown fish, parrot fish, lion fish, butterfly fish, banner fish, reef sharks and turtles if you're very lucky. Old friends all.

My mind flashes back to the good omen I received from the ocean on my first dive from the Only One Centre in January this year. My whale shark.

'Ciao, Jim!' Andrea is beside me. He is suited up and his teeth are glinting as he gives me his widest grin. 'Shall we dive!'

'Let's dive!'

Andrea will be my safety diver today. This means that he will dive down and meet me at around thirty metres as I return. Should our timing go wrong, he will have to wait there until I arrive. He cannot touch the line that I will be descending on as it is a record attempt, so he will have to use energy suspending himself in the blue while he looks down into the darkness, searching for the first glimpse of the white airbag bringing me back to the surface. Should there be anything wrong when I arrive at thirty metres, he will need to assist me. So it's vital that he does as careful a warm-up today as I do. He may also have quite a long dive ahead of him.

Three good warm-up dives. Swim to the platform.

Rasta is sitting on the platform with his official yellow AIDA T-shirt. The second judge, Angela Ambrosi is in the water by the sled. The crowd of tourists around the dive site is growing. Rasta gives me an OK sign and asks if I'm ready to start the five-minute countdown. I give a silent OK sign back and put my head into the water, breathing through a snorkel, and back into the peaceful world beneath the surface of the sea. I feel good, very strong, very relaxed and focused, very serene – in the zone.

I swim over to the sled and push my feet through the ropes that will secure them. It takes a few attempts as the sled is bobbing up and down in the swell. Once I am secure I nod at Rasta. 'Two minutes!' he cries to me and the crowd and presses his stopwatch.

My torso is loose.

My breath is long and powerful. My stomach expands. My ribs expand. I exhale fully, contracting my belly to a tiny, seemingly impossible size. I can feel my diaphragm working underneath me. The Kundalini yoga and the dive training have left it strong and very flexible. It will need to be flexible because in less than two minutes it will be pulled into my chest cavity to compensate as my lungs decrease in size.

'Sixty seconds!' Rasta's call is loud but I hear it in the far distance now.

My muscle control feels good. I'm only using the minimum amount of muscle tension required to keep myself upright on the sled. I can feel everything else relax; I can feel the sea support me. My eyes are closed and my eyelids are relaxed. The old tune is playing loudly in my head and is all that I can focus on now. 'Aad Guray Nameh' – long and slow, repetitive, magnificent.

'Fifteen seconds!' It's a dim noise, but I'm aware of it. I lift my chin and look at the heavens, at the blue dome, fill my abdomen and chest with warm air, close my mouth, hold my nose, bring my chin to my chest feeling the usual involuntary inflation of the air space in my ears. Rasta knows the sign and releases the sled.

Adjust from the stillness to the pace of descent. A slow pace at this depth, it will increase rapidly as we get deeper and become more neutrally buoyant. Chin is tucked in, head looking downwards. A bright star is there that I haven't seen before. It takes a few more seconds before I'm close enough: Debbie and her camera. I travel past her.

Complete solitude. The massage begins as the sled accelerates. Just me and the sea for another seventy metres. Focusing on equalising, concentrating on letting every muscle in my body enjoy the hug and the rippling massage of the sea caused by the pressure on my body and the speed of descent through the water. Amazing.

The muted beep of the computer in my hood – forty metres. Fill my mouth with air from my lungs. Seal my nose, mouth and larynx. Applying just enough pressure to keep the air secure. If I release my larynx at this depth, the air will disappear into my lungs to fill the vacuum being created there. I will not be able to make the depth.

The quiet hum of the friction of the sled against the rope harmonises with 'Aad Guray Nameh' again. At fifty metres I can feel that there is still air left in my lungs and I want it. I want it in my mouth to be sure that I have enough to keep my ears equalised down to 101 metres. I break all the rules, open my larynx and feel the air come into my mouth. An extra, unexpected gift. Invincible now.

And down. Close my eyes. Wait for the clank of the sled as it hits the steel plate at the bottom of the line.

Incredible pain. I've run out of air to equalise, I don't know why. I don't know how. I must nearly be at 101 metres so I ignore it and descend. But it won't be ignored. I pull the brake on the sled and bring the thing to a halt. It is too dark to look at my computer. The pain is intense. I jiggle up and down on the sled hoping to dislodge the bubbles in my lungs into my mouth. The clock ticks. No bubbles. No relief from the pain. Such pain!

How has this happened? It didn't happen in training. I must be just short of the platform. I release the brake and descend. The pain reaches unbearable levels. I'm shouting out involuntarily – there is no sound; no bubbles. There is no air. I stop the sled again, I have to relieve the pain by heading up.

I have failed.

No.

I could leave the sled, ascend a few metres on the line, decrease the pain in my head and maybe find some air in my lungs after all. I take my feet out of the ropes and leave the sled. Why is my arm stuck? The lanyard which attaches me to the sled pulls taut and holds me. The effect of this brings me to my senses. I have been at extreme depth already for way longer than I should have been. I must be approaching two and a half minutes by this stage. I am still somewhere near 100 metres. It enters my head that I am now experiencing nitrogen narcosis. A kind of pleasant, relaxing intoxication brought about by depth. Pleasant – but deadly if it impairs my judgement at this critical point in the dive. I give up. Open the valve on the tank to inflate the airbag. Adopt the ascent position on the sled, dangling from the foot rest, body completely relaxed. For once, I don't enjoy the massage as I race towards the surface.

Failed.

I break the surface to the crowd above. They come as a surprise. I have forgotten that all these people are here. I need to know whether I've reached the depth and in the glare of the sunlight I look to my Suunto computer immediately. Eighty-four metres. It's impossible. Makes no sense. Too shallow.

A huge failure.

The judges wear confused expressions on their faces. They don't understand why I have not completed the surface protocol. They are hoping that I have been to 101 metres. They know that, if I have been there, I've now blown the dive by failing to observe the protocol.

'Eighty-four. I want to try again.'

My voice sounds odd to me – I've been alone in my head for too long. The dive has taken over three minutes and twenty seconds with far too much of that time spent at extreme depth.

The judges confer and tell me that I am clearly suffering from nitrogen narcosis. They refuse to let me dive again today.

In silence, I collect an oxygen cylinder, descend to five metres and stay there for six minutes. This is usual procedure after a deep dive and is not related to the failure of this one.

As I bob up and down in the shallow swell, holding on to the line, I look back up at all the faces above me. A whole group of people just staring at me. I want to move away from their gaze but it is impossible. I feel like a caged idiot.

I have failed. I didn't follow the basics under pressure. The sensation of air I thought I felt coming into my mouth was in fact air leaving my mouth. How could it do otherwise? My compressed lungs formed a vacuum and by opening my larynx I caused the air in my mouth to be sucked into my lungs. I didn't follow Rule 9 when I needed it most, on record day. I forgot the basics and tried to be clever.

I don't want to do this again. I'll take tomorrow off and arrange a flight home for the next day. I am thinking of giving up. At five metres. When the Tiger is loudest, Rule 10 – never, never give up – is hard to find.

By the time the six minutes are up and I return to the surface, I am alone with Rasta and Andrea. The boys have worked very hard for me over the past eight months. They are disappointed as well. Silence as we swim to shore.

28 August 2010. I have rediscovered Rule 10. I will dive again. It is Groundhog Day. Sunrise, yoga, off to the centre. Except that today I have committed to following the basics brilliantly. Today I will dive by the Rule 9 basics.

'Fifteen seconds!' It's a dim noise, but I'm aware of it. I lift my chin and look at the heavens, at the blue dome, fill my abdomen and chest with warm air, close my mouth, hold my nose, bring my chin to my chest feeling the usual involuntary inflation of the air space in my ears. Rasta knows the sign. He releases the sled.

I look out for the star at thirty metres and there is Debbie with her camera. Forty metres – alarm – mouth-fill – seal larynx, nose, mouth – descend. It feels good. It feels so good. The massage is intense, the relaxation almost exhilarating. The sled and I accelerate. 'Aad Guray Nameh' swells in my head.

Clang.

The sled hits the steel bottom plate fixed to the rope.

One hundred and one metres. I raise my tongue to squeeze out what remains of the air in my compressed mouth cavity. Is there any air left in here? Can I go deeper next time? Bubbles appear from my mouth. I could have equalised for many metres more. I didn't even pack extra air in on the surface – just went with a lungful. This is good news for the future.

I may be at 101 metres, but if I don't ascend efficiently and carry out the surface protocol it won't count as a record. As the last bubble leaves my lips I open the valve on the tank, reposition myself on the sled and enjoy the ride. Fifty, forty, thirty metres. My lungs begin to open again as the trapped air expands. Beautiful.

I reach Andrea at thirty metres; he looks me in the eye questioningly. I give him an OK sign and, without taking his eyes off my pupils as we ascend together, he gives a victory dance underwater. We swim up eye to eye, following the discipline, in case of any blips during the final huge pressure changes after a deep dive. We reach the surface. I carry out the surface protocol.

The judges confer in Italian and look back at me with serious faces.

Then their faces burst into smiles. Rasta lets out a roar and holds up his white judge's card. He is shouting:

'British record! British record! Britain's deepest freediver! The British have passed 100 metres!'

I take the oxygen tank and descend to five metres for my six-minute rest. I was here yesterday feeling that I had let everybody down, considering going home. I am now the deepest freediver in British history, the first to pass the magic 100-metre mark.

Rule 9, Create disciplines, follow the basics brilliantly, and Rule 10, never, never give up, have secured me the record twenty-four hours after defeat.

Time to celebrate!

What are the rules that you need to put in place for yourself if you really want to get there?

Before we look at Rule 10, let's finish our examination of Rule 9 with two deceptively simple questions for you. Thinking about the story you want to write, the life you want to lead and the opportunities that you have no intention of missing in the future (as you may have missed them in the past), what disciplines do you think, had you put them in place ten years ago, and had you practised them faithfully on a daily basis, would have most positively altered the position that you are in today?

Another question. If you put those disciplines in place for the next ten years, starting from today, how much of a difference do you think you would create in your life as a result of the sentence in your life story that you are writing in your head at this precise second?

Do it now. Have a little think.

If you can make time for thirty minutes' TV a day, you could make time to become a very handy pianist in a couple of years, or to be person who takes thirty minutes exercise every day and weighs many pounds less. It is the everyday thing that matters. And it is the sticking with it.

The plot of a good book or film turns on a sentence, and this is your moment for sentence writing. Don't miss your moment. It may not return for a long time.

Over to you.

Things the Tiger wants you to forget about Rule 9

Rule 9: Create Disciplines – do the basics brilliantly

Behind every moment of glory that you witness in any field, there are many thousands of heroic decisions to defer gratification, not to take the easier path.

It is the apparently mundane, daily personal tasks that deliver the moment of public triumph.

There are no extraordinary people – just ordinary people doing extraordinary things. These things are the basics and disciplines.

Look out! When you think of ways of avoiding basics and disciplines, the Tiger may well be at work. It may use lines such as:

- 'It's easy for them – if I were playing for those high stakes, I could be disciplined too.'

- 'Obviously discipline and basics are important for a top sportsperson/businessperson, but they make no difference to me.'

Are you going to let yourself be motivated away from the minor discomfort of practising your disciplines and basics or towards the goal that inspires you, towards being the person you wish to become?

Now log in to the Campus at tamingtigers.com and watch the film: '5 Metres'. You can also watch the video of the successful dive there.

Twitter: @jim_lawless
Web: tamingtigers.com
Facebook: facebook.com/pages/Taming-Tigers.

Case Study 9:
James Le Brocq

During 2005, I was one of the Commercial Directors at a global financial services provider. We were facing significant market pressures, and to succeed in our many challenges it was clear that we needed to support our people to increase their level of personal leadership and accountability. So we asked Jim and his Ten Rules for Taming Tigers to help us achieve this. Watching the teams be introduced to Taming Tigers was like watching light bulbs go on.

I chose to take the Ten Rules to heart also and they have helped guide my decisions since. For example: are any concerns and fears I have about acting boldly merely the Tiger working to diminish my story – or is there a legitimate concern to address?

I am now engaged in the biggest challenge of my career. As Managing Director of O_2 Money, within the mobile telecoms company O_2 part of the global telecoms giant Telefonica, I am leading the project to revolutionize what mobile payments are all about: how they are done and how customers interact with their other financial products. We are establishing our own, brand new, payments business as part of this charge.

Mobile operators have already got involved with banking but always through the traditional method of partnering with an established bank. To my mind (a view shared within the O_2 leadership and my team) this is not bold enough to create a revolution; it is merely providing a new platform for traditional banking. I'm not sure that, in the eyes of consumers, traditional banking or traditional bankers are covered in glory after the global financial crisis and ongoing economic challenges.

There is no certainty in what we are doing. We are at the frontier. Central to our approach is to follow Rule 6 – 'There is no safety in numbers'. We have decided to be out there on the track. O_2 is the only TelCo to have hired bankers, created a new infrastructure for them and sought its own e-money licence. Critically, we have immersed our bankers in a fast-moving, consumer-focused mobile phone operator and not left them within a traditional banking structure.

My team and I have have fleetness of foot now. We don't have the great hierarchy and infrastructure of a bank to deal with. We are building, from scratch, a company fit for its 21st Century purpose and not reshaping a legacy from the 19th Century. The flipside of all that is that it is untested, it's new, nothing is certain – it's risky – I am exposed and accountable. It's great – but the Tiger roars!

Jim speaks about the Tiger's bared teeth when we challenge our Rulebooks and head into uncertainty: he is correct. The Tiger has roared at us in a very real way. But I believe that all progress and innovation has been achieved by individuals choosing to push through this. I want to be a part of that.

By taking the entire contents of the wallet and the purse and putting it on the customer's phone – along with a set of other services, we are not only challenging our own, and O_2's Rulebooks, we are challenging the Rulebook that has governed financial services for generations. But we have a strong purpose – we have Rule 3 – we keep heading in the direction of where we want to arrive and that keeps us steady when the Tiger appears.

Interestingly, people have different views of me at present. I recently spent time with the CEO of a global payments network who seemed rather jealous of the opportunities that O_2 and I have and the path we are walking. Days later I sat on a steering group preparing a major Financial Services conference and found myself on the receiving end of a very dismissive attitude from a senior member of the traditional banking community. What is it that Jim says about getting criticized from the grandstand once you are out on the track for all to see? Rule 6 in action.

I thought hard about this role before I committed to it. Why? Because the Tiger roared – it was a huge personal risk. I have a wife and three children. I had spent 26 years in banking and was moving into a new industry. If I wanted to return to the banking sector at some stage, people would say 'What the hell did you do that for? You're mad – why would we take you back?' So it could, possibly, at some nebulous stage of the future, be seen as 'career limiting'. If we win, however, it will be the most incredible prize. The stakes were high. I had to tame my Tiger before committing but I am delighted that I did. As Jim says, who is writing my story? Me or the Tiger? I couldn't turn down this opportunity just because there are no guarantees of success. That would be the Tiger talking.

I decided to act boldly and commit. I do not believe that we will fail but, if we do, I will have learned a great deal and have been true to myself. That I can live within the nursing home. I have a bigger story to write than fleeing from imagined risks several years away. In the meantime, I am having the time of my life. I have the opportunity to be creative, lead other great people and be at the spearhead of delivering advances for the customer in the industry I have served for my whole career.

Who would have thought I would be doing that from within a mobile phone operator?

Never say never – whatever the Tiger might tell you.

Part Four

The Growth Rule

Never, Never Give Up

'Aren't you ready to ride in a charity race yet?' I've been riding for about five months and Marcus Armytage, Gee's brother, *Daily Telegraph* Racing Correspondent and winner of the Grand National in 1990 on Mr Frisk, was coming up with an idea.

Unfortunately, Gee was within earshot. Within thirty minutes, my fate was sealed. I was riding in a charity race in four weeks time at Brighton Racecourse.

For those of you who don't ride, six months into your lessons is about the right time to consider moving from trot to canter on a 'nice old boy'. It is a bit of a stretch to gallop on a racehorse in a public race – at a racecourse. Still, I am in a hurry to win my challenge, so certain luxuries must be sacrificed.

Unlike most racecourses, Brighton does not run a complete circuit; it is shaped like a warped horseshoe. This is not good for the novice whose horse may well bolt on the way to post. The runaway horse does not run wildly around a circuit until it exhausts itself. No. The horse runs to the end of the track where it meets 'the cheese grater'.

The jockeys in the pub had had a glint in their eyes as, over a mineral water, they told me about 'the cheese grater'.

'It's like the big white wooden screen thing they put behind the batsman on a cricket pitch,' they said. 'If a horse has lost the plot, they just run straight into it. Basically, if you get run off with on the way to post, you smash through the cheese grater and you land up falling into the grounds of Roedean School for Girls. But if you can't pull up fast enough at the end of the race, you go through the other cheese grater and land up on the beach.'

The week before, Gee had taken me to Newbury racecourse and introduced me to everything I needed to know about procedure at the races. She made me stand on the scales in the weighing room and, to the delight of the bored security guards watching over the otherwise empty racecourse, she had me come out and place my whip and hat silk on to the table in front of an imaginary Clerk of the Scales. She then had me sit on the scales (until very recently most scales at British racecourses had a chair on them upon which the jockey sat holding all his tack) and solemnly announced my weight to me. And she made me hand my tack to her (as she ran round to become the trainer rather than the Clerk of the Scales) and then go back into the weighing room for an imaginary cup of tea until she came in to call me for the race. Then we marched out to the empty parade ring together to leg me up on to an imaginary horse.

So, I am prepared for all eventualities. Except for Frankie Dettori and Jamie Spencer coming out of the weighing room in their silks for their last race as I walk in to change. Frankie gives me a nod as I head in and it all becomes perfectly clear to me.

I have no right to be here!

The Rulebook goes bananas and the Headmaster is screaming at me to go back home. Gee has gone to speak to some people so the 'tools' for Taming Tigers are nowhere to be found and the idea that there is anything more scary to be done today than walking into this changing room (full of people who have become my heroes in these short months) is ridiculous.

But there are greater challenges ahead.

'Jockeys please!'

Time to go out. The wind catches you as soon as you leave the weighing room, especially by the seaside. Everybody else is in a coat but we are in silk. Gee has not mentioned the wind. Perhaps it is different for girls.

I meet Gary Moore for the first time. He is a gentleman and puts me at ease. The bell rings and Gary legs me up. Gary Moore, one of the finest trainers in the country, has just legged me up on to a racehorse at Brighton races and I am being led out on to the racetrack by one of his team. I am tempted to shout for joy but then I remember the cheese grater. Theatre of Life is already jig-jogging along and I have to get this racehorse steadily all the way to the start – a canter of one and a half miles – and then stop him. Or it's Roedean School for me.

As we go down the chute (the little narrow path between the parade ring and the racecourse) there is a commotion behind us and our groom lets out a scream. This is unusual around racehorses. I follow her eyes behind me in time to see a rearing, riderless horse (the jockey is flying, colourfully, backwards towards the crowd) break free of the groom leading it up and start to bolt down the chute.

Theatre of Life, my groom and I are creating a cork in a narrow bottleneck. We try to get Theatre of Life to move forward but the horse has planted himself as if he is curious to see what will happen next.

What happens next is that both beasts and I go upwards and then downwards. I remember a sensation as like being in a washing machine, hitting the ground and then curling up into a tight ball and wondering if stuff like this ever happened to Frankie. I uncurl slightly to take a look at what is going on around me and see an eight-legged beast with shiny, sharp metal shoes on flailing about beside me.

I take the ball option again.

Horses are not at their daintiest when they are on their backs, tangled up with each other and trying to get up off the ground. Especially not when doing it fully tacked up and in a panic. I am aware of a few thuds on my body and a few cracks and I somehow find myself standing up and looking into the eyes of a beautiful person.

'What's your name?' she asks me.

'Jim,' I reply. 'What's yours?'

'Don't be cheeky,' comes the reply. And as I start to focus more clearly, the big green letters on her armband begin to form into the word 'DOCTOR'.

She holds up fingers for me to count and then she asks me to follow her index finger as she moves it in front of my face. Finally, she asks my name again to see if I will give the same answer as before. Stupidly, I do. Big mistake.

'Well, Jim, I pronounce you fit to ride.'

'Sorry. What did you say?'

'It's good news,' she says. 'You're fit to ride!'

Clearly this new relationship isn't going to work. She has a very different idea of 'good news' to mine. I don't reckon I could take her 'bad news'.

Gee appears over the horizon, jogging over to us. Gary appears beside her. Clearly seeing that hesitation to follow Rule 1 and 'act boldly' could lead to her man bolting for Brighton Pier, she grabs my left ankle and chucks me on to the horse's back. Gary takes the leading rein and we are out on the track before you can say 'cheese grater'.

As I take Theatre of Life down to post, another horse comes up on our outside. The rider is in trouble. The horse is bolting and he is swinging off the back of the thing. Theatre of Life and I have been going at a nice steady canter until that point but that sets my boy alight and off he goes. I ease my weight back and begin to pull on the reins, hoping that he will come back to me but, as I do so, the reins slip through the fingers of my right hand. Weird. I look down.

The fact that I have to look at my hand to understand how it is operating should have been a warning sign.

Theatre of Life comes back under control but I watch the other fella bowl off in the direction of Roedean School for girls. The horse performs an emergency stop with his nose inches from the cheese grater. The jockey keeps on travelling, hits the thing with arms and legs outstretched, and seems to be momentarily suspended on it, like a cartoon character, before sliding to the ground several feet below. That's one less competitor to worry about.

Well, to cut a long story short, we did not come home in a blaze of glory after this first race. Theatre of Life was very slow to start (who could blame him?) and we came home 'tailed off' at the back. After the presentations I was off to hospital, having never been so utterly terrified in all my life.

I sat there in hospital wondering if I should continue. I had been on a special diet for six months. I had lost nearly a quarter of my body weight. I had ridden out every morning and run every the evening. I had moved house and pitched up in Lambourn telling everybody that I was 'going to be a jockey in a year' and not everybody had reacted well to my clumsy cockiness. And now I wanted to quit – more than anything.

I had not bargained on this. I had fallen off a lot at home already. If you learn to ride on racehorses, you hit the ground frequently. But nothing had been as alarming as this incident. It was a reality check. I was calculating which way to go, whom I would be letting down, who would mock me if I stopped. I was looking for a way to justify bailing out on everybody – and on myself.

The phone rang. It was Richard Dunwoody.

I had first met Richard in Lambourn and again as a fellow conference speaker. We had become friends and he had also ridden upsides me on the gallops to give me some coaching. For those of you who have no knowledge of racing, Richard won a couple of Grand Nationals, a Champion Hurdle, a Cheltenham Gold Cup and had been Champion Jockey on three occasions. He also partnered Desert Orchid, perhaps the most famous and best loved horse in European racing, to some of his greatest victories.

I told Richard that I was thinking of giving up. 'Fair enough,' he answered, 'but remember that giving up has a consequence. You'll sit on your sofa and you'll watch your race go with somebody else riding your horse and living your moment, writing your story. If you're OK with that thought, fine – stop it today. If you don't like that, go on holiday, get well and get back on the horse.'

It was simple! It was not about whom I would offend or who would laugh or anything else. It was very simple: did I want to ride in a race on a racetrack under Jockey Club Rules, live on the TV and prove my Ten Rules in the process or not?

If I did, then I should get well and get on a horse as soon as I was able. If I did not, then I should move back to London and stop it all. I did, so the path was clear, the worrying could stop. I could get on with tomorrow.

And that is how Rule 10 was added to the Ten Rules for Taming Tigers.

Rule 10: Never, never give up

We don't give up on the good days. We give up on the bad days. We give up when it is grey and rainy and we doubt ourselves. When we fool ourselves that we have been deserted and are alone and unsupported. We give up when we face criticism and other obstacles. In this moment of weakness we contemplate giving up. Giving up on writing our story, on taming our Tiger, on inspiring others, on growing, learning and living.

Rule 10 of the Ten Rules stands alone as the Growth Rule. It was the last rule that I discovered. I'd always been aware that 'staying power' might be important, but I had thought that this sat within Rule 4 (It's all in the mind), dealing with setbacks and choosing your attitude. I was wrong. There's something more fundamental and visceral about the dogged determination that's necessary truly to tame your Tiger and write your unique story. I was taught this during my racing year through encounters with some of the inspirational people I was lucky enough to meet. I also learned it when my own Tiger threatened to diminish my own story with its roars.

The growth rule

Rule 10 is the Growth Rule. Rule 10 is about promises. Keeping your promises to yourself and to others – right through to the end. In the workplace this is the mark of success; this is the habit of the respected, the rewarded, the trusted, the leaders of today and of tomorrow.

Rule 10 creates growth not because we achieve the prize, but because we conquered the Tiger and went through the stages of fear and discomfort necessary to win the prize. That, and not the prize, alters us. It makes us stronger and more understanding of others' fears.

The point is that we said it (perhaps only to ourselves), we worked at it and we did it – whatever the Tiger threw at us along the way. And, in the process, learning to become – and knowing that we are – the kind of person who keeps their promises to themselves or others even when the path is rocky. This is growth.

Seeing the thing through wins us greater self-esteem and self-confidence.

It wins us esteem from others also. The world is full of grand-stand jockeys. The world is full of people who could change the world if they only had this or that on their side. The world is not full of the people who commit to doing something and then see it through to its conclusion to the best of their abilities, taming unknown and unseen Tigers along the way. We need people like you. Other people know that it's tough. And that is why you gain the respect of others through Rule 10. After all, which of your heroes, the people who have really influenced you, have a reputation for leaving the job half done?

Rule 10 is the finishers' rule. It's the rule that separates the men from the boys, the women from the girls. It's the rule that is understood by people who've had to stand alone, when all around doubted them, to make their unique contribution to the world. They've stood firm – not arrogant, but firm. You have done this also. Are you ready to stand firm again, on a higher level?

PERSISTENCE, NOT INSISTENCE

There are two caveats to be made to Rule 10 to save any readers from knocking their heads against the same wall until it hurts.

First, there is a big difference between giving up and changing course. We might change course many times, perhaps radically, in order to reach the intended goal. There is no disgrace at all in coming down the mountain a few hundred feet in order to find a safer, smoother route to the summit.

Secondly, the universe is beyond our control. Other people are beyond our control. Events can unfold that are beyond our control. To believe that we can always accomplish exactly the thing we set out to accomplish is the stuff of trite self-help books; it is a comfort blanket thrown to protect us from the reality of being human. There is no certainty. Our motto should be persistence and resilience but not foolish, desperate insistence.

TIMES WHEN WE SHOULD DEFINITELY NOT BE GIVING UP

In any attempt to tame your Tiger there will, by definition, be times when the Tiger has the upper hand. There will be bad days. These are the times when the Tiger picks up the scent of victory and could chase us off the track to the grandstand. The times when both you and I will be tempted to settle for mediocrity rather than the story we have set our hearts on.

If you give up when you're feeling the emotion or fatigue that comes from a run of bad days, you are giving up under the wrong circumstances.

It may be that it *is* time to give up, but don't take the decision on a bad day. Buy some time, make some excuses, sit by the beach, walk in the park, review these rules, very, very carefully.

Do you need to take a bold action to create some energy (Rule 1)? Are other people's Rulebooks causing you pain, conflict and doubt (Rule 2)? Are you biting off more than you can chew just at the moment? Is the plan clear or in need of tightening up to give you a better chance? Do you need to give yourself a break and take smaller steps (Rule 3)?

Is the Saboteur or the Headmaster running wild in your head? Are they persuading you to do things under pressure that you're going to regret for years to come (Rule 4)? Are there people around you to whom you could be going for support? And could those people give you practical, tangible support in your project that the Tiger is scaring you away from (Rule 5)? Are you being scared into running with the crowd? You know that there is no safety in numbers and yet you are beginning to feel a little too exposed out there (Rule 6)? How long will it be before the crowd starts to move in your direction, to follow you, if you stay on the path that you're on?

Are you doing something scary every day? Are you examining, measuring, recalibrating, stretching and flexing your risk muscles? Are you understanding how your brain and body react when you're put into a risky situation (Rule 7)? Have you thought through what, in real life, is at stake for you? What is the worst that could happen?

Have you thought about the consequences of giving up? Have you carefully thought through what you will be investing your time in if you're not investing it in getting this particular return? What's the return you'll be settling for instead (Rule 8)? Is it acceptable? Is the grass actually greener on the other side if you spend your time doing the other thing?

When the heat is on, it may be time to rely upon your old friend, the basics. Have you identified your disciplines? Are you practising them every day? Can you rely upon those by instinct when you are on the long run-in after the last fence, head to head with someone else, and they are all that you have to rely upon (Rule 9)?

Which brings us back to Rule 10, 'Never, never give up'! Or, at least, never give up until you've stared the consequences long and hard in the face, visited that nursing home by the sea and imagined yourself looking in the mirror and either congratulating yourself for having the wisdom and foresight to have stopped pursuing an impossible dream (that's if you're sure it was impossible) or whether you're wishing you could turn the clock back and take this decision all over again.

Some Specific Signs That It May Not Be the Right Time to Give Up

If any of the following apply, giving up at this point may not be the right thing to do:

- you still have a big gut feeling that you are on to something and there is just a chance you could pull it off

- you have allies, people whose opinion you trust, who are urging you to continue

- you've taken advice, you've received feedback – again, from people you trust – and they rate your chances of success at odds that are acceptable to you

- rather than losing faith in the project itself, you are being lured by something specific – the 'next big thing' is calling you. Are you using this apparently greener grass to give yourself permission to take the pressure off yourself, to let yourself off delivering on the thing that you committed to deliver now that it is getting tougher?

IF YOU REALLY MUST GIVE UP

If you really, really must give up, then give up on a good day. Give up with your head held high, when the sun is shining and those you value and admire are applauding you for your achievements. Then at least you will have waited until things improved before deciding that you were making the correct decision.

Most of us don't give up on a sunny day. Most of us give up on a stormy day. We give up when the clouds are black and our friends are doubting us and we have to get up at 5 a.m. and the rain is horizontal and our partner lies beside us asleep in the bed, and there are doughnuts downstairs. And they look good!

But if we give up on that day, if we take the easier, more inviting path, if we take all the pressure off (as is our right) then we must go to that nursing home by the sea to play dominos not knowing.

Not knowing what our real story was!

Not knowing whether it would have been a year, a month or just a week before we cracked it, before it all came good. We walked off the track, we gave in, we joined the throng of people seeking 'safety in numbers' and sat in the grandstand, telling everybody our view of the other fellas but never getting involved in the action.

The question to you is this: who is writing your story? You? Or the Tiger that you have created? The Tiger that we each create to keep us safe from the fear and discomfort of trying.

COMMITTING TO THE DESTINATION

There is a very special moment in a freedive. The moment when you take the final breath and commit yourself to the dive. At that moment, it is vital that you commit to the depth you are going to – 101 metres – or you will fail.

Why? Well, if you were to stop at eighty metres and have a little think, you would find yourself in a place where:

- it is dark, cold and very quiet

- you are eighty metres away from your next breath of air

- you are fifty metres away from the last human being you saw – a cameraman at thirty metres. There is no safety diver with a supply of air ready for you – it would be extremely risky to start breathing compressed air at eighty metres anyway

- your lungs are the size of golf balls and your diaphragm has been pulled into your lung cavity to compensate for this

- you are experiencing pressure equal to nine times the atmospheric pressure at sea level and that pressure has changed in just over a minute – and you are contemplating increasing that to eleven times the atmospheric pressure at sea level.

In short – there is room for fear and discomfort at eighty metres. If you do not commit to the destination at the outset, if you leave room for doubt, if you stop at the point of potential discomfort and have a little think about whether or not to push on, you spook yourself, turn early and fail.

It is the same in any endeavour. If you leave yourself an exit other than the finishing point, the Tiger will chase you through it when you meet the point of greatest discomfort, when the going gets tough.

Keep Your Promises

It is impossible for me to describe the feeling of achieving what you were told, bluntly, you could not achieve. A thing that, on many occasions, you also doubted you could achieve. A thing that you and a select crew of talented people and, by now, good friends, decided to commit to nonetheless. You have either felt it yourself, or you haven't - yet.

We can all do it – every one of us – if we are willing to see that the Tiger, for all its ferocious noise, has no teeth.

It is easy to keep the promises we make to others. We find it harder to keep the promises we make to ourselves. But these promises are the stuff of which our story is made.

I'll leave you with the closing chapter of my twelve months working to get to the racecourse. I raced three times under Jockey Club Rules to prove to myself that the first was not a fluke. The day of my first race was one of the most memorable and rewarding days of my life. Given all the people who had helped me to get there, it was also one of the most humbling. If you have had similar experiences, you will understand that. If you are awaiting that experience, tame your Tiger and claim it!

Make your promise to yourself, keep it and write your bestseller of a story.

My first televised race under Jockey Club rules

21 November 2004, the night before my first race, I feel like a condemned man. In fact, probably a little worse than a condemned man – at least he gets a last meal, and I am not going to be having much of a dinner.

I pack my bag for the morning, and get a childish satisfaction from, for the first time ever, putting a bag containing saddle, stick, silk breeches, body protector, skullcap, shiny new permit to ride under Rules, medical book and so on by the door for the morning. A jockey's kitbag.

I go to bed nervous but I wake up with my heart in my throat. The race is at 12 p.m. at Southwell, an approximately four-hour drive. I have arranged to pick Gee up at 6 a.m. so that we'll have time to walk the track. On the journey, we make the mistake of picking up the *Racing Post* to see if they are writing about me. They are, and it is a very kind and encouraging piece, but it is the wrong time to read it. The pressure is mounting.

We arrive at Southwell Racecourse and park in the jockey's car park (another first) and I get my bag from the boot and stride with Gee towards the weighing room. All the track staff, stable staff, trainers and jockeys seem to know Gee and they are nodding at her and waving. It's like walking through Leicester Square with Madonna! We get to the weighing room and I sign in.

I say 'hi' to Marmite, who is my valet today and whom I had met at Brighton and I put my things by my peg. I meet Gee outside and we walk the track together.

As we walk around the fibresand surface Gee exudes confidence in me. I don't know why she does – but I am very glad and grateful. It helps. We go through, once again, the key things to remember. Grab hold of the mane as the stalls open. Leave him a nice long length of rein so you don't jab his mouth. Have you agreed the race tactics with Charlie? Don't stop riding until you pass the finishing line whatever you do. Don't be put off by the Tannoy when you come into the home straight. Don't be tempted to use your stick – don't even pick it up on your first race, I've seen people fall off. Hands and heels all the way. And then we're past the finishing line and I'm heading back to the weighing room.

I get changed and sit on the wooden bench under my peg. I thought I had time on my side, but everything's happening more quickly now. Marmite wants me to do a trial weigh out, to check how much lead I'm going to have to carry. Charlie's arrived with the silks and Marmite's put the white silk on my hat and draped the jacket over my peg while we've been walking. I get changed to do the trial weigh out, and Marmite asks if I want any elastic bands.

'What for?' I ask.

He laughs: 'Because your silk is too long for your arms! You don't want it falling down over your hands!'

'OK. Elastic bands, please.'

I weigh out, and I've never been so pleased to see Charlie's face; he's standing in the weighing room by the scales. He gives me a broad grin and a wink as he picks up the saddle and weight cloth and heads off to saddle up Airgusta.

Back to the wooden bench in the weighing room. Nerves have kicked in quite hard now. A lot of people I don't want to let down have poured their heart and soul into making this day arrive. I think through the phases of the job. First, the parade ring, then the chute, getting down to post, keeping him calm at the start, loading up and jumping out of the stalls. And then there are the different personalities of the race itself; jockeying for position, sticking pretty much tight in that position as the race unfolds, and then either dictating or reacting as you begin to come into the home straight. And then hell for leather for the finish.

I'm sitting on the bench, lost in these thoughts when I hear my name called out. I don't recognise the man in a suit who's calling my name, and he's looking blindly around the weighing room without a clue who I am. I put my hand up and say, 'yes', and suddenly realise that I look like a schoolboy. He asks if he can have a word and we go outside to the Clerk of the Scales' table together. Now I do feel like a schoolboy following the headmaster outside and it is not easing my nerves.

'I'm the Starter,' he introduces himself, 'and I want to speak to you about the procedure down at the start to make sure you understand it.'

Now we've been through this at the British Racing School, and Gee and I have gone through it together a hundred times at home, but I'm surprised at how happy I am to hear him say this. He talks me through everything from arriving at the stalls, loading, and then he begins to describe what he'll do to start the race.

'So I'll call, "Jockeys!" and then, if there are any blindfolds, I'll call "Blindfolds!", and then you'll see my flag drop and the stall gates will open. Is that clear?'

'Clear, thanks. Except... hold on! What if there are no blindfolds? What will you shout then?'

'Then I'll just shout, "Jockeys!" and the next thing will be that the stall gates will open.'

He's making me nervous. In one situation he'll shout the equivalent of 'Ready, Steady, Go' but if there are no blindfolds, it's going to be the equivalent of 'Ready – Go'. And I'm still going to be waiting for 'Steady!' He's sees my problem and understands it without me saying anything more.

'Okay, Jim. Whatever happens today, I will shout, "Jockeys! Blindfolds!" And then it's the flag. Happy?'

I resist the urge to give him a hug and, instead, reply, 'Happy.'

And I'm back on the wooden bench waiting.

'Jockeys for the first, jockeys for the first!'

I feel my stomach lurch, get up and walk out of the weighing room. To my amazement I'm getting some good luck shouts from the other lads, and a massive smile and a raised clenched fist from Marmite.

I'm just adjusting to the feel of nakedness that silk trousers in November give when I see Charlie and Gee standing in the middle of the parade ring. They have great big grins on their faces as I walk over. Caroline is leading Airgusta round the outside and he looks a picture. Charlie asks me if I can remember the tactics. We're running Airgusta, a two-miler, over a mile simply because the team want to help me win my bet. This race is a year to the day since I met Gee and it all started. I repeat the plan back to Charlie.

'Yes. Use him up as fast as I like, get to the front as quick as I can, stay there and kick out all the way home, because he doesn't have any turn of foot [no acceleration]. He only has one pace, so we need to use it all the way.'

'Spot on.'

The bell rings and Caroline brings the horse round to us. Gee, rather than Charlie, legs me up – she's my lucky mascot today – and Caroline leads us out on to the track.

Airgusta's on his toes and moving sideways down the chute, but this is nothing that he hasn't done walking on to the gallops at home, so I'm not too worried. In fact, I'm amazed at how much happier I am sitting up here in the saddle than I was in the parade ring. Perhaps it's down to that Rule 4 tool: 'get lost in the task rather than analysing it' – that we spoke about all those pages ago. We canter past the grandstand, pull up, turn around and canter round to the one-mile start.

We load up. Airgusta is first in, and he loads like an angel. The gates shut behind us and he stands alert but still, waiting. And I am waiting also. And the strangest thing to me, as I sit in the stalls waiting, is the view that I have. I've sat in the stalls often enough at school in Newmarket and at home in Lambourn, but I have never sat in them on a racetrack before, and I find myself totally unprepared for the different view. In front of me now, instead of a grassy field with some trees at the other end that I'd better pull up in good time to avoid hitting, I have the back straight at Southwell Racecourse. Far to my left is the grandstand with the faint noise of the commentator. The truck with the TV camera mounted on it is sitting ahead of us on the inside of the track, and another camera is mounted on a crane at the turn, about two furlongs ahead. It is the first race of the day, so the track is freshly harrowed and looks like a beach after the tide has gone out and the sun has dried it off. It's not Goodwood, but to me at this moment it's an amazing view and, perhaps for the first time, the race itself becomes very real.

In a few seconds, we'll get to make the first hoof prints of the day on the deep fibresand and, if the plan goes right, I'll be tight against the rails at the front. In a horserace. What'll it be like? What will happen?

We've drawn stall one, which gives our plan a better chance of success. It's very unlikely that Airgusta would be able to beat the milers that he is lined up against. The bookies have us at 50-1 for that very reason (perhaps not helped by a new rider on his back), but if I can jump off smartly enough and get him up to a pace that no miler will want to be at just yet, we've certainly a chance of landing mid-division or better.

One of the lads calls out, 'Who's making it?' (setting the pace from the front of the field).

'I am,' I call back.

I turn my head around and there are three left to load and they are all being led forward. Maybe five seconds unless one refuses. I can feel my heart beating against my body protector, but everybody else looks as though they're having a day at the office. I've never been in the stalls with more than one other horse, and, as they load, the whole structure begins to move as different animals behave in different ways in their stall. My legs are tight up against the side, so every time a horse makes the structure move, my leg gets crushed against the wall. It's not that it hurts, it's just that it's weird and not what I'm expecting – I'm miles outside my safety zone. I'm amazed to find that all I want to do now is get out of the stalls and get on with the race.

'Two to load! One to load!'

The stalls handlers are calling to each other, the starter and the jockeys as they load each pairing. They keep emerging from the front of the stalls beneath us and running out to the side as each horse is led into position.

'Loaded!'

Breathe. Long rein. Grab the mane. Take the weight into my feet but don't leave saddle.

'Jockeys! Blindfolds!'

I can sense some of the jockeys looking round a bit puzzled – there's not a blindfold in sight. Then there it is. That familiar snap of the gates. Familiar from all those trips down to the start, familiar from Newmarket and from Lambourn.

And there it is. That acceleration. But it's faster, much faster than anything he's done at home. And I'm riding him already, scrubbing along and shouting in his ear to get him up to speed, just as I've done so many times on the equicisor in the gym in Lambourn with Jason Cook, simulating getting the horse up to full speed in the early part of the race. Gee has had us working on this ever since we knew it was going to be a mile race on a two-miler. Once I am in the lead and hugging the rails I can 'sit' still on him and let him bowl along at this pace for me.

The noise! I've never heard anything like it before. The thunder of hooves after the thwack of the opening gates is so sudden. I've watched this at the racecourse, I've heard the noise but it is momentary when you are a spectator. It is gone in seconds as the field accelerates from you. As a rider, it grows louder as we accelerate.

We reach the first bend tight against the rails with a lead of a length and a half, cruising nicely, and for a moment I stop to enjoy it. For a moment it's very simple, very peaceful and, for a deluded second or two, I even get the feeling that I know what I'm doing here. Out in front at Southwell, all I can hear is the sound of Airgusta's hooves and the sound of wind. I can't hear any other horses behind me now that I have the lead, just the wind. It's like hurtling downhill on a bicycle with a skullcap on that doesn't cover your ears and, again, it's a noise that I've never experienced before. Even that first rush of wind that I felt as Victor ran off with me at Jamie Osborne's, and which seemed so loud at the time, turns out to have been a gust compared to the tornado that's going past my ears now. I even have time to notice how deep the track is at Southwell. The hollow of

Airgusta's hoof is making a thud into the sand as it hits the ground.

But the thudding is now getting decidedly louder. We're on the long, sweeping turn, and in a matter of seconds we're going to be on the home straight. It is a complete delusion, after all. I've been distracted, perhaps for less than two seconds, by all of the new sensations, and that's not allowed in a horserace. I'm about to get punished for it. First there's one, then there's two, suddenly three horses are upsides me. We're almost touching. Down in the saddle, change hands, Airgusta picks up the bit and does his best to go with them, but we're on the milers' home territory now, and I should have been working him far harder from far earlier round that long, sweeping bend. The horses with two gears are using them to our disadvantage.

He's working really hard (I thought I was, too, until I saw the video after the race, and was very disappointed at how weak I looked in that first race), but one's got past us, now two. For the first time in the race he's got kickback – his muzzle, his eyes and my face are beginning to be covered in sand. I look down to take a quick gasp of clean air and spit out some grit before coming head-on again, this time to be met by the noise of the Tannoy; another unexpected sound. Two horses upsides us now, three in front, the Tannoy beginning to be much louder than the hooves. Five in front now, fourteen in the race, perhaps I can hold sixth?

Then another strange sound: the roar of the crowd. Nothing prepares you for this, even at Southwell. I cannot imagine what it must be like to ride into this sound as you come up the home straight at Ascot.

The two red lollipops are getting closer and I need them now. To be honest, Airgusta could probably do this for a little while longer. I probably haven't made as much use of him early on as I should have done, but my thighs, despite all the work on the equicizer, are on fire.

'Don't stop riding until you've passed the line'. And I don't

And it's done. I'm trying to pull him up. I stand up in my irons and ease my weight back and I'm amazed to find that my legs are working just fine. I've seen newcomers buckle as they try to stand up and it's not something I wanted to do. Thanks, Gee, and thanks, Jason.

And then it strikes me. We've done it.

We've bloody done it!

Airgusta, the two-mile horse, and I, the newcomer, take 7th place from 14 horses. The bookies had us at odds that suggested we should have been tailed off. We haven't won, but we've done well.

And I'm not the only one who's realising this. As we turn and canter back to the chute, ease into a trot and finally come to a walk, Gee and Caroline are jumping up and down and beaming where the chute meets the track. And seeing their reaction sets me off too. Absolute elation! None of us can quite believe that we have finally made it. Gee beams up at me and I try to speak to her.

Then I realise that I can't. It's not that I'm welling up here, it's that my mouth has simply never been this dry – the mixture of nerves and sand means that I am completely unable to speak. It's welded shut.

The journey back to unsaddle and eventually the walk to the weighing room is quite surreal. Strangers are waving at me and saying 'well done'. I guess they've seen the paper or heard the commentary and have been wishing me well. As I walk back past the *At the Races* commentary team's position for the day, Simon Mapletoft and Jason Weaver ask if I'll come straight back out when I've dumped my kit and talk to the cameras. Now that I hadn't expected at all, and given the fact that I'm not actually able to speak at this moment this sets me back into another stomach clamp of nerves.

In the weighing room there are lots of congratulations for me and I'm really touched by everyone's reaction. Racing really is an extraordinary place. I place my saddle and skull cap on my peg and turn round to find Marmite giving me a big, broad grin and telling me he wants those elastic bands back.

I get a plastic cup of water from the jug on the table, swill it round my mouth to get rid of the sand and see if I can get my tongue to come back to life before going out to talk to the TV presenters.

And as I do so, in the first real quiet moment since the race ended, it dawns on me at last that calling up a raft of strangers and asking for help, moving house, losing almost a quarter of my body weight, getting as fit as a flea, learning to ride, breaking bones at Brighton Racecourse and getting up at 5 a.m. every day have all been completely worthwhile.

We won the bet. We did it!

We formed an amazing team, Gee, Bos, Sarah Bosley, Charlie Morlock, Tina Fletcher, Jason Cook, Michael Caulfield, so many others and me. And we formed friendships. And we did it.

And, along the way, the Ten Rules for Taming Tigers were proven.

Things the Tiger wants you to forget about Rule 10

Rule 10: Never, never give up

Rule 10 is the Growth Rule – it is about keeping our promises. Not our promises to others, that is easy. Our promises to ourselves.

Rule 10 does not deliver growth because you achieved the prize, but because you went through the battle, stayed the course, negotiated your fears and discomfort and defeated the Tiger.

It is OK to change route to achieve the goal – that is common sense.

Events are beyond our control. Things change and there is no certainty. Our motto should therefore be persistence and not desperate insistence when it is clear that to ontinue will cause us harm.

If you are considering giving up, look at the Ten Rules again. Is there a Rule that you should be using?

You should not consider giving up when:

- You have a big gut feel that you could achieve the thing

- You have allies still willing you on and full of (educated and considered) faith in you

- Your advisors and mentors still believe that you can succeed

- You are being lured by greener grass

Commit to the destination. If you commit merely to 'giving it a go', you will walk off the track at the point of maximum fear and discomfort. You can push through this.

And if you do push through the hard days, the prize is huge. The prize is your growth, becoming the person you want to become, *writing your own unique story.*

Now log on to the Campus at tamingtigers.com and watch the film entitled 'Promises, promises . . .'

Twitter: @jim_lawless
Web: tamingtigers.com
Facebook: facebook.com/pages/Taming-Tigers.

Tiger-Free Living

Taming Tigers is not about 'how to be a success', although its principles, practised with discipline, will make you such. It is about liberation. Liberation from fear. Granting yourself the freedom to live your life.

'So, first of all, let me assert my firm belief that the only thing we have to fear is fear itself — nameless, unreasoning, unjustified terror which paralyzes needed efforts to convert retreat into advance.'

So said Franklin D. Roosevelt. It seems that FDR was a Tiger tamer, too.

This liberation from the Tiger, from our fear of fear, is an awakening. You may well find that there are areas of your life beyond work that are impacted by this awakening. That comes as no surprise, does it? The Tiger suppresses your true Self. What does your true Self desire when you finally come face to face with him or her?

- to live in accordance with our values

- to seek meaning in our lives

- to have purpose in our lives

- to find true, authentic connection with other people (to be 'real' with others who themselves are 'real')

- to grow – have a sense that we are still 'becoming', that we can transcend our current reality

When you release your true Self from the Tiger's constraints, there will be many wonderful consequences.

You may find that your word becomes more important to you. Keeping promises to yourself is no mean feat. Keeping promises to others is easier, but many still fail. 'Flakes' is our lovely word for them. Breaking our word is seldom something to be valued.

You may find that you wish to have – and without the Tiger you can have – honest and authentic conversations at home that lead to a richer and more fulfilling relationship with your partner, friends or children.

You may find that you wish to treat your body with more respect, to eat well and exercise well. Why? Because this is the vessel for your story now and no longer just there to bear the brunt of addictive behaviours.

You may find that once you can see the Tiger at work, you have the freedom and the courage to face any addictive behaviours that have been distressing you. To take bold action (Rule 1) and seek help (Rule 5). It need not be a part of your Rulebook (Rule 2) that you have these thorns in your life or that you inflict them on those around you. Addictive behaviours mask our fears. If you are human you have fears and, possibly, addictive and harmful habits to ease the pain of those fears. These can range from misusing substances to spending money you don't have to controlling and manipulating others.

I stress that *Taming Tigers* may lead you to address these behaviours and may give you strength for the change, but it does not set out to equip you for this process. In the Taming Tigers Campus there are details of organisations that can assist you, if you wish to take this courageous step and liberate yourself and your loved ones.

Finally, you will be free to choose what to write in the next chapter of your story and be able to use the Ten Rules to write that chapter successfully. Despite the Tiger's roar, it will be *your* story.

If you are confused about what to write in the next chapter of your story, don't worry. Tame your Tiger today and tomorrow in small ways, aim for small goals. Through the confidence and growth you achieve in doing that, your purpose will emerge from underneath all of that Tiger-created behaviour and thinking.

Your meaning and purpose become clearer over time as fear of fear subsides.

If you know in your heart what you need to write, I wish you every possible success. I know that many other successful Tiger tamers do also.

You are writing the story of your life

You are writing the story of your life. You must be, mustn't you? Who else could possibly be holding the pen? Decision, action, result. You are writing a sentence of your story now, as you finish reading my book. I am writing a sentence of my story now, as I write these final words to you. Our stories have converged. You and I are very similar when we come to the subject of the Tiger, as we have discovered. We can both tame it, too.

'Did I write my story? Or did I let the Tiger dictate my story to me?'
Over to you.

Appendix

The New Economy: join the revolution and claim your prize

Taming Tigers is a vital tool for you in the New Economy. If you have not yet been asked to tame your Tigers, become more 'accountable', become a 'leader' and prepare for 'change' at work, you soon will be.

The entire world of work is changing rapidly. We cannot wait to be told any more. We need to contribute, and proactively. None of us has a job for life. We are all entrepreneurs, mini-businesses, only as good as our last contribution. You know this is true; you have experienced the world of work changing around you.

This is seen as a threat by most but as an opportunity by some. The other side of the coin is that there is a tremendous hunger from businesses for those who can contribute fully. Not work longer, not work harder – just engage and contribute more fully. Those who do will be rewarded in many ways. The biggest reward will be freedom to act, freedom to live, freedom to create fun and adventure at work.

What has happened? To understand the shift, we need to go back a bit.

The four economic ages

In the beginning we were hunter-gatherers. This was the first economic age. We went out and hunted meat and gathered fruit and vegetables.

This could be hard and dangerous work, so we invented the second economic age. The agricultural age. We fenced off land and we raised animals for meat and grew fruit trees and vegetables. This had its disadvantages – feudal lords and property lawyers, for example. But it had advantages, too. We didn't have to face wild beasts to get our dinner and the legend of Robin Hood was born.

Then came the industrial age. Now people were required to become thinking cogs in the new machines – factories. These 'thinking cogs' were required to act in a certain way in order to keep the machine working. For many tasks, opposable thumbs were the advantage that human beings brought to the manufacturing process. The ability to think was not particularly welcomed. It was often safer to 'know your place' if you wanted to keep the job that fed your family.

People were managed in order to perform predictably as part of a manufacturing machine. They were placed on the profit and loss account as a cost – not on the balance sheet as an asset.

Now we have entered the fourth economic age. In this book I will refer to this as the New Economy. It is a very exciting place. Opportunity abounds and meritocracy is vital for survival. For the first time, many more people are able to find meaning and purpose in their work. Hierarchies are being broken down – innovation and vital contribution can come from all ages or 'ranks'. Lifelong learning is the norm, access to information and to people is freely available.

There is a challenge, though. Many leaders only understand industrial age management theory – they are terrified to change, trust others, let go of command and control. Most employees still act as though they were employed in the industrial age – it can feel quite safe and unexposed back there. Both sets of people have to change fast to survive in the New Economy. This is the change that we are all feeling

The new economy

What is different in the New Economy and how has this change come about? Here is a very brief description.

BRAND INTEGRITY AND TRANSPARENCY

The biggest change is that the consumer is demanding integrity and transparency from companies that he or she considers doing business with. This has changed the nature of the brand. A brand is no longer something that appears, carefully presented, on TV. The brand is on trial every time the consumer interacts with the people, products or processes of a company. And the consumer *can* now demand integrity and transparency. Consumers now have a major research tool – the internet. They can broadcast their findings through a megaphone – the internet. Companies like Amazon know this – look at how they provide you with megaphones at every opportunity on their site!

Are you still dubious? Try this: Procter & Gamble was founded in 1837. It has advertised Fairy, Ariel and many other brands to you since you were a child. And yet it launched the first advertising campaign about itself as a company – as opposed to its brands – in 2011. Why?

Think about it. Consumers want to know what the company stands for, not just buy the brand messaging any more, and P&G have a great story to tell about themselves. Now is the time to tell it!

Can you name the CEO of Apple? Can you name the CEO of General Electric? Which has the higher market capitalisation? Clearly there are other elements to Apple's success, but the answers to these questions are indicative of a shift. Who is the leader of Virgin Group? Which brand in the UK is considered to be the consumer's champion?

This is a powerful force and a major change. It gives employees of any company a new and higher value. The employees, collectively, create that brand experience – not the leaders. They create it every day at the point of contact with the consumer; they often understand the interaction far better than the leaders. If the interaction with Virgin staff is not as we were led to believe it might be by following Sir Richard Branson's adventures and statements – his brand promise to us on behalf of Virgin has been broken.

Your leaders need your integrity, energy and ideas as never before.

PACE AND SCALE OF ACTIVITY

The other creator of change is pace and scale. Things move too fast now for a business to have time to get advice and approval from the top. Agility is vital. Things move so fast that businesses need innovation opportunities to be grasped – and shouted back up the line quickly if investment or approval is required. We cannot wait for a quarterly brainstorming session in some hotel followed by a 'cascade'. Similarly, as organisations grow the size requires that the leaders either produce a massive structure of hierarchy to take decisions for the staff and police their obedience or empower the staff to make their own decisions. Given that the middle management layer brings its own difficulties and slows pace, the latter option is often preferable.

EMPLOYEE NEEDS

The final major shift is in the people seeking to go to work. Like the consumer, they demand a certain integrity now. Talent has choice, and seeing as people generally have all they need to satisfy their lower requirements on Maslow's Pyramid of Human Motivations, (safety and physiological needs) they are looking for community, engagement, increasing self-esteem, a sense of purpose and meaning. Company's expecting to command and control 'thinking cogs' cannot recruit such talent and they know it.

Tame your tiger and seize your prize

This shift represents the start of the most exciting step forward in working conditions in history.

I receive over one hundred briefings from board members of companies each year before delivering keynote addresses to their staff. Three years ago, the briefs used to vary. Now they are all variations on a theme designed to deal with one problem in particular: 'Please help my people see that we need them to step up to the challenges, take personal accountability and demonstrate leadership – and help them believe that only they can make a real difference to this business.'

Leaders are shouting out: 'We need you to take control of your areas – innovate – advise us – make things happen – don't wait for us, be entrepreneurial and come to us with ideas.' Some leaders are further ahead with this than others, but the opportunity to be creative, innovative and highly valued is getting greater each day.

The bad news for most businesses is that many employees are not in a hurry to engage with this exciting change just yet – largely because of the Tiger. The current Rulebook for most employees is rooted in an education and early job experience designed to be fit for the old industrial age. But the Tiger roars at the thought of change.

But the fact that many employees are not in a hurry to engage with this exciting change yet – largely because of the Tiger – is great news for you. You are already working to tame your Tigers.

You are facing opportunities to negotiate your own agenda and to be entrepreneurial in making things happen within your organisation that have never been presented before.

Don't let the Tiger steal this from you. Join the revolution and claim your prize.

FURTHER READING AND PROFESSIONAL HELP

To access the Taming Tigers Reading List, please visit the Campus at tamingtigers.com.

If this book has prompted you to consider areas of your life such as addiction, relationship issues, the impact of your childhood or adult traumas upon your current thinking patterns and the impact of any of these upon your personal story and your work life, you will find a list of resources and organisations that can offer professional assistance in the Campus.

If you, your team or your organisation have cultural changes to make, goals and direction to set and achieve, and would like to know how Taming Tigers can assist, please contact Jim and his team through enquiries@tamingtigers.com. You can read testimonials from clients of Taming Tigers on the website.

May the long time sun shine upon you
All love surround you
And the true light within you
Guide your way on

Sat Nam

Index